The *Trees*
Won't Tell

LYNN TERRELL

CHAPTER ONE

The old man moved slowly through the trees, stopping frequently to catch his breath. It was not a long walk from his cabin to the falls, but the terrain was unstable -- even treacherous at times. And the heat on this day was stifling.

It was not yet eleven o'clock, and the temperature was already in the mid-eighties. High humidity made it feel ever warmer. But, this was typical July weather in the Western Carolinas, the old man reminded himself.

And as he neared his destination, he was encouraged by the sound of rushing water. The falls were straight ahead. He was in his eighties, but he appeared even older. Once tall and erect, he now was stooped and frail -- his proud step replaced by a cautious shuffle. His long silver hair hung down in thin strands. And his wrinkled olive skin bore the ravages of prolonged exposure to the elements.

When he moved to these mountains, he had had the eyesight of a hawk. Now, his steely blue eyes were blurred by cataracts. And the clamor of small animals scurrying through the forest no longer reached his ears.

Weary from the arduous walk, the old man paused in the shadows of the creek and basked in the cooling effect of the fast-moving water. He took a seat on a nearby boulder and watched the churning stream for several moments. He removed his yellow straw hat and used his handkerchief to wipe the moisture from the sweatband. As he sat there, a gentle wind rustled through the trees overhead. The breeze felt good to his exposed skin. From his shady perch, he gazed up through the leaves at the relentless sun. The glare caused his eyes to fill with moisture, and he blinked repeatedly.

The sensation of heat and humidity suddenly transported the old man back in time -- back to his boyhood on the family farm in Montana. Memories of baling hay in the open fields with other family members were still fresh in his mind. Then, as now, the heat was oppressive. He vividly recalled his sweat mixing with cuts from the sharp hay stems, causing his skin to itch and burn. Baling hay was one of the reasons he had hated life on the farm. As soon as he was old enough, he had told himself, he'd leave and never look back.

Just thinking about that long-ago experience caused his skin to itch. It was one of those sensations that never left a person's consciousness -- like sand crunching beneath bare feet on a beach, or the sound of fingernails scraping across a slate board.

After resting for several minutes, the old man rose to his feet, adjusted the straw hat on his head and continued his journey. It only took a short time for him to reach the precipice of the falls.

Once there, he stood silently and watched the cascading water as it dashed violently on the rocks below. The maelstrom created a blowing mist that swept over his arms and face. For a brief moment, he had the urge to roll up his pants and wade into the inviting water. But, that was unwise. The slippery rocks beneath the surface made for treacherous footing.

The old man had visited this site so many times before. And each time he had come here, it was as if he were seeing the falls for the first time. This had become his special place in the forest -- his nirvana. Here, he could dismiss troublesome memories and escape from every day cares and pain. Here, he could be free in spirit again.

After standing for several moments, he made his way to the sloping rocks just to one side of the falls. One of the boulders was his favorite. It was much larger than the rest, and its flat top made it an ideal spot for relaxing and enjoying the view.

The old man carefully eased himself onto the boulder and settled into a sitting position, his legs crossed in front of him. He sat for considerable time, watching the rushing water below and relishing the refreshing mist hanging in the air. Finally, he removed his hat and ran his fingers through his thin hair. With his eyes closed, he stretched his neck backward and turned his head toward the sky. He was totally relaxed.

Just then, a sharp pain gripped his chest, and he leaned forward in agony. His eyes were now open. What is happening to me? he asked himself. At that moment, another pain raced down his left arm, and he suddenly felt weak and dizzy. Once again, his gaze turned skyward. His last sight was of white clouds floating against the rich blue sky. Slowly, his vision faded and his consciousness ebbed. He fell backward and his head slammed against the big boulder. His now limp body shifted momentarily, then rolled from the big rock and fell to the ground. As he lay there, life slowly drained from his body. It all ended that quickly.

The old man's time in the mountains had come to an end. There would be no more hiding -- no more secrecy. There would be no more feelings of fear and vulnerability -- no more living life in total seclusion -- no more looking over his shoulder wherever he went. None of the things that had become routine in his life -- none of the things from his checkered past -- mattered any more. Now, they all were just footnotes in history.

As a younger man, he had served his country with distinction in far-away wars. But, there would be no service to honor his gallantry -- no military funeral to pay tribute to his life. He had abandoned that right by severing all ties with the past and moving to these mountains.

Earlier in his life, he had been a good citizen, a good neighbor and a good friend. He was a hard-working and loyal employee. He married and lived happily with his wife. And he had been a good husband to her. When she died, he grieved over her loss.

After that, he made a choice that totally changed his life and his fortunes. It was a choice that gained him notoriety -- even transformed him into a celebrity of sorts. Countless newspaper and magazine articles were written about his exploits.

In the final analysis, this man had become one of the most famous - yet mysterious - people in the country. Some now considered him a folk hero, and they assembled each year to toast his memory. They even told stories about his daring feats. Later in life he had found love again, but that, too, had ended in sorrow and emotional loss.

Now he had died alone in the woods. There were no children or relatives to grieve his passing. There were no friends to remember his life. There was no one at all to mourn his death. Here in the mountains, his legacy and his life had ended quietly and un-noticed. But, somewhere in these mountains, another life had begun.

CHAPTER TWO

Fall settled early over North Carolina's western mountains. It was only the first week of October. A frigid air mass had slammed down from Canada, and temperatures across the area dropped to near freezing. Summer was over.

Plant life responded to the cold by shutting down the flow of water to far-reaching branches and foliage, effectively ending the growing season. It was a ritual that was as old as the earth itself. The absence of moisture drained the chlorophyll from leaves, robbing them of their rich green color and exposing the underlying pigments. Virtually overnight, peaks and valleys in the surrounding Nantahala National Forest were transformed into a kaleidoscope of color. Magnificent poplars, maples and chestnuts were now resplendent in brilliant shades of red, yellow and orange.

On this morning, beams of sunlight penetrated the forest's lush cover, further highlighting the already dazzling foliage. Some of the leaves were beginning to fall, floating slowly down to form a colorful quilt on the forest floor.

This unexpected cold spell had caught the forest's black bears by surprise. Throughout the mountains, the big furry creatures paused in their foraging and immediately set about finding suitable shelter to sleep away the winter. Other signs of the approaching cold season were evident, as well. Overhead, flocks of Canadian geese could be seen in their familiar V-formation, moving relentlessly toward the southern horizon.

Against this backdrop, Mitch Conner stepped onto the deck of his rustic little cabin and took a deep breath of the chilled morning air. He glanced out over the bluish peaks of the surrounding mountains, which protruded through the blanket of fog obscuring the valley below. Hidden beneath the haze, some 2,000 feet down, was Bryson City, NC.

As Conner looked out over the horizon, he was keenly aware of the calm that hung over the area -- particularly at this time of day. The only sounds he heard were those of the forest and its inhabitants. From a distant perch came the lonely cry of a hawk. And there was the hushed whisper of the wind rushing through the trees. Otherwise, all was quiet. There were no sounds of traffic. No neighbors yelling at neighbors. No horns blowing. No car radios blaring. This serenity was one of the reasons he had moved here to Bryson City, he reminded himself

Conner had only lived in the mountains four months, moving north 150 miles from Atlanta. But, he already looked like he belonged. His cheeks had a healthy reddish glow, the result of spending increased amounts of time outdoors. Subtle creases around his eyes further added to his rugged appearance.

And his shock of salt-and-pepper hair was full, extending slightly below his collar in back. It was longer than he'd ever kept it. But, long hair provided added warmth against the mountain cold. Conner also had grown a modest beard, which was mostly white, and he kept it short and neatly trimmed.

Women considered Conner appealing and fun to be around. He was just over six feet tall, and 185 pounds were spread over a lean, muscular frame. His features were well-defined, and his serious green eyes and dimples transformed his face when he smiled. He also had a strong jaw line and a slightly crooked nose, a souvenir from high school athletics.

Acquaintances were immediately impressed with Conner's intelligence and persuasiveness. Some even felt he had a little boy's shyness. But, at the same time, he could be confident and bold when the situation called for it.

It was ironic he now found himself alone in the mountains at 46 years old. But, he was alone because he and his wife of 21 years had divorced. And the passing of time had not yet healed the psychological wounds. Susan had remarried almost immediately, and their two teenage children now lived with her. Conner wanted to marry again. He missed the love of a good woman and the fullness that came with marriage. But so far he had not found the right person.

When Conner began his search for a home in Bryson City, a property agent listened to his needs and wishes, and without much hesitation, drove him to the top of a nearby mountain peak just minutes away from the center of town. As soon as they arrived at the site, Conner sized up the modest little dwelling, and his eyes then swept the view of the surrounding valleys below.

"This is where I want to live," he told her.

The quiet little town of Bryson City, which now had become Conner's adopted home, was nestled in the very heart of the Blue Ridge mountains -- only 20 miles east of the point where the North Carolina, South Carolina and Georgia borders merged. It was where the Blue Ridge Parkway began its 500-mile journey through the scenic valleys of Carolina and Virginia -- following gorges shaped long ago by the James and Potomac rivers.

Conner's cabin had the appearance of a summer cottage, which in many respects it was. And it was not that well insulated. The only source of heat was an oversized stone fireplace. So, when he moved in, he purchased a wood-burning stove, which was a great addition. Now, he had to be careful when he stoked it. Otherwise, the cabin could get too hot inside. Overall, the modest little house was solid, but not fancy – just the way he viewed himself.

Conner didn't own the whole mountain -- just an acre and a half at the very top. It was enough to accommodate his small home and a summer garden -- even room for possibly expanding at a later date.

But, this spot clearly was prime cut -- the center of the melon. And it gave him a million-dollar view of his surroundings. Given the choice, who wouldn't take the top of the mountain? he often asked himself.

There were a few neighbors, farther down the mountain. But, you wouldn't know it. The nearest house was quite a distance away, and it was virtually invisible during the summer months, with all the leaves on the trees.

Conner took one more deep breath of the crisp air on this morning, then glanced at his watch. It was getting late, and there was work to be done. He re-entered the cabin, and the wood-burning stove was now at peak efficiency. The warmth felt good to his face. Conner plugged in the coffee pot and pulled out the makings for breakfast. He'd be spending most of the day in the cold, and he needed to fortify himself against the elements. With the coffee on, he headed for the shower.

Mitch Conner's life had changed dramatically during the short time he'd been in Bryson City. He had traded a high-profile management job at a major Information Technology company in Atlanta for working as a self-employed wildlife photographer in the woods of North Carolina.

But he was no newcomer to photography. Even as a child, he was smitten with the magical nature of cameras and film. It was a passion that began with the old photos he took with his "Brownie" box camera. And that passion had grown as he expanded his knowledge of the processes for capturing images on film, and having the images developed, and then printed – first in black-and-white, and later in color. And he remembered the considerable time he spent in darkrooms, learning how to change sometimes ordinary pictures into great photographs, through, dodging and burning.

As an adolescent, Conner was awe struck with famed landscape and environmentalist photographer Ansel Adams – not a baseball player, not a football player nor a race car driver – but a widely acclaimed black and white photographer, Conner often pointed out. Adams, helped develop a process known as the Zone System, which utilized tonal range, exposure, negative development and specialized darkroom printing techniques to maximize photographic imagery. During the mid-1900s, Ansel Adams was one of the most celebrated photographers in the world.

Later in life, he worked closely with the U.S. Department of Interior, photographing the beauty of public parks, and history has remembered him for helping expand the National Park System through his pristine work. For his lifelong work, Ansel Adams was given the Presidential Freedom Award by

President Jimmy Carter, Conner liked to say. Conner also liked to tell friends and acquaintances the cost of buying an original Ansel Adams photograph these days would run about $100,000 or more.

But, the application of artificial intelligence had added a whole new dimension to the art of photography. Conner felt this new trend, in a sense, was cheating. It was more animation than photography. And he had no interest in it.

Photography also had been a fundamental element of Conner's undergraduate college courses for a degree in journalism. And he applied those skills at the time by working on the side as a newspaper photographer. But his opportunities as a writer had taken him in a different direction during a successful, 25-year career with IBM, mostly in Atlanta. Looking back at those early years, in some ways Conner felt he saw many of the things he achieved later in life, through the lens of a camera.

Now, after only a few months in Bryson City, he had developed quite a reputation for the creativity and artistry of his work, which he shared through area art galleries, at county fairs, festivals and at other public gatherings. And people were willing to pay good money - 100 dollars or more - for original copies of his pictures. Based on what he had already achieved, he was convinced he still had the eye for this game.

Conner's move to Bryson City also had caused other "image" adjustments. It had taken him less than a week at the cabin to realize his stylish sports car from his time in Atlanta wouldn't cut it in Bryson City. His second trip up the difficult road to the cabin was the final determinate. He needed a vehicle that could tackle these rough-and-tumble hills, the unpaved and pothole-filled dirt roads, and the underbrush-strewn mountain trails.

Luckily, a couple of new acquaintances told him about Eddie Chatworth.

Chatworth owned an Exxon station and auto repair shop on the outskirts of Bryson City. "He's the best mechanics in these parts," one of the acquaintances had said. "And he occasionally sells used vehicles he's rebuilt."

The other man claimed Chatworth, or Fast Eddie as they called him, came up with the popular line: "If it ain't broke, don't fix it."

In their first encounter, the mechanic nodded and smiled as Conner introduced himself. Eddie looked exactly like a mechanic should look. He hadn't shaved in a few days, his shirt had multiple oil stains, and his hands bore the dirt and grime of a man who worked with his hands. He was stocky, with curly black hair and a slightly olive complexion. He also had the forearms of a bar-room arm wrestler, Conner thought.

And when Eddie felt under pressure, or frustrated in some way, he stuttered.

Overall, Conner's impression of Chatworth was very positive. He seemed to be a personable and honorable man. And he was likeable. Conner explained his situation to Chatworth, who rubbed the stubble on his chin a bit before responding.

"Well, I got this old Bronco here. Ain't much to look at, and it's got a lotta' miles on it. But I just rebuilt the engine. Everything works. Brakes are new. Got good tires. And it's got four-wheel drive, which is right handy in these parts. It'll take anything you can throw at it."

Chatworth paused briefly in thought.

"I can let you have it for thirty-five hundred."

Conner smiled at the mechanic who peppered his comments with a slight stumbling of speech.

"You ever have any trouble with it, bring it back, and I'll fix what needs fixin'." Chatworth added.

Before responding, Conner smiled again, then walked slowly around the old Bronco gazing inquisitively as he walked.

You wanna' drive it?"

"Sure," Conner replied.

"Key's in it."

Conner slipped behind the wheel and twisted the key. The old machine immediately jumped to life, and the roar of the engine was that of a young colt ready to run. Conner changed gears and the transmission immediately propelled the Bronco into motion. As he turned the vehicle onto the roadway, the steering was tight and responsive with no wobble. Conner drove for about ten minutes, then headed back to the station.

Chatworth was inside his office when Conner returned. The owner met him and stood inquisitively as Conner climbed from the vehicle.

"You got a deal," Conner said, smiling.

The next morning, Conner got an early start on the day, which he planned to spend exploring the forests up near Cashiers. He had spent nearly an hour carefully packing his gear into the Bronco. And as he entered the cabin once more, he turned and looked back at his new transportation, the unsightly old Ford Bronco. It probably was at least 20 years old or more. But after a couple of months' use, it was doing just fine.

There was no way of knowing how many times this old antique had dragged its tired frame up these hills, through these woods and along the area's challenging roads.

This model of the Bronco was on the all-time list of classic American vehicles, one of the forerunners of the SUV, and a monster on wheels, owners of the vehicle liked to say. To this day, it was still the quarter horse of utility vehicles. And its ruggedness and durability were legendary. In fact, the Bronco had developed something of a cult following. Owners and aficionados held regular rallies, published newsletters and operated a sophisticated network for used and rebuilt parts. There even was a comprehensive home page on-line for Bronco owners.

Conner remembered chuckling the first time he saw the vehicle, which he now called "The Beast." It was so ugly, he found it appealing.

It had no major dents or flaws, but it's dark blue color had long since faded to a streakish color that was more gray than blue. This old warhorse would probably serve his immediate needs, he told himself. And he could always upgrade when the time was right.

With everything secured in the Bronco, Conner made one final trip to the cabin. From a bedroom drawer, he retrieved his 9-mm Walther and tucked it inside the small holster attached to the inside of his belt. This gun, in Conner's view, was the perfect choice for self-protection. It was accurate and light-weight. It had a 10-round clip and not much of a kick. It also was a proven weapon – a popular choice for both law enforcement and the military.

There were black bears in these woods. And if he found himself face-to-face with a bear, he didn't want to coax it with a candy bar or chase it with a stick. Besides, there were other types of creatures out there – both two-legged and four-legged. And he believed in playing it safe.

Convinced he was ready for the day, Conner slipped behind the wheel and pulled onto the road leading down the mountain. There were occasional lanes leading off the roadway for neighboring houses. Otherwise, the road was just over a quarter-of-a-mile and, at best, a rough ride.

The road base was a combination of crushed gravel and slag that was infrequently graded by the county. There were occasional rough spots and potholes, and Conner made himself a mental note to visit the Swain County Highway Department to try and get something done about the road's current condition. The good news was the cabin was located in Swain County and Bryson City was the County seat.

When Conner reached the base of the mountain, he pulled over and poured a cup of coffee from his big, red thermos. A little caffeine hit always helped jump-start his senses. Or so it seemed. The truth was, the caffeine in coffee just caused the heart to pump faster. And that probably wasn't good for anybody.

When he still worked in the corporate world, Conner drank coffee throughout the day. And it was standard to have a couple of cups before going into important meetings or before making presentations to high-level executives.

The mere thought of those days -- with all of the pressures, anxieties and frustrations – brought a frown to his face. But all of that was now in the past. That part of his life was over. But, he reminded himself there were good memories, as well. He had a number of friends who still lived in Atlanta, and he tried to keep in touch, at least by phone. Conner took a long sip of coffee and forced a smile as he pulled onto highway 28 leading into downtown Bryson City.

As he drove, his thoughts about Atlanta lingered. It was only about a two-hour drive away. But he didn't have any plans for making that trip any time soon.

But for many people in North Georgia and Western Carolina, Atlanta was still the place to go for serious medical attention, access to major league sporting events, big time cultural attractions and national and international travel.

Conner frequently used a well-known parable to describe his former home in Atlanta and what he called the southern experience. The parable was narrated by a lady with a very pronounced southern accent, and she was describing for a stranger the differences between various cities in Georgia:

"When you go to Au-gusta, they ask you what your grandmomma's name was. When you come to Atlanta, they ask you what business you're in. When you go to Macon, they ask you what church you go to. And when you come to Savannah, we ask you what you want to drink."

During the 1970s, the 1990s and into the 21st century, Atlanta had become the Alpha or Mega City of the South. Its population had increased from just over two million in the 1990s to almost six million by 2020.

And as the home base for Delta Airlines, Atlanta's airport also had become the largest and busiest in the world, servicing some 225,000 passengers a day. There was a popular saying that "if you died and were on your way to heaven, you'd have to change planes in Atlanta."

Conner had lived through this Atlanta transformation. And he was not real pleased with what had happened to this once chivalrous and genteel –

maybe even sleepy - little southern town. The change had come gradually, but it had changed nevertheless. Conner realized early on, that having hundreds of thousands of new residents pouring into the city each year would deeply affect Atlanta's persona and appeal. And he was right.

In Conner's mind, the changes were manifested in the way people interacted with one another… with the way they drove their cars…with the way they talked to each other…with the loss of certain courtesies…and with the possible loss of patience and tolerance among different ethnic and social groups.

Most importantly to Conner, this runaway growth could end up driving people away who no longer wanted to live in a much larger and busier Atlanta, as it did him.

It all started as a steady stream of refugees from cold weather states in the northeastern U.S., who moved to Atlanta for its moderate weather. This included people from states such as New York, New Jersey, Connecticut, Pennsylvania – even Massachusetts and New England. Others from the Rust Belt and Midwest were attracted to the growing number of new job opportunities in the South, and the moderate weather in Atlanta was just a bonus.

Being a native Southerner, Conner subconsciously took exception to this invasion and what was happening to the place he considered home. He also took exception to these newcomers' responses when asked how long they had lived in Atlanta.

All too often, they replied: "I've lived here for 10 years, I'm practically a native." When he heard that, which he often did, he wanted to say, "no, you're a native of New York…not Atlanta," but he never called anybody out. That would have been uncivil and rude. So instead, he typically smiled.

In a lighter sense, Conner also took exception to the unintentional attack on Atlantans' quaint dialect or Southern Speech. In Conner's mind, southerners tended to talk noticeably slower than most folks. And they frequently added additional syllables to words, and in some cases, they even eliminated syllables. And sometimes their pronunciation of words was inconsistent with how non-Atlantans or non-southerners pronounced things.

In the mid 1800s, Atlanta named a major street after Spanish explorer, Juan Ponce De Leon. And generations of Atlantans had grown accustomed to pronouncing the street Ponce De-leon. Much to Conner's dismay, the interlopers from other states began calling the street, Pon-ce-Da-Le-on.

And since Atlanta was home to the Coca Cola Company and its founder, the beverage of choice in the city was "Coke," or CoCola as locals called it. And these northern outsiders insisted that Coca Cola be called what it was back in their hometowns, simply a "soda."

Finally, those tasty nuts that are grown mostly in the south were called "Puh Cahns" by northerners, though locals prefer "Pee Cans." That pronunciation, as well, was probably headed for the dumpster, Conner thought. And despite his resentment toward these continued attacks against southernisms, the issue was both outrageous and unavoidable. And once again, all he could do was smile. Besides, there were other battles to be fought. That, too, brought a smile to his face.

Conner was not a native Atlantan, but he was a native Georgian. He was born in the coastal town of Savannah, which was about 250 miles down the interstates southeast of Atlanta. He had lived his early childhood in Savannah, where his father owned a dairy of some 70 milk cows.

But when he was 10 years old, his family – all of whom had southern accents -- moved to Atlanta, where they remained for several years before moving to Ohio. It was in Ohio that Conner lost his southern accent, though he never lost his kinship with the South.

CHAPTER THREE

It was nearly dusk when Conner stopped at his mailbox down by the highway. It had taken him a couple of months to get straightened out with the Bryson City Post Office. But now he was on an assigned delivery route. Still, after a few weeks with the Post Office, he concluded he shouldn't have made his presence known. It seemed like most of what he got was junk mail. And junk mailers were the cockroaches of society. Regardless where you went, they always found you and crawled back into your life.

Most of Conner's communications with family and friends was done by email or phone. Otherwise, there was an occasional magazine, greeting card or bill he received by mail.

But, for the past couple of weeks, he'd kept an eye out for a note from Western Carolina University. A few weeks earlier, he'd submitted a resume and his personal educational profile to WCU regarding a possible teaching job. It wasn't that he needed the money. He was doing pretty well financially. His early retirement package had included an immediate pension. And his hobby turned business had become pretty lucrative. He also was having great fun working as a photographer and doing what he'd loved to do. But he didn't know how long he'd be able to climb hill and dale chasing photographic opportunities.

He also was too young for total retirement. He knew several people who'd taken early retirement, only to become totally bored and had gotten back in the work-a-day world again. He felt lucky to have options that involved doing things that were compelling and fun. And there were other things he wanted to do in his life

For years, he had toyed with the idea of teaching writing in some form – whether creative writing or journalism. After all, it had been one of the reasons he obtained a master's degree. He often pictured himself in a university setting, wearing a tweed coat and smoking a pipe. But, after earning his degrees, he chose higher paying jobs in business. And he never took up smoking, and certainly not smoking a pipe, Nor, did he ever own a tweed jacket. Looking back, he had no regrets. But now, the idea was appealing to him again.

But the thought of becoming a professor also was a bit unsettling. At this point in his life, teaching represented a major new career move and starting over again.

He wasn't sure how he'd adjust to such dramatic change. And he was concerned about meeting everyone's expectations, including his own.

Would he be good at teaching? Conner frequently asked himself. In his mind, he was convinced he could do as well as most of the instructors he had in college.

Maybe better. And he reminded himself the same things that made him successful in business would serve him well in the classroom.

But, a major issue had evolved with the news media in this country. Freedom of the Press was clearly guaranteed in the U.S. Constitution, and the media's oversight or watchdog roles were often cited as being fundamental to the effective and transparent functioning of our government:

"Congress shall make no law respecting an establishment of religion, or prohibiting the free exercise thereof; or abridging the freedom of speech, or of the press; or the right of the people peaceably to assemble, and to petition the Government for a redress of grievances," was the way the Constitution spelled it out.

But in recent years, the media had blatantly dismissed these responsibilities. Instead of providing objective oversight for the people to judge, the media had joined special interests groups and big government to advance their own personal agendas - thereby becoming both judge and jury.

Such blatant role changes went against the grain of Conner's conscious-ness. And if he did become a journalism professor, he would do it to crusade for the media to reclaim its public reputation and trust, thereby embracing policies that served the citizens of our country again. Such an effort would have to start with reaching the hearts and minds of neophyte journalists who had not yet been corrupted by the system. And assuming he'd receive a response to his inquiry to WCU, he'd have to explore these ideas with some-one at the University.

In the meantime, he hoped to begin his new career by teaching in WCU's Continuing Education program, which was a "not for credit" offering. Such courses were generally held in the evenings and were popular mostly among housewives who were bored with their lives and had nothing better to do in the evening, Conner had heard before. Nevertheless, it would be a good first step to getting involved with the university system. And by making his inquiry with WCU, he had cast his lure. And it was time to see if there'd be any bites.

Everything Conner had heard and read about WCU was very positive. The University traced its beginning to the 1890s when it was established as the Cullowhee Academy. And in 1953 it became Western Carolina College.

In 1972 WCU was recognized as a constituent in the University of North Carolina system. In the past 10 years, the institution had become one of the fastest growing schools in the southeast, with a student population now of some 13,000.

Conner retrieved everything from the mailbox before gunning the Beast for the steep climb up the hill. When he reached the cabin, he turned on the lights and tossed the mail on the table. After discarding his coat and stoking the fire, he plopped down in the big leather chair and reached for the stereo.

The room came alive with the sounds of Beethoven's Ninth Symphony. Conner threw his head back and closed his eyes. The powerful music swept over him, washing away his thoughts, just as an ebbing tide erases footprints in the sand.

After several minutes of relaxation, Conner reached for the mail and began thumbing through the stack. He separated the throwaways from the keepers, putting the materials of interest on the top and the automatic throwaways on the bottom. As he neared the bottom of the stack, a letter caught his eye. It was from the Office of the Dean of Fine Arts, Western Carolina University. Conner immediately felt a rush of excitement.

He quietly stared at the impressive white envelope and its embossed lettering. The stereo reached one of his favorite parts of the Symphony, and he closed his eyes and devoted his attention to the music. After a few more moments, he raised the envelope to eye level again and took a deep breath. He was now ready to accept whatever was inside the letter. Carefully, he tore a strip down one side of the envelope, tapped the letter out and began to read:

"Dear Mister Conner:

Thank you for your letter regarding the possibility of joining Western Carolina University as an instructor in our Continuing Education program. I think your resume and credentials are impressive and your experiences appear to reflect a person with considerable communications skills. I must say, I'm also impressed with the thoroughness of your plan to enroll in our Advanced Degree program.

As for our Continuing Education program, it's quite vibrant, with a current enrollment of more than 250 students involved in a diverse range of courses, from accounting to creative writing. And your field of interest is one of the more popular of these offerings. Because of the discrete skills required for Continuing Education instruction, we routinely request an in-person interview, which would be our next step in this process. If this is acceptable to you, I suggest you call my secretary at the number below for a time that would be mutually convenient. I look forward to your reply.

Dr. Harrison Frees, Dean of Fine Arts, Western Carolina University."

A big smile crossed Conner's face. He threw his head back and dropped both hands over the arms of the chair -- the letter now dangling just above the floor. Conner lifted the letter and read it again, this time savoring the good news. This was a positive twist on his new experience in the mountains.

Looking back on his life, he had been blessed with considerable good fortune. Fresh out of the military, he had applied to and was accepted at the university of his choice. During his junior year, he was named editor of his college newspaper. And following graduation, he received a partial scholarship to a prestigious university for his master's degree.

The cabin was now filled with strains of Mendelssohn. In the background were the cracking and popping sounds of burning logs..

Conner returned his gaze to the wood burning stove and indulged himself in the warmth it radiated into the cabin. Just then, he felt very secure in this little cabin. He sat for several more moments, relishing this feeling of well-being.

Then, with the letter still in his hand, Conner pulled himself up from the big chair and stepped out onto the deck. He braced at the cold air, taking several deep breaths. As he looked through the darkness at the lights down below, he held up the letter and began to speak:

"Brace yourself Western Carolina University, Mitchell Conner's in town," he announced to the darkness.

CHAPTER FOUR

It was about nine o'clock when Conner emerged from the cabin. On this day, he planned on spending several hours exploring the forests with his cameras and capturing the wonder of fall in the mountains. The leaves were at their peak. And there was a cornucopia of waterfalls, cascading rivers, bubbling streams, sculptured rock formations and other examples of nature's beauty waiting to be shared. The possibilities were endless.

And his new gear was a far cry from what he used as a child and later as a student, he thought to himself. The cameras were all digital and electronics, with much better optics and built-in sensors that virtually eliminated constantly adjusting lenses and exposures to prevailing lighting conditions. There were exceptions, but the drill now seemed to be, point and shoot.

Once in downtown Bryson City, Conner turned east toward Sylva which was about 15 miles away along the Smoky Mountain Expressway. This first leg of the trip was mostly divided highway, and since moving here, he had become very familiar with this stretch of road. It seemed that wherever he headed, the trip always began down the road to Sylva. But it was a pleasant enough drive, meandering through the foothills of the mountains.

But, the next leg of the drive – from Sylva to Cashiers -- was a different story. This stretch was very narrow and winding. Along some portions, the outer drop-off was a couple of hundred feet. He always made a point to keep his eyes on the road and not look down. Most people considered this route from Sylva to Cashiers as hazardous, particularly during the winter months.

But, in Conner's view, the biggest threat on this road was the tourists. They didn't have a clue about driving in the mountains. And, for the most part, they certainly weren't qualified to drive under icy conditions.

After reaching Cashiers, Conner headed east for about three miles toward the iconic Whitehead Mountain, which was located in the Nantahala National Forest. That would be his final driving destination on this day.

Whitehead was one of the most scenic attractions in the Smoky Mountains, which was a sub-range of the Blue Ridge and Appalachian Mountains.

Whitehead got its name from the jagged, ivory-colored cliffs that rose more than 2,000 feet above the forest floor. The mountain's summit was more than 4,930 feet above sea level. And the south face was about 700 feet. In Conner's mind, this was another example of the magnificence of nature in this part of the country. And it was virtually in his back yard.

Just before he reached Whitehead, Conner pulled off the main highway and eased onto an old logging road. The abandoned road was beginning to blend in with the rest of the forest. Young saplings were quickly taking over. If allowed to grow unchecked, these young trees would soon render the road totally impassable.

As Conner drove into the unwieldy thicket, it occurred to him all the hand-wringing environmentalists who decried the loss of trees these days didn't give nature enough credit. Leave a field untilled or a roadway unused, and a forest would quickly re-assert its natural rights. Even if a road were paved, grass and seedlings would force their way through cracks and crevices to destroy these man-made encroachments. He had seen countless examples of that over the years

Conner followed the sandy road for about 300 yards. But the thickening ground cover made it impractical to continue. He parked the Bronco in a small turnaround and grabbed several pieces of equipment, which he transferred to a backpack. Using the backpack would make it easier for him to assault the underbrush and uneven terrain, using both hands if necessary.

Before leaving The Beast, Conner retrieved the 9 mm from its holster and checked to make sure the weapon was loaded and on safety. It was. He tucked the gun back inside his belt, grabbed the sling of his thermos and began making his way into the forest. Rising majestically over the tree line was the hazy image of Whiteside Mountain. He estimated it was about four miles away.

Conner's brisk pace and quick movements were those of a man younger than 46. For years, he had run at least three miles a day, four days a week. But now his exercise regimen consisted mostly of walking these hills on a regular basis and doing aerobic exercises. As he saw it, age was in the mind. And in his mind, he was only 21 years old. But when he expressed that view, people often gave him a rather peculiar stare.

After walking for about 10 minutes, Conner came upon a pristine mountain waterfall. The combination of sunlight and colors was spectacular. This would be the starting point for his shoot.

Conner slipped the knapsack from his back and took a seat on a fallen tree. It took a few seconds to attach a wide-angle lens to his camera.

Next, he made a slight adjustment and instinctively glanced up at the sky. With the sun popping in and out, he would probably have to make a few adjustments as he worked. It was the preparation and attention to details that separated good photographers from bad, he felt.

Conner began moving in an arch around the falls, snapping photos as he went. Nearly an hour passed. Satisfied that he had captured this setting from every conceivable angle, he packed up his gear and moved on. His camera was now suspended by a strap around his neck. As he walked through the trees, he was struck with one beautiful sight after another. And with each new opportunity, he paused and clicked off several exposures.

As Conner continued, he was venturing into areas he'd never explored. The trees were closer together, and the foliage was thicker. At one point, he began to struggle with the underbrush, and a passage from James Thurber's Thirteen Clocks came to mind: "The brambles and the thorns grew thick and thicker in a ticking thicket of bickering crickets. Farther along and stronger, bonged the gongs of a throng of frogs, green and vivid on their lily pads. From the sky came the crying of flies, and the pilgrims leaped over a bleating sheep creeping knee-deep in a sleepy stream, in which swift and slippery snakes skidded and slithered silkily, whispering sinful secrets."

Conner smiled at the imagery of the verse. Funny how the mind worked, he mused. He had not read Thurber in ages. Still these lines were etched in his memory. It was one of his favorite passages -- so descriptive, so lyrical.

Just then, something caught his eye. It was movement of some kind. He hesitated briefly, then slowly moved forward, choosing each step carefully. When he reached an open area, he stopped. The source of the movement was in plain view.

About 50 yards straight ahead was a white-tailed deer, grazing in a grassy meadow. Slowly, Conner raised the camera from around his neck and quickly snapped off several exposures. The doe's sensitive ears picked up the clicking, and her head shot up. With lightning speed, she bolted into the woods and disappeared. Another photographic opportunity had been short-lived. Being prepared for targets of opportunity was another asset in photography, he reminded himself.

Conner secured his camera and continued walking into the woods. With each step, he was careful to avoid the sharp and bristly ends of tree limbs, which could cause serious eye damage. Fortunately, he did not have to worry about the prickly thorns and briars. His clothing not only protected him from the cold, it totally insulated him from this intrusive underbrush.

He discovered very early that dressing appropriately was one of the prerequisites for living and working in these mountains. Whenever he worked in the woods, he wore camouflaged army fatigues and a three-quarter-length, all-weather coat. It was not only warm; it was moisture proof. The bulky coat had a polyester outer shell and an attached hood for really bad weather.

But, he seldom wore the hood. It restricted his visibility. He preferred a woolen stocking cap. His heavy-duty, waterproof boots were double-insulated and fleece-lined. They had the look of leather turned inside out. Sturdy and comfortable, they afforded protection in virtually any setting. In that respect, they were rather like ski boots. It was almost impossible to sprain an ankle with these babies.

Conner's gloves also were polyester, which he preferred over leather. Polyester was warmer than leather. But, the gloves were too cumbersome for operating a camera. So, when he worked, he stuffed them inside the big pockets of his coat.

The sun was now rather high on the horizon. Conner estimated the temperature to be around 40 degrees. He paused and looked at his watch. It was almost one o'clock. Climbing these hills had made him hungry.

And the exercise had elevated his body heat. He removed his coat, settled onto another downed tree and retrieved lunch from his backpack. It consisted of a cold chicken sandwich and an apple, which he washed down with another cup of coffee. This time, it wasn't the caffeine that he enjoyed. It was the warmth of the liquid. He tossed what remained of the apple core to the ground for some forest critter to enjoy.

With lunch over, Conner put his coat back on, grabbed his backpack and continued into the woods. He guessed he had travelled about four miles from the spot where he left the Bronco. He was now well beyond the range of tourists and hikers. That was good.

Every few minutes, something new caught his eye, and he stopped to snap off a few more exposures. Now and then, he also paused to reorient himself and get his bearings.

The last thing he needed was to get lost. But he had a pretty good sense of direction. Still, he made a mental note to buy a small compass at the next opportunity.

The combination of a full stomach and the cold crisp air were making him sleepy. For the next several minutes, he fought off the urge to find a pine straw mound and take a nap. Attractive as that idea sounded, it was out of the question. There were too many unknowns in these woods to take a nap. He forced himself to think of other things. This sleepiness would soon pass, he told himself.

The circumstances brought to mind an earlier period in his life -- the two years he had served in the U.S. Army. At age 19, he was drafted and shipped to Fort Knox, Kentucky for basic training. It was the middle of winter and temperatures hovered around the freezing mark, sometimes much colder. Each agonizing day, he and three hundred of his closest friends would assemble at dawn for breakfast.

Shortly thereafter, they would march off to a rifle range, a bivouac area or an infiltration course. It was not unusual for the recruits -- including himself -- to begin nodding off while sitting or standing in sub-30-degree temperatures. At least the Army had taught them to sleep in a variety of unusual settings, including the outdoors. He smiled at the thought. On the whole, being in the military had been a beneficial and positive experience. It had given him a sense of responsibility and taught him how to get along with others.

As Conner proceeded through the woods, he continued to fight off drowsiness. And his mind continued to wander. His thoughts now returned to a subject that was a frequent companion. It was the idea of being alone -- the idea of living and working alone.

For the first few days in the mountains, he had awakened in the middle of the night and questioned his decision. Funny how thoughts of uncertainty and insecurity invaded one's consciousness at night -- or when you were alone.

But after a few weeks in his new surroundings, the change in lifestyles had grown on him. Living here quickly felt comfortable. He was now convinced that he had done the right thing. He was happier now than he'd been in a long time. And his little house on top of the mountain truly seemed like home.

Still, living out here was not without its risks. It clearly was living life on the edge. He'd just have to accept the hardships and inconveniences that went with his choice. Up here, there were none of the conveniences that people in big cities took for granted.

There were no fancy movie theaters. Barbershops were scarce at best. There were no public restrooms. Even gas stations were few and far between.

If you ran out of gas up here or had car trouble, you probably were in for a long walk.

And, what would happen, he often asked himself, if he had a medical emergency? He consoled himself with the thought the worst that could happen was that he would die in the woods. That was not a bad way to go -- passing away among the chipmunks, the squirrels and the mountain laurel -- lying face up amidst the beauty of nature and gazing up at a quiet, peaceful sky.

In fact, such a fate was not without its advantages. If he died way up here, his soul wouldn't have as far to travel. That is, if it were travelling in the right direction. Again, he smiled.

Just then, Conner's thoughts were interrupted by the sound of rushing water. There was a stream up ahead. Maybe even another waterfall. As he continued, the rushing sound increased to a near roar. He was approaching the precipice of a small canyon.

He continued his advance, and finally spotted the source of the sounds - a raging stream dashing over rocks and boulders and pounding its fury into a churning pool of water. The force of this stream created a mist that rose to the top of the canyon walls. It was a spectacular view, and Conner stood for several seconds admiring the sight. This was all new, and he instinctively grabbed his camera and began shooting.

After several seconds, Connor paused and looked around. He had no idea where he was. But, his creative instincts kicked in, and he began looking around for a different angle to photograph. Some 30 yards above and to the right was a rocky ledge that jutted out over the falls. He turned and carefully climbed toward the ledge. Once there, he slipped the knapsack from his back and settled onto a huge rock. He sat for several minutes, catching his breath from the climb.

Conner then lifted the camera and swept it around, assessing the surroundings through his viewfinder. Slowly, his eyes focused on an object partially obscured by another boulder some 50 feet away. Out of habit, he lowered the camera to let his eyes take over. But, he had seen the object better through the viewfinder.

Once again, he peered at the object through the viewfinder, focusing the lens as he looked. His mood quickly changed from excitement to anxiety. Slowly, he removed the camera from around his neck and placed it carefully on the rock next to him.

He then stood erect, his eyes straining toward the spot he had just seen through the camera's lens. Conner then walked hesitatingly toward the big boulder.

His mind was now struggling with the image before him. Were his senses playing tricks on him? No. What he had seen was real. He paused at the big boulder and stared down. Lying before him were weathered pieces of clothing and what remained of a human body. This wasn't happening, he told himself. But, it was happening.

Based on what remained of the clothing, it appeared to be the body of a man. The exposed skull, with its jaws partially open, appeared to be staring straight at him and crying out some message of despair. Conner felt a queasiness in his stomach. He had only seen an exposed dead body one time in his life. And it had been a distressing sight. Now, as he stood over these remains, his mind vividly recalled that first experience.

What had happened here? Had this person died a natural death? Or had he been murdered? What should I do? he asked himself. Instinctively, Conner glanced around at the surrounding forest. Was he being watched? Was there anyone else out here – was there someone he could reach out to? Was there anyone else who could tell him what had happened? Anyone who could tell him what to do?

"Hell! I'm alone in the fucking woods. Who else would be crazy enough to be out here?"

"Sunovabitch!"

He continued looking around, mostly out of frustration. Nervously, he brushed his hand against his belt to assure himself the 9-mm was still there. The bulging presence of the weapon gave him comfort. Conner then returned his eyes to the sight before him.

After a few more moments of thought, he returned to the nearby ledge and retrieved his camera. Over the next several minutes, he took pictures of the remains from every conceivable angle. He also snapped close-ups of the skull from different angles. As he did so, he lowered the camera from his face and looked into what had been the man's face.

He then returned to his work, taking pictures of the surrounding area, including wide angle shots of the rocks and waterfall. These photos might be helpful to the police, he told himself. Conner then retrieved the rest of his gear and slipped the knapsack on his back. His photographic outing was over. He took one final look at the site before retreating from his lofty perch and re-entering the woods. The return trip to the old logging road would take him at least an hour.

CHAPTER FIVE

The following morning, Conner pulled the Bronco into the small recreational complex just east of Bryson City. It was a few minutes past seven o'clock, and the sun was just appearing over the mountains. He poured a cup of coffee from his thermos and glanced out at the baseball field straight ahead. That was where the chopper would land. And as he sat in the early morning mist sipping coffee, troublesome thoughts ran through his head. He had only been in the mountains for a few months, and he was already involved with the police.

"Damn! I don't need this," he muttered.

Conner consoled himself with the thought that he wasn't the reason for their visit. Nevertheless, he was still implicated. And he guessed this whole thing might be time consuming. When he moved to the mountains, he had sworn he would not get involved. Not with anybody. Not with anything. He swore he would solve his own problems and let other people solve theirs. He had come here looking for solitude. But now this. For Chrissake, this was precisely the kind of thing that had driven him from Atlanta.

Over the years, he had taken pride in being a positive person. He felt being born an optimist was a gift. And being optimistic about things thrown at you was a distinct advantage. In fact, he tried, as much as possible, to avoid people who were worry warts… people whose glasses were always half empty.… people who wouldn't cross the road because trouble may be on the other side. He felt people who think like that are often heart attacks waiting to happen. And he liked the admonition: "You spend all your time watching out for the ants, and the elephants will step on you."

Conner was convinced something positive would come from this experience, and he vowed to himself to dial it back a few notches and put this whole issue in the rear view mirror.

Just then, Conner's thoughts were dashed by the unmistakable sounds of the approaching helicopter -- the familiar thumping noise of whirling blades sending shock waves through the air. As it drew nearer, the chopper's presence was telegraphed by the high-pitched scream of its powerful engines. Conner looked in the direction of the approaching fury just as the chopper darted into view above the tree tops.

The North Carolina Air National Guard helicopter was an Apache AH-64A gunship, a Vietnam-era fighting machine.

Its rocket canisters were empty. But it still carried twin 50-mm cannons that could spit out 500 rounds a minute. The chopper's approach was an image he'd seen many times before -- in newsreels, on television and in person. And although its role on this morning was peaceful, it was still a menacing looking machine.

After clearing the nearby trees, the helicopter banked into a turn and nosed toward the center of the baseball field. A cloud of dust whipped up as the chopper settled onto the baseball diamond. It reminded him of a giant hen reclaiming her nest. The screaming of the chopper's engines subsided, and the big blades slowly ground to a stop. Almost on cue, the side door slid open, and two Macon County sheriff's deputies climbed out.

Each held on to his wide brimmed hat. The two men were dressed in gray uniforms and each wore distinctive Macon County Sheriff's Department patches and sidearms. Once outside the downblast of the blades, the deputies turned and walked toward Conner. Almost reluctantly, Conner climbed from his vehicle and met the two officers approaching him..

"Mister Conner, I'm deputy John Eassel, and this here's deputy Rife Bramley."

Conner nodded to the two and reached his hand out in greeting.

Deputy Eassel was short, no more than five feet eight. But he was powerfully built. He had gray hair and green eyes. His face was weathered, but he had a pleasant, almost scholarly look. Eassel appeared to be in his early fifties. Conner's first thought was that the deputy looked more like a teacher than a cop.

Conner's glance then shifted to Deputy Bramley, who was tall and gangly. What a contrast between the two men. Bramley had big hands and big feet. He also had red hair and a long, crooked nose. But his demeanor was friendly, almost like that of a big puppy. He was much younger than Eassel, probably no more than 35.

The three men stood and talked for several minutes. Deputy Eassel gestured freely with his hands. The other deputy stood silently, nodding his agreement with what was being said. When the conversation ended, Eassel turned and led the way back to the helicopter. Conner and Bramley followed. As they reached the chopper, the deputies instinctively grabbed their hats -- even though the big blades hung lifelessly overhead.

Eassel held the door, and the other two climbed aboard. There was a brief exchange inside the aircraft as Eassel introduced Conner to the pilot, Major Jonathan Worley. The major wore the familiar khaki flight jumpsuit of all Air Force pilots. He removed his headset and reached out to shake Conner's hand, flashing a friendly smile as he greeted his new passenger.

Worley was of average build, had bright blue eyes, well-defined features, and his light brown hair was noticeably receding. His manner and personality gave him an aura of intelligence and serious competence. Conner was immediately impressed. He liked doctors and pilots who had an intelligent look about them.

The major watched closely as his passengers climbed into their seats. Satisfied that everyone was buckled up, the pilot replaced his headset and turned back to his responsibilities in the cockpit. Instinctively, he glanced to either side and to the rear of the chopper. The surrounding area was clear.

He then deliberately reached for the control panel and began flipping switches.

Slowly, the powerful engines screamed back to life, and the giant blades began to revolve. Within seconds, the rotors were a circular blur and the chopper shook with restrained power. Once again, the major glanced outside before changing the blade pitch and pushing the yoke forward. The chopper darted off the ground, and they were airborne.

Conner had been in helicopters a couple of times. And the flights had not been altogether pleasant. After all, he wasn't particularly fond of heights. In fact, he suffered from acrophobia.

As a child, he had not relished carnival rides that suspended him high above the ground. And helicopters brought out the worst of such feelings. He remembered the first flight he'd ever taken in a helicopter. Friends had talked him into it. It was a sight-seeing excursion in Hawaii. As soon as he sat down in the chopper, he knew he had made a mistake.

The helicopter was one of those little glass bubble machines that looked like a giant light bulb. The flooring was Plexiglas, and he could look straight down at the ground.

The initial part of the flight was not bad. After lifting off, the pilot proceeded toward a large mountain range straight ahead. He was flying at no more than 300 feet, skimming just above a giant field of sugar cane. Workers in the field looked up as the noisy chopper passed overhead, and Conner could clearly see their faces. At this height, the flight was almost exhilarating.

But, the pilot banked to his right and nosed the chopper skyward. Conner looked down and the ground started receding quickly.

Suddenly, he felt an uneasiness in his stomach. The chopper climbed to about 5,000 feet and leveled off. Conner looked nervously back at the other passengers and tried to make small talk. But his mind was clearly on the ground below.

This was a very un-natural state. There were no wings to glide them back to earth in the event of a mechanical failure. And there was a constant vibration from the spinning rotors, reminding them that they were defying the laws of gravity. He felt like he was being suspended on a string.

The flight got worse as they neared the mountain peaks. Winds sweep up the mountain from the valley below, creating turbulence that buffeted the little aircraft like a balloon in a thunderstorm.

For a fleeting moment, Conner considered asking the pilot to set down on top of the mountain so he could walk back down. But, he gained control of his emotions and gutted it out. Still, he swore that he would not get into another helicopter any time soon. These thoughts ran through his head as he looked down now at the trees of the Nantahala Forest. Conner estimated they were flying at about 1,000 feet. At this height, he did not feel uncomfortable. The cushioning appearance of the trees below were giving him a false sense of security.

At deputy Eassel's urging, Conner provided Major Worley with in-flight directions for reaching the remote waterfall. The major flew to nearby Highlands, largely proceeding along the main surface roads to accommodate Conner's sense of direction. As they neared Cashiers, Conner identified the old logging trail he had used to reach the site.

The rest of the search was not as easy as Conner thought it would be. From the air, his orientation was less definite. Still, he knew the direction he had taken on foot from the logging road.

And he knew how long it had taken him to reach the waterfall. The major made a rough calculation, comparing flight time to walking time. He then flew a northeasterly course for about five minutes and spotted a stream down below.

The major then banked the helicopter to the right and began following the stream toward its source. After a couple of minutes, Conner spotted the waterfall, though it was partially obscured by the giant trees surrounding the area. Again, Major Worley banked the chopper and began flying an elliptical pattern so that Conner could get a better view. This definitely was the waterfall, all right. Conner could not see the boulder that obscured the remains. But, he pointed out the general area to Deputy Eassel.

Major Worley circled the area for several more minutes, both for his benefit and for that of Deputy Eassel. The forest here was too thick to even consider a landing. It would be up to Worley to find a spot where they could put down later.

Again, at deputy Easel's request, Worley continued circling, giving Eassel time to clearly mark the area on his topographical map. With this done, Worley banked the chopper and headed back to Bryson City. Conner had done his job. It would now be up to the Macon County Sheriff's office to physically visit the site, retrieve any evidence and remove the remains.

Conner offered Deputy Eassel the photos he'd taken at the site. He also asked the deputy if he'd keep him informed of what they found. The deputy told him he would.

When the chopper landed back at the baseball field in BC, Conner was the only one to exit. He nodded his head to the others, and walked away in a stooped position to avoid the big rotors turning slowly overhead. Standing well away from the chopper, he returned the pilot's wave and quickly walked toward the Bronco.

There was a sudden burst of sound, and the chopper lifted off again. Conner turned and looked back. He watched as the aircraft hovered momentarily, then disappeared above the tree line.

As he stood there alone, he told himself his role in this incident was over. He had met his civic responsibilities by calling the police. The matter was now theirs to handle. But there was something about it that still bothered him. Maybe it was just a matter of his curiosity, and the fact he had a lot of questions and no one to ask.

He shrugged off the thoughts with a sigh. There were other things to be done on this day. He then retrieved the Beast and headed home.

CHAPTER SIX

Nearly a week had passed since Conner accompanied the Macon County deputies on the flight to Cashiers. So far, he'd heard nothing more about it. He wasn't particularly concerned. He tried to dismiss the entire experience, but it continued to nag at his consciousness. Day and night, vivid images of what he'd seen flashed through his mind. Maybe if he found out who the guy was -- or if he knew the circumstances surrounding the man's death -- he could put it behind him. In the meantime, all he could do was busy himself with his work.

On this day, Conner spent most of the morning and afternoon taking photographs of the Cullasaja River, which twisted and turned as it made its way from Highlands to Franklin along highway 64. Along this stretch, the Cullasaja swirled around rock formations and spilled over cliffs -- dropping nearly 3,000 feet in elevation as it raced to Franklin some 30 miles away.

The combination of churned white water and cascading falls provided visitors with spectacular views that were Mother Nature at her best.. It was breathtakingly beautiful. But the roads that followed the river's path were treacherous. And for those responsible for driving along this road, the focus was totally on the dangers that hovered on both sides, not the surrounding beauty. In some sections, the drop off along the narrow road was more than 300 feet. Driving on this road was clearly white-knuckle time.

It was now a few minutes before five, and the sun was drawing close to the horizon. The amount of available light was too low to get decent exposures. Conner packed away his gear, loaded it into the Bronco and drove back to Bryson City.

When he pulled to a stop in front of the cabin, it was almost six o'clock. The temperature had slipped back below freezing, and a light snow was beginning to fall. The fading sunlight -- mixed with the swirling snowflakes -- created an eerie glow in the sky. It was a beautiful sight and Conner lingered for a few minutes, admiring the view. Before stepping inside, he gazed down at the valley below. Here and there, he could see trails of smoke rising from chimneys. The thought of crackling fires in those homes gave him a secure feeling that all was right with the world.

Once inside the cabin, Conner moved about turning on lights. It was a little chilly, and he instinctively rubbed his hands together. Time to stoke the fire, he told himself. He retrieved a few logs from the stone hearth and banked them in the stove. Simmering coals were still glowing from the morning's fire. In a matter of seconds, the dry logs erupted in flame. Conner then reached for the stereo and the room was suddenly filled with classical music.

He threw his coat on the hall tree and slumped into the big leather chair just across the room.

After unlacing his boots, Conner used one foot at a time -- toe against heel process -- to dislodge the heavy shoes. He then eased back and closed his eyes. Over the strains of Mozart's Eine Kleine Nachtmuski, (A Little Night Music), he listened to the logs crack and pop as they continued to burn in the wood stove.

It would be easy, he told himself, to sit here and fall asleep. But that was out of the question. He was hungry. And besides, it was Friday. He was not in the mood to spend this evening alone.

He forced his eyes open and pushed himself out of the chair. He turned up the stereo volume and headed for the shower just off the main bedroom.

Conner's cabin was virtually square. On the south end was a combination living room and breakfast nook. Together, the two areas occupied about half the cabin's floor space on this level. At the far end of the room was a big picture window that provided a spectacular view of the mountains.

A door next to the window opened onto the wooden deck, which he'd added after moving in. Conner had plans for an addition to what now was the kitchen. That would allow expanding the living room area to cover the whole fireplace wall and increasing the size of the picture window overlooking the valley below.

And mounted in the corner of the "front door" wall was a large screen television set, primarily for watching college football and old movies. The flooring on the main level was all hardwood, which he also had installed. There was the big stone fireplace against the outer wall. But, it was now obscured by the wood-burning stove, with its venting pipe extending up into the chimney. Conner didn't miss the fireplace. It couldn't match a wood-burning stove for heating efficiency. Besides, the stove was something of an anchor point in the room.

Dividing the breakfast nook and the small kitchen was a narrow island counter. A short hallway at the rear of the kitchen led back to two modest bedrooms in back. Off to the left of the hallway was the stairwell for a large room downstairs. Conner used the room for storage. There also were two doors on the lower level. One opened to the back yard. The other was for the carport just underneath the living room.

After taking a shower, Conner slipped into a navy blue sports shirt and a pair of jeans. He then grabbed his brown leather jacket from the hall closet. The jacket was one of his favorite items of clothing. It was casual but dressy. And it gave him an air of respectability, he thought.

Before leaving the house, Conner adjusted the stove's flue to reduce the heat. The fire would now smolder for hours. He then turned off the stereo and most of the lights. As he walked to the Beast, big wet snowflakes brushed against his cheeks.

The snow was coming down harder now, and the ground was covered with a blanket of white. There weren't too many sights prettier than falling snow, he told himself.

Conner climbed behind the wheel and headed down the mountain. As he drove through town, he gazed casually at the shops and commercial buildings along Main Street. It was not yet seven o'clock. But everything in Bryson City was closed tighter than a drum. The only businesses open were Billy's Shell station and the UGA supermarket.

Bryson City, or BC as Conner occasionally called it, was a town of about 2,000 people. They were honest, blue-collar folks who left their doors unlocked and attended church regularly. Their strong faces reflected pride and determination, in Conner's view. Here, a man's word was his bond. And most people considered it their responsibility to help their neighbors.

But life was hard.

Many residents tended small pieces of land and sold fruits and vegetables to friends and neighbors to make a little extra money. But most held down full-time jobs in nearby Sylva or Waynesville. Some even drove 40 miles away to Asheville, where they were employed in machine shops or in processing plants. And since money was hard to come by, bartering was commonplace.

Tradesmen had no problem swapping their skills for other goods and services. It was a tradition that traced its roots back to the turn of the century.

Most residents of Bryson City also owned guns, whether for hunting or recreational use. Crime was virtually non-existent. Ten years had passed since the last murder was recorded. That involved a jealous husband who shot and killed his wife's suitor.

The town's police force consisted of a chief, Daryl Parsons, and six officers. Police activity typically involved traffic control, patrolling the highways and responding to an occasional drunk-and-disorderly call.

Bryson City also had a volunteer fire department, which was housed on Main Street in the same public safety building as the police department.

The downtown area was dotted with a mixture of small businesses and retail establishments. There was the usual collection of clothing, hardware, automotive and grocery stores. The restaurants were mostly fast-food places.

During the summer months, a flashback tourist train from the 1940s ran between BC and Sylva twice a day. The Great Smokey Mountain Railroad was originally a part of the Southern Railway system, a major passenger and freight carrier prior to World War II. The four-hour train excursion took tourists back in time over tracks that traversed a tunnel and multiple old bridges that forged river gorges, including the legendary Nantahala gorge.

The train had become a favorite subject for Conner's cameras, with several photographs he'd taken of the old steam engine now very popular with tourists. But most of the visitors who walked through Bryson City's streets, including those who had taken the excursion, left little behind in the shops and stores there.

When asked about the summer tourists, one store owner confessed to Conner: "They buy a few ice cream cones and take a leak. That's about it."

When Conner reached the north side of town on this evening, he turned into the gravel driveway leading back to the Fryemont Inn. In his view, the Fryemont was something of an oasis. It was elegant and urbane -- a striking contrast to the surrounding area. From its lofty perch on the side of a hill, the Inn looked down on the scenic Tuckasegee River, which wound through the center of Bryson City.

Conner discovered the Inn shortly after moving to the mountains. It was a great place to relax, unwind and have a couple of drinks. And the food also was very good.

Many items on the menu were regularly featured in gourmet magazines and in cookbooks. Specialty dishes included venison, trout, steaks, prime rib, homemade soups and a variety of fresh-baked breads and pastries.

The first time Conner stopped at the Fryemont, he was struck with the staff's friendliness and hospitality. Here, guests were guests, whether they were having a cocktail, a lavish seven-course meal, staying at the Inn or simply stopping in to ask directions. Newcomers immediately felt welcome.

Fryemont's main lodge featured 37 chestnut-paneled bedrooms, with private baths, and luxurious appointments. There were additional cottage suites in adjacent stone and cedar buildings.

All of the rooms had large windows that could be opened for guests to enjoy the crisp mountain air or listen to the sounds of the wilderness at night. In the main lobby, double French doors opened onto a sprawling rocking chair porch, providing a magnificent view of the mountains. Just beyond the porch was a large swimming pool nestled in a grove of hemlock, dogwood and poplars.

During his first visit, Conner read a promotional flyer which described the Inn's history. The Fryemont was listed on the National Register of Historic Places. It was designed and built by Amos Frye, a wealthy resident who made a fortune in the timber business during the late 1800s.

Frye's dream was to share the natural beauty of the Smokies by creating an alluring mountain retreat for tourists. Guests of the Inn, Frye boasted, would experience true southern hospitality, impeccable accommodations, unparalleled service and elegant dining.

For the construction, Frye used the finest chestnut, oak and maple trees he could find. And he covered the exterior with natural bark siding from huge poplar trees. He wanted the structure to blend in with its magnificent surroundings.

The Fryemont opened for business in 1923, and it was an immediate success. It was everything Frye had hoped for. Guests flocked in from across the eastern seaboard, arriving mostly by train at the Bryson City railroad station. There, they were met by carriage and transported to the Inn.

In Conner's mind, Frye's passion for quality workmanship had contributed to the Inn's longevity through the years. Physically, the structure was as sturdy today as it was when it was built.

There also was the matter of the surrounding area's appeal. Those things that lured tourists in the early days were as compelling now as they were then.

They included the wondrous beauty of the Blue Ridge Mountains, the area's moderate summer temperatures, and the many nearby attractions -- including parks and wildlife preserves. Plus, the surrounding brooks and streams offered some of the best trout fishing in the country. In short, this section of the mountains was a nature lover's paradise.

But, most importantly, the management and staff had maintained a passion for service over the years that contributed to its success. The Inn was now in its second century of operation, and there weren't many businesses that could lay claim to that.

As Conner entered the Fryemont on this evening, he paused in the foyer and glanced out over the big dining room to his right. Except for waiters putting final touches on place settings, the room was virtually empty. The dinner crowd had not yet begun to arrive.

The dining room had spacious paned windows and gleaming hardwood floors. All of the tables were covered with white linen cloths, sparkling silverware and folded napkins protruding from crystal glasses. A lighted candle and fresh flowers made up the centerpieces.

A huge, stone fireplace dominated the entire wall at the rear of the room. The fireplace was big enough to accommodate logs up to eight feet in length. Virtually all year long -- with the exception of the hot summer months -- the big hearth was stoked with a crackling fire.

As Conner gazed at waiters scurrying about, delectable aromas of food cooking on stoves in the kitchen wafted out over the big room. It was wonderful. He lingered for another moment, then turned and walked into the lounge just to his left. The dimly lit room had vaulted ceilings and was separated from the foyer by several oak columns, connected by railings. A number of large green plants provided additional privacy for lounge patrons.

The room was richly appointed, starting with the black marble top on the bar and its rich walnut base. Plush green carpeting covered the floor. Behind the bar was a long, smoked-glass mirror, with rows of liquor bottles tiered in front. Three brass and wood paddle fans turned slowly overhead.

Pin lights suspended from the ceiling provided minimal lighting along the bar – but enough to read labels on beer bottles. In Conner's view, that was all the light that was needed in a bar.

During his travels in Europe, Conner had discovered that Europeans -- particularly the French and the Germans -- had a penchant for bright, harsh lighting in their pubs and restaurants. He didn't understand that. In his mind, bright lights were for doctors' offices and police interrogation rooms, not bars. People went to bars to have a couple of drinks and mellow out. They didn't go there to read.

On this evening, there were only a few patrons in the lounge. Most of them were seated at tables in the open area. A young couple, waiting to be seated in the dining room, sat at the far end of the long bar. Conner slipped onto a chair about half way down the bar and smiled at J.D. Stricker, the bartender.

"Whatta ya' say, J.D."

"Hey, Mitch! Nice to see ya.'"

Conner nodded and smiled as he settled on a chair right in front of Stricker.

The bartender reached out and gripped his hand. Then, without breaking eye contact, Stricker lifted a bottle of Dewar's from the well and looked expectantly at his customer. Mitch nodded his approval. Stricker then skillfully poured the amber liquid over an ice-filled glass and slid it across the marble top. The glass was one of those big, man-sized tumblers that Conner liked -- not one of those dainty little things you'd find at a woman's tea party.

The first time Conner had visited the Fryemont lounge, he got the impression Stricker was unfriendly -- maybe even arrogant. Contributing to this were his sophisticated manner and his outspokenness. In a couple of instances, Stricker appeared to be rude with some of his customers. But Conner's first impression turned out to be wrong. Stricker was just an intelligent and well educated person. And he didn't have a lot of patience with stupid people, who seemed to be in abundant supply in some bars.

Stricker also was very cautious. But, once you got to know him, he could be very friendly and engaging. And he had a good sense of humor. Conner guessed the bartender to be in his mid-fifties. He wore a typical uniform: a black vest, black pants and a bow tie. This gave him a rather formal appearance. He also was tall -- about six feet two. And he had sharply chiseled features, hazel eyes and a ruddy complexion. His receding gray hair was combed straight back.

Though Conner had talked to Stricker on several occasions, he knew very little about the man's personal life. Stricker simply wasn't one to offer much about himself. But he did say that prior to becoming a bartender, some six years earlier, he worked at a major bank in Chicago.

With Stricker looking on, Conner swirled the Scotch around in the big glass for a few seconds and took a long sip. As he savored the taste of the cold liquid, he held the glass up before him and looked squarely at Stricker, who was standing in front of him.

"Ya' know, I don't know why I drink this damn stuff. It tastes terrible."

The bartender chuckled. As he responded, he began wiping water spots from freshly washed wine glasses, intermittently holding the glasses up to inspect his work.

"Yeah. is pretty nasty-tasting stuff. Makes you wonder if the people who concocted it intended it for human consumption. But, I guess it's another one of those things that you gotta' develop a taste for. Kinda' like marriage."

Conner chuckled and took another sip. Before he could respond, Stricker leaned forward with both hands now on the bar.

"I remember the first time I had a martini. I hated it. I still don't like the taste. But, it's a helluva' drink. If you wanna' get a quick buzz, or tie one on real quick, a martini's your poison. It's the alcoholic version of overdrive."

Conner smiled and looked down at his drink.

"Yeah. I know what you mean about those things. Drinking a martini, in my mind, is like blasting off in a space rocket. Once you realize you've had too much, it's too late. It gets worse."

Stricker chuckled and paused briefly,

"Hey, you seem a little pre-occupied tonight."

Conner paused before responding.

"I've had a rather interesting week."

"Interesting? That could mean a lot of things."

Conner smiled and looked up from his drink.

"Yeah. I guess it could."

Again, Conner paused before continuing..

"I was working up near Whiteside a few days ago. Stumbled into something I didn't bargain for... found some human remains out there in the woods."

"You found a dead body?"

"Yeah. What was left of'em, anyway? Far as I could tell, it was a man."

Before Stricker could respond, Conner continued, his voice now intense.

"You ever see a dead body before? Not just in a funeral home. But, somebody who's been dead for a while," Conner asked.

"Well, no. Not exactly."

"This was the second time for me. The first was when I was in college. I was working part-time for a small newspaper. Green as a grass snake. My editor heard over the police radio they found a body, and he sent me over to check it out. When I got there, police chief Grubb took me aside. Asked me if I'd ever seen a stiff before."

"I told him no. He laughed and sent me upstairs. The guy was on the floor of his bedroom, and he apparently had died of a heart attack."

"The body had been there for several days, and it was three times the normal size. The smell was awful. I couldn't eat for a coupla' weeks."

Stricker nodded his understanding without responding.

Conner continued: "That experience reminded me the dignity of man is just a term. And it gave me a reality check about our mortality."

Again, Stricker nodded and looked intently at Conner.

"That's pretty heavy stuff," Stricker said, before continuing his questions.

"What'd you do about the body in the woods?" he asked.

"When I got home, I called the Macon County Sheriff's office. Next day, they picked me up in a helicopter, and I showed them the site where the remains were."

"I'll bet flying in that helicopter was a kick."

"Not for me."

Stricker smiled.

"They find out who he was?"

"I doubt it. As far as I know, it's still a work in progress. I haven't heard anything more about it, and they told me they might need to ask me more questions."

"You'd think something would have been in the papers or on TV. I haven't seen anything."

"No. Me either."

"How long you think the guy was out there?"

"I have no idea. But it was a while. Wasn't much left but a skeleton and the remnants of some clothing."

"What's your guess? You think he was murdered?"

Conner was surprised at the question.

"Murdered? I don't have a clue. But, nothing surprises me anymore. There weren't any shell casings or axes nearby, if that's what you mean."

Stricker shrugged. There was a brief silence, and the bartender resumed wiping water spots from the wine glasses. He glanced quickly at the couple at the end of the bar and then looked back at Conner.

"You know, the odds are they'll never find out who the guy was."

"Whatta' ya' mean?"

"Well. There are some people around here who don't want their identities known. They'd just as soon go unrecognized. In fact, I've run across a few characters that I swear are in the witness protection program."

"You serious?"

"Dead serious. Actually, they're pretty easy to spot. They seem out of place, and they don't ever talk about their past -- even if you ask. Course, it helps that folks up here don't pry into other people's business. They respect privacy."

"In fact, there appears to be to be an unwritten rule around here: 'Don't ask me any questions, and I won't ask you any.'"

Conner looked at Stricker and shrugged. Before he could respond, the bartender continued.

"If a guy were looking for somewhere to hide, this would be the perfect place."

Conner thought about the statement. When he re-established eye contact with Stricker, there was a smile on his face.

"J.D. You've just described your own situation. You're not in the witness protection program are ya?"

The bartender laughed out loud, rolling his head back. He then leaned close to Conner and smiled, his eyes sparkling.

"If I were, I wouldn't tell you about it. Let's just say there are some people I'd just as soon not see anytime soon. Besides, If I were trying to hide out, I wouldn't be working as a bartender. In this job, you're exposed to too many people."

"Maybe the people you're hiding from don't come into bars."

Again, Stricker laughed.

"Good point."

The bartender returned to wiping glasses. He then looked back at Conner.

"There's another thing I've discovered about folks up here. If somebody's in a jam, these people will help out with few questions asked. These days, you don't find that too much."

Conner looked intently at Stricker without responding. He lifted the Scotch to his lips and took another long sip. Again, the bartender leaned forward and spoke in a near whisper.

"Remember that young guy who was running from the FBI several years back? The one who was wanted for the bombings at the Olympic Games in Atlanta?"

"Rudolph I think his name was. There musta' been two hundred agents climbing these mountains, looking for him. And they couldn't find a trace for quite a while. Now, you can't tell me he escaped all those cops on his own. He had to have had some help. But, he was in friendly territory. People up here understand what it's like to be under the gun. Or maybe they just like to defend the underdog. Who knows? But, in my mind, somebody gave that young man lotsa' help."

Stricker leaned back, a wry smile on his face.

"Yeah. You're probably right," Conner said.

Stricker walked away to care for another customer, and Conner's mind drifted in thought. He vividly remembered the fugitive from justice the bartender mentioned. The guy had killed several people and injured hundreds of others with those bombs he planted, first at the 1996 Olympic Games and later at other sites in Georgia and Alabama.

The bomber eluded police – including nationwide efforts by the FBI – for about five years. Authorities suspected the suspect had possible ties in Western Carolina and that he probably was very familiar with the area and its terrain. It was only by accident the guy was discovered and arrested in 2003. He was found rummaging food from a grocery store dumpster in Murphy, NC, only 40 miles from Bryson City.

Some sources were convinced the suspect, indeed, had assistance from sympathetic locals, though officials denied such a link. Conner smiled to himself and stared at his now empty glass on the bar.

"The truth is probably somewhere in between, he thought to himself. It usually is."

Without prompting, Stricker grabbed another glass, filled it with ice and poured a generous amount of Dewar's on top. He placed it deliberately in front of Conner who returned the bartender's gaze.

"Don't you live near Cashiers?"

Stricker hesitated momentarily. There was a vagueness in his reply.

"Yeah. Actually I'm closer to Tuckasegee. But I spend a lot of time in Cashiers. Highlands too."

Conner smiled thoughtfully.

He was just about to ask another question when a middle-aged man and woman entered the lounge and took seats down the bar to his left.

Conner gazed at the pair briefly. The man had dark hair that appeared to be dyed, and a paunchy face. His noticeable girth was concealed by a well-tailored, brown plaid sport coat. On the little finger of both of his hands were gaudy pinky rings.

The woman had bleached blond hair, and she wore too much makeup. She was attractive, but her appearance was one of a woman trying to hang on to the past.

The man and woman did not appear to be locals. Conner guessed they were tourists. Probably man and wife. The man smiled at Conner before turning his attention to the bartender. The woman was already busy giving details on what she wanted to drink. Conner continued to stare curiously at the pair.

Just then, Conner's attention was diverted by two women who entered the bar and took seats to his right. He glanced quickly in their direction and then returned his gaze to Stricker, who was in the midst of preparing drinks for the middle-aged couple at the other end of the bar.

The lounge was starting to get busy. And the conversation with Stricker was probably over, he told himself. Conner still had other questions he wanted to ask the bartender. But they'd have to wait. There were too many customers around to engage in small talk now. Conner glanced back to his right. The two women were deeply engaged in conversation.

The one closest to him was very attractive. Conner guessed her to be in her late thirties or early forties. The woman had high cheek bones and a rounded face.

Her features were less than perfect, but she was well groomed, and she had beautiful skin.

When she talked, her green eyes sparkled. She also had an ample figure and was well dressed. Her light brown hair was tied up in back, and it bobbed back and forth as she moved her head. There was a sensuousness and sophistication about her that Conner found compelling. And he could tell by her movement she knew she was being watched.

The woman's companion was less attractive. But, she too was well dressed, and she had a cultured appearance. She had plain features, somber brown eyes and long black hair that hung down to her shoulders. She wore oversized, horn-rimmed glasses. She also was shorter than her companion, and she appeared to be a little overweight. This woman looked rather melancholy, he thought.

Conner always found it interesting to look at strangers and try to guess what they did for a living. These two could be anything, he told himself. Bankers. Lawyers. Sales representatives. Corporate executives. Maybe even doctors. Or they could be high-priced hookers, for that matter. One never knew. The absurdity of the thought caused him to chuckle to himself. They weren't hookers.

As Conner gazed at the women, the one closest to him turned and smiled. He returned the smile and then looked away. He did not want to come across as prying or being intrusive.

Stricker then appeared before the two women and initiated a playful conversation. Both of the women were amused by the bartender's friendliness. Both laughed openly at his comments and flirtations. Clearly, Stricker was playing to the more attractive one. It occurred to Conner that he didn't know if Stricker was married or single. But, it didn't matter. The bartender was just being friendly with his guests.

Conner could not help but overhearing every word of what was being said. To his surprise, the woman next to him ordered a Beefeater martini with a twist. The other woman ordered a glass of Chardonnay.

Stricker then turned and began a flashy display of bartending skills for the women. Conner looked on as an amused observer. First, Stricker pulled a bottle of uncorked Chardonnay from a refrigerated cabinet and poured a sample into a chilled wine glass.

He pushed the oversized glass toward the second woman, who looked at him and smiled. She raised the glass, took a modest sip and nodded her approval.

Stricker then dashed the contents of the bottle into the glass until it was three-quarters full. The woman thanked him in a soft-spoken voice.

Next, Stricker retrieved a martini glass from an overhead rack and filled it with ice. He added water and set the glass aside to chill. He then grabbed a metal tumbler and topped it off with more ice. From an overhead shelf, he retrieved a bottle of Beefeater gin and began pouring the clear liquid into the tumbler, raising his hand high in the air to create a long stream of alcohol. As he poured, his female customer's eyes grew wide at the amount of gin being dispensed. She looked shyly at her friend and giggled.

Stricker then reached for another bottle and added what appeared to be three drops of vermouth. After topping off the tumbler, he held it in the air, shaking it vigorously as if it were a maraca -- first above one shoulder and then the other. Picking up the martini glass, he dashed its icy contents to the floor and raked a lemon peel around the top edge.

He then dropped the peel inside the glass, removed the tumbler lid and reverently poured the martini into the chilled glass. When the last drop fell from the tumbler, the glass was filled to the brim. It was a work of art, in Conner's view. It made him want a martini himself.

Stricker gingerly placed the drink in front of the woman. Her eyes grew wide, and she again looked at her friend and giggled.

To avoid spilling any of the precious liquid, she leaned forward and sipped the contents as it sat on the bar. She then leaned back, laughed and held her chest as if her insides were on fire. And they probably were. Both of the two women and J.D. laughed heartily. The attractive woman then turned and looked at Conner, seemingly embarrassed.

"I don't drink these very often. But, tonight's a special occasion. We're celebrating."

Conner smiled at the woman and held up his glass in a toast.

"To whatever it is you're celebrating."

The woman touched glasses with her friend and then raised her martini toward Conner.

"Cheers!"

"Cheers!"

It was Stricker who spoke next.

"If I may ask, what are you celebrating?"

"I'm moving here and taking a job at Western Carolina University."

The remark hit a chord with Conner. He turned and looked pointedly at the woman.

"Western Carolina?"

"Yes. Are you familiar with it?"

"You betcha! You can't live around here and not know about WCU."

Again he smiled at her. She returned the smile, which lit up her entire face. This was one handsome woman, he told himself. Just then she extended her hand to him.

"I'm Cynthia Henchel, and this is my friend, Gwenn Peterson."

"Nice to meet you Cynthia...Gwenn. I'm Mitch Conner."

Conner nodded to both women, who smiled and acknowledged his greeting. Before they could respond, he continued.

"I have to tell you that I was already impressed with the faculty at Western Carolina. They have a high ratio of PhDs for a school of that size. But after tonight, I have to say I'm even more impressed."

"Thank you, Mitch. And now they have one more PhD."

"What about you, Gwenn? Are you on the faculty as well?"

The woman laughed and looked at Stricker before turning back to Conner.

"Heavens no. Nothing that exciting. I'm a physical therapist in Baltimore. Just came down to help Cynthia settle in."

"Well, the world needs physical therapists, too."

"Yes, fortunately."

Conner then turned his attention back to Cynthia. She took another careful sip of the martini and wrinkled her nose at the bitter taste.

"You don't appear to be a regular martini drinker," Conner said.

"I'm not. Can't handle it. But, they're great for special occasions."

Conner smiled and nodded his approval. Cynthia turned back to her friend, and the two chatted briefly before Conner spoke again.

"Are you moving to the area?"

"Well, I'm actually taking an apartment in Asheville temporarily. I had to spend some time at the University today, and we decided to stay here for the night rather than drive back to Asheville. A colleague at the University recommended the Inn."

"Well, I don't think you'll be disappointed. But, it looks like you're going to have a pretty good commute each day from Asheville."

"Yes. But I don't mind. I'm only staying there until I decide where I want to live. And it's such a pretty drive. I'm actually looking forward to it. At least I won't face the traffic I did in Washington. And hopefully, it won't be for long."

Conner nodded his agreement. Cynthia then looked thoughtfully at him.

"What do you do, Mitch?"

"Well, at present, I'm a photographer. Took an early retirement from IBM. But, I just moved here myself just a few months ago. In fact, I've recently communicated with the University about getting involved in their Continuing Education Program – possibly teaching business writing."

The young woman nodded her understanding and smiled as she took another sip of the martini.

Conner paused and watched her briefly before continuing.

"I have my masters, and I'm giving some thought to working on a PhD there, which would allow me to join the for-credit program. But, we'll see."

"Oh really? What would be your course of study?"

"I thought maybe history I'm something of a history nut…particularly military history."

"Oh really. I've always enjoyed history, too."

Conner chuckled at her response.

"What about you? What's your discipline?"

"I'm an associate professor of psychology."

"Well, I think you'll find this to be very fertile ground. There are a lot of interesting characters in these mountains. Including the bartender here."

Both Stricker and the women laughed.

"Well, I'm not a clinical psychologist. I confine my work to the classroom."

"Too bad."

Again Cynthia chuckled.

"Did you teach in Washington?"

"Yes. At American University."

"I have a friend who attended A. U. That's a good school."

"Yes. I loved it there. But, this was a promotion for me. And I wanted to be closer to my grandmother, who lives in Knoxville."

Conner nodded understandingly and smiled at Cynthia.

"Tell me something. I assume you have a close relationship with your grandmother."

"She's the best."

"What is it about the relationship between grandparents and grandchildren? I know several people who grew up hating their parents but adored their grandparents. As a psychologist, you must have the answer. What goes on?"

Cynthia smiled, her green eyes sparkling.

"I don't think I have the time to answer that. In fact, I'm not even sure I know the answer. But, I know when I was growing up, my grandparents were great to me. That's not to say I didn't love my parents."

"But, I think it has something to do with age. I have a friend who was the youngest of seven. She's always said her parents were different to her than they were to her older brothers and sisters. They wore more strict with the older ones."

"But the parents mellowed out. And didn't try to run her life," She recalled. "But they were always there to support her."

"I think the same thing can be said for grandparents. They don't try to run your lives. But they're always there when you need them."

"Sounds like a pretty good answer to me. And it makes sense."

Conner paused briefly and looked at Stricker before returning his attention to Cynthia.

"Listen, I'm keeping you and Gwenn from your celebration. It was nice meeting both of you, and good luck in your new job."

"Thank you Mitch. And good luck to you. Maybe we'll run into each other on campus sometime."

"I look forward to it." Conner said, smiling.

Conner exchanged brief comments with Gwenn and Stricker and paid the check. As he walked toward the maitre'd, he gazed out over the dining room. It was now half full, and several guests were standing in the foyer. As he stood and waited for a table, he gazed back into the lounge. The two women were engaged in conversation again. Cynthia glanced briefly in his direction and smiled. He returned the smile and repeated her name several times. He didn't want to forget it

CHAPTER SEVEN

Conner was still living in Ohio during the late 1970s. And at that time, the outside world was generally unaware of the naturalist wonders to be found and explored among the hills and valleys of North Georgia and the western Carolinas.

Conner included himself among this group of people. But, after moving back to Atlanta as an adult, it didn't take him long to become a major supporter of the area, its potential and possibilities.

And, helping that process along, in his view, was the building of Georgia State Route 400 in the 1970s, 1980s and 1990s, connecting Atlanta to this wondrous area. The creation of Route 400 was an ambitious project, and it took quite a while to complete. The plan's objective was both to help deflect the explosive growth of Atlanta and to provide straight and high-speed access to the mountainous area just to the north.

And even before the project was finished, it began to show the impact this new access route was already having. It became so successful that as soon as a new extension of the roadway was completed, efforts were underway to expand the number of lanes already handling both north and southbound traffic on the divided highway.

Finally, when the Route 400 project reached its original goals in the mid 1990s, it had significantly reduced the driving time to the northern-most borders of Georgia, cutting it from almost four hours to just about two hours. It was a project that never seemed to end, in Conner's view as a resident.

The new corridor's construction continued to promote North Georgia's and the Western Carolinas' potential for residential, recreational and commercial development. It was an enlightening project, aimed at in-state residents, as well as national and international audiences. But the initiative also began to attract unexpected benefactors with vested interests in the scenic beauty and appeal of the region.

In July of 1970, German-born, high-wire daredevil Karl Wallenda chose the spectacular gorge, waterfalls and canyon at Tallulah Falls, Georgia to perform his death-defying high wire act. In addition to live national media coverage of his feat, there were 30,000 spectators watching on-site as Wallenda walked 1,000 feet across the gorge, some 800 feet above the canyon's raging waters and rock formations. Wallender had conquered yet another formidable adversary, and the world had gotten a close-up look at some of the many scenic treasures in North Georgia.

Less than two years later, Hollywood released the blockbuster movie, Deliverance, which was filmed along the Chattooga River, less than 15 miles north of Tallulah Falls.

This action-packed thriller also chronicled the scenic beauty of that area, including the waterfalls, rugged rock formations, and the powerful rapids of the Chattooga as it rumbled between Clayton, Georgia and Salem, South Carolina.

Conner liked to tell newcomers to the area about the State of Georgia's topographical gems. They were growing in popularity, and the state was quickly becoming responsible for more on-location filming and in-state movie production than Hollywood.

One of the first North Georgia cities to benefit from the completed Route 400 project was a small place called Dahlonega. That city of 7,000 residents was just a little over an hour's drive from Atlanta and about a 45-minute drive to Bryson City. Dahlonega was an historic, 1820s gold rush mining town that now had become the gateway city to the Blue Ridge Mountains. It was a great place to hear local entertainers and for enjoying surprisingly good restaurants that served a variety of good food.

Other towns within a 50 to 60-mile radius of Bryson City included Asheville, NC, the largest city in the region with 90,000 people. Conner had visited Asheville on several occasions, including trips to the city's regional airport. Asheville was a major tourist attraction and was noted for its vibrant arts community, sophistication and historic architecture. The city was home to the Basilica of St. Lawrence Cathedral, which was consecrated by Pope John Paul II in 1993. Ashville also was home to the much heralded Biltmore Estate and its priceless art collections – including paintings by masters such as Rembrandt and Renoir.

There were scores of other little hamlets scattered throughout the area, most of them small. Included were Gainesville, Clayton, Dillard and Lake Rabun, GA; and Cullasaja, Cashiers, Franklin, Cullowhee and Highlands, NC. In his short time living in the mountains, Conner had already visited many of those places, attending state fairs or holiday celebrations and festivals.

Highlands, NC, in particular, had become something of a popular summer retreat for people with permanent residences elsewhere.

Because of its elevation (4,100 feet above sea level), Highlands tended to be noticeably cooler than other southeast locations during the hot summer months, which made that city very appealing. Highlands, much like Asheville, was another place that offered sophistication in its shops, attractions and accommodations – even for transient visitors, Conner found.

But, although Conner now lived in North Carolina, his heart would always belong to Georgia. It was the best, in his view. And it seemed to have something for everybody.

Georgia's people, on the whole, were friendly and hard-working, trusting and good natured, Conner felt. It had a moderate climate and an abundance of natural resources.

And it was blessed with major rivers and streams and got ample precipitation to water its rich and fertile soil in the production of diverse crops and textiles – everything from blueberries and peaches to soybeans and cotton. Such commodities helped Georgia become a major supplier in the nation's food supply and textile chains..

The state also had an illustrious and proud history. But most importantly, North Georgia's beauty and topographical diversity placed it right up there with the most desirable locations in the nation, in Conner's view.

What's more, there were other locations in Georgia that had unique and notable attractions, and Conner was well versed on them all. In the southern part of the state, there were beautiful beaches along the State's Atlantic Ocean shorelines.

Cumberland Island, the heralded barrier island just off Georgia's southeast coast and major destination for wedding ceremonies, had protected wildlife preserves, a maritime forest and a sanctuary for loggerhead turtles and feral horses.

And just a few miles up the coast, Savannah's old historic district boasted one of the most impressive collections in the country of old Victorian homes and public buildings that had been restored and preserved. Many of these treasured old structures dated back to the late 1700s and were of historical importance.

And the city's major seaport, already one of the busiest in the eastern U.S., had become one of the fastest growing ports in the country. As a result of these historical and logistical assets, Savannah had become one of the most significant tourist attractions in the southeast. And Georgia also had become a major force in international transportation and world trade.

Scattered around the middle of Georgia were numerous other historical sites, interesting terrain and various wildlife preserves and sanctuaries -- including the famous Okefenokee Swamp located near Waycross in the southwest section of Georgia.

CHAPTER EIGHT

It was the middle of October. Snow was in the air. And so was college football.

Conner was a University of Georgia football fan — some would say nut - and he seldom missed a game, either by attending in person or by watching the Bulldogs play on television. On this Saturday afternoon, Georgia was playing its arch rival, Florida, in Jacksonville - which was referred to as the world's largest outdoor cocktail party.

Conner had attended several of these games in person over the years. But, today, he would sit in a friendly local setting -- at a bar in town - and have a couple of beers — and maybe a few wings - as he watched the game. There was a popular sports bar in BC. Previously a gas station, the festive little bar was called the Universal Joint.

The Joint had good sandwiches, tasty finger food, and a wide selection of cold beers. And there were several large screen TVs tuned to the games of different schools on football weekends. But, because Georgia was a local favorite, most of the sets today would be tuned to the Georgia game. Besides, the bar owner was a Georgia graduate.

The Universal Joint had both indoor and outdoor seating, which was weather dependent. But, some people just liked the outdoors, regardless of the temperature or conditions. Those people could sometimes be found outdoors, even when it rained. The bar also had entertainment most of the time. But there would be no entertainment on this day. It was a football weekend, and people were here to watch football and drink beer.

Conner liked the Universal Joint because locals frequently brought out-of-town visitors, which contributed to more interesting conversations. He also liked the bartenders, most of whom were young women who were playful and good natured. But most importantly, they were very efficient and attentive to their customers. Conner felt that good bartenders tended to have excellent peripheral vision and could see everything going on around them. And these ladies seemed to have an abundance of such vision.

Conner still didn't know very many people in town...but on Georgia game day, that didn't matter. After the game was underway and you had a couple of beers under your belt, even total strangers became your best friends.

Conner had played football in high school, making the team as a wide receiver. He wasn't the fastest guy on the team. But he had great hands.

There were few better at catching the football than he was. He'd go up for the ball in a crowd and more often than not, come down with it. Coaches liked him because he was a hard worker, and he never gave up.

Conner also was a pitcher on the baseball team and that was his sport of preference. People said he had a good fastball, with a lot of movement. That made it hard to hit.

Shortly after graduating from high school, Conner was drafted into the U.S. Army and spent nearly a year serving in the U.S. Army Occupational Force near Seoul, South Korea. When his entire unit was transferred to Southern Japan, he tried out for and made the baseball team at the U.S. Airbase in Itazuke, Japan.

One of his teammates on the team also was an assistant coach back home, and he offered Conner a baseball scholarship to Florida State University. But Conner was focused on getting his college degree and moving on with his career. He respectfully declined the offer and never had any misgivings about that decision.

Growing up, Conner was often told he was a good writer. And with just a few weeks left on his two-year military obligation, he applied for admission to Kent State University and to Ohio State University. Kent State's journalism school had a good reputation, and Ohio State was a close second on that list. But, Kent notified him of his acceptance first, and he quickly took the offer.

Kent also was just a 45-minute drive south of Cleveland, which is where other family members lived. After graduating from Kent, Conner went on to earn a master's degree in journalism from Northwestern University.

Conner knew the Universal Joint would be busy for today's game, so he made a point to get there early. But when he arrived, the place was already packed, even though it didn't start for another hour. The seating options were few. Conner sighed to himself as he looked around the room. He spotted a couple of seats at the bar and began making his way through the mix of noisy conversations and laughter. As he proceeded, he returned smiles to happy faces and nodded to other friendly patrons. But unexpectedly, his concentration was dashed by a nearby voice:

"Mitch?"

Conner stopped in his tracks. He turned sharply to his left in the direction of the voice. He waited for his mind to catch up with what his eyes were seeing. Sitting in the middle of the room was Carolyn Briggs, an employee at a Bryson City art store that processed most of Conner's photography and supplied the dressy mattes that made his pictures ready for framing. The store was one of Conner's early discoveries in Bryson City.

It was called The Scarlet Letters and it was a perfect match for Conner's needs. It not only provided photo services, it sold and serviced photographic equipment. The store had a small café and reading area. Based on the name, the fact they had a café and a reading area, Conner guessed the owner of the store would be a woman. And he was right. The owner was Gretchen Dunner, whom Conner got to know and like.

The art store employee, Carolyn Briggs, was with a female friend. Carolyn had the look of a cheerleader, in Conner's mind. She had an athletic body and nice legs. Conner thought she probably looked great in high heels. Carolyn was a quintessential blond, with long yellow hair and blue eyes. But her best feature was her smile, which lit up her entire face. Carolyn appeared to be in her late 30s or early 40s.

Her friend Susan was small, and soft spoken. She wore horn-rimmed glasses and tended to bow her head in respect after making statements to others. Susan was Oriental, and she had beautiful skin and big dark eyes. She was very cute, in Conner's view. But Conner didn't think she was a first generation American. She had no trace of an accent. But he bet during her upbringing, she had gotten a lot of guidance and supervision from parents or grandparents, who followed strict cultural and ethnic traditions and behavior.

Conner was locked in on to his target and began moving in her direction. When he spoke, it was with some hesitation:

"Carolyn?"

"Hey guy. I didn't expect to see you here."

Conner smiled a big smile and looked a little flushed by the unexpected encounter.

"Now, I don't know whether that's a friendly greeting or a warning."

Both of them laughed.

"No. No. That's not what I meant. I just didn't expect you to be into Georgia football."

"Well, if you knew me better, you might be surprised at some of the other things I'm into."

Carolyn smiled at the thought, seemingly ignoring the remark as she continued:

"Why don't you grab one of those chairs over there and join us?" she asked.

"I don't want to intrude."

"You're not intruding at all. Susan and I were just cooling down with a beer after running a few miles. Now is that a contradiction, or what?"

As Conner took a seat at their table, he realized Carolyn and Susan both were wearing shorts and running shoes.

Carolyn's voice took on a little more serious tone as she continued.

"Mitch, this is my friend Susan Tarayama. We know each other from WCU. She's on the staff, and I got to know her when I was getting my master's there."

Conner nodded at Susan and responded, extending his hand to her as he did so.

"Nice to meet you Susan."

Susan's face lit up with a big smile, and she bowed slightly.

"But, we didn't realize Georgia had a big game today.....until we stepped inside," Carolyn added.

"Yeah. Both teams are undefeated. A lot at stake today. And yes, I'm a big fan of Georgia, even though I didn't go there," Conner said.

"Where did you go to school?"

"Kent State and Northwestern."

Carolyn pursed her lips and nodded at the names.

"Those are both good schools," she said.

Conner smiled and nodded.

The three continued to share personal information and stories. But Just as the game was about to begin, Carolyn glanced at her watch and looked around the room.

"Susan, I don't know about you, babe. But I've got to run," Carolyn said. "I've got some errands to do and I have plans for this evening."

"I've got to get going, myself," Susan added, smiling.

Carolyn pushed away from the table and reached out to Conner.

"I'm so glad we ran into you," she added, squeezing Conner's hand. "I think I know more about you now than I learned in months working at the store."

As she stood, she reached down for her check, as did Susan. Conner quickly moved both checks to his side of the table, and he stood, out of courtesy to the ladies.

"I'm buying tonight 'cause I have a good feeling about Georgia," Conner said, smiling. "Maybe next time we see each other you guys can buy the beer."

Conner continued standing and watched as the two women walked through the crowd and left. In consideration for other patrons, Conner abandoned the table and moved to an empty seat at the bar.

"It' showtime," he told himself.

When the game ended, Conner stood and did a fist pump.

"Yeah!"

He exchanged pleasantries with the bartenders and with several people at the bar, before paying the check and heading out. It had been a good day for Georgia. They had beaten Florida decisively. And it had been a good day for Conner, with the chance meeting of two new friends. He found the longer he lived here, the more places and things he discovered that he liked.

As Conner stepped outside, he hesitated and looked up. A light snow had begun to fall, and it was accentuated against the darkening sky. It had been a long day, and it was time to get home.

CHAPTER NINE

Snow continued to fall across the Carolina mountains. On Sunday evening, weather forecasters issued a winter storm advisory for western Carolina, eastern Tennessee and northern Georgia. The combination of snow and sleet could make driving in the area hazardous, they said. But, for Conner, the snow and sleet were more of an opportunity than a threat. A blanket of snow covering the area presented him with winter wonderland type photo possibilities.

Before going to bed that evening, Conner set his alarm for five thirty. He wanted to get an early start on the day. If the skies cleared, the sunrise could be spectacular. And he wanted to be in position to get shots of the sun as it peeked out over a snow-covered landscape.

Several times during the night, he awakened and glanced expectantly at the clock. He felt like time had reversed itself. What seemed like hours were actually minutes. And minutes had turned into seconds, He thought about getting dressed and heading out into the woods. But that was silly. The sun wouldn't be up for some time yet. And he couldn't shoot in the dark. Still, he was anxious to see what wonders nature had sculpted overnight.

As he laid in the dark, his mind raced with images he hoped to capture -- including snow-covered Douglas Firs, their limbs drooping awkwardly under the weight of accumulated snow. But, he'd just have to bide his time and try to get some sleep.

When the clock radio finally came on, Conner was already in the shower. As he stepped back into the bedroom, the wood stove had done its job, and the temperature throughout the cabin was perfect. Once dressed, he moved to the living room and turned on the FM radio, which was set to National Public Radio.

Since moving to Carolina, NPR had become a regular part of Conner's daily routine. At this time of the morning, the format was all news. But, during the late morning and evening, NPR aired a great selection of classical music. And he loved classical. It was a balm, a fresh breeze on a summer's day -- a refuge from life's harsh realities.

But NPR's news broadcasts throughout the day did little more than raise his blood pressure. The network had a history of passing off leftist points of view as unbiased reporting. This was an outrage. How could a radio network supported in part by taxpayer money be so one-sided in its presentation and analysis of the news? It was a question he couldn't answer. In fact, it caused him great consternation each time he thought about it.

But on this morning, Conner's focus was on preparing breakfast, which consisted of grits, eggs, ham and pancakes. As he moved about the kitchen, the radio broadcast was nothing more than background noise. Normally, he ate sparingly in the mornings. But today, a hearty breakfast was in order. He'd burn up a lot of calories walking through the mountains in the heavy snow.

With breakfast over, Conner packed several pieces of photographic gear in a small backpack. And he chose three lenses, a medium-range lens, another for wide angles and a third for close-ups. Next, he filled the thermos with coffee, and retrieved several pieces of fruit from the refrigerator, placing them in the knapsack. He would only be walking distance from the cabin. But he didn't want to trek back up the hill unnecessarily. He then grabbed his all-weather coat from the hall closet and headed outside.

Conner paused momentarily on the porch. It was still dark -- too dark to see the full beauty of what stretched out before him. But, as his eyes adjusted to the outdoors, he could see that everything was covered with a blanket of white. Limbs on the big tall fir trees around the house slumped helplessly beneath their white overload.

It had stopped snowing for the time being. But more frozen precipitation was forecast throughout the day. From the faint glow in the sky, it was evident the sun would be rising soon. He glanced briefly at the Beast. It had a layer of snow some four to six inches deep.

Cautiously, Conner stepped from the porch into the ankle-deep snow. The experience caused his mind to drift back to an earlier period in his life. But, those pleasant memories were dashed by a sudden interruption. The phone was ringing inside the cabin. Should he answer it? he asked himself. Or, should he just let the answering machine pick up?

"Damn!"

Reluctantly, Conner re-entered the cabin and grabbed the phone in the kitchen, his voice laced with frustration.

"Yeah!"

"Mister Conner?"

"Yes."

"Deputy Eassel here, with the Macon County Sheriff's office."

There was an awkward pause as Conner's mind reeled to make the connection. He had not expected this voice. And he had not expected this call -- certainly, not at this time of day. It took him a few seconds to collect his thoughts. Before he could respond, the deputy continued.

"Hope I didn't disturb you callin' this early."

"Nah. No problem."

"Well, Mister Conner, the reason for my call is to see if you could meet with us sometime today. We'd like to ask you a few questions."

The statement caught Conner by surprise.

"Questions? What kind of questions?"

"Just routine stuff. We haven't been able to turn up much on that John Doe you found. And we thought you might be able to shed some light on it for us. Anything at all that you could tell us might be helpful."

Again, Conner paused. He was not only caught off guard by the call, he was getting a little perturbed by this intrusion. He didn't know a damn thing about that guy. He'd only found him in the woods. When he responded to the officer, there was a trace of sarcasm in his voice.

"Deputy, have you looked outside?"

"Yessir. Not the best of days, weather-wise. But, we thought this would be the perfect day to catch you at home. All the schools are closed. Many businesses, too. Course, we don't expect you to come over to Franklin. We'd be happy to drop by your place. For our vehicles, weather like this is no problem."

"Well, my business is not closed. I was just getting ready to head out in the mountains to take a few pictures. It's what I do for a living, as you may recall."

"Yessir. I remember. But, we only need a few minutes of your time. Maybe we could get together later this afternoon, if that would be more convenient."

There was silence as Conner considered the request. His mood had suddenly changed from one of anticipation to one of reality. The last thing he wanted to do was come across as uncooperative.

"What time did you have in mind?"

"You name it. We'll be there."

Again Conner paused.

"Let's make it four o'clock."

"That'd be fine."

Over the next couple of minutes, Conner gave the deputy directions on getting to his house. When he hung up the phone, he stood motionless for a few minutes. Then, out of frustration, he began muttering to himself.

"What the hell is happening here? I don't know jack about this guy. I just found the poor bastard in the woods."

Conner recalled one other time in his life where an innocent set of circumstances led to a very frustrating encounter with the police. It was when he was married to Susan. He had just returned from a two-week trip out of town.

It was a Saturday morning, and there was a knock on the door. When he answered, a deputy sheriff served him with a subpoena. He was being charged with a hit-and-run accident.

"What?"

According to the summons, his car reportedly hit another vehicle in an inner city neighborhood very late at night and left the scene. Conner knew he couldn't have been involved in this thing. He began to ask himself whether his wife had been driving his car in those neighborhoods while he was out of town. Nah, that was absurd.

He called the police and told them there had been some mistake. At the time of the accident, he had been in Hawaii. And he had scores of witnesses. The police told him to ignore the citation and assured him it would be handled. Nevertheless, a couple of weeks later, he received a call, advising him to appear for a deposition.

He was now extremely upset, and he called an attorney. It's probably just a bureaucratic snafu, the attorney said. He assured Conner he'd take care of it. A few days later, the attorney called back to tell him he'd have to give the deposition as directed. "It's routine," he advised.

"Routine? I'm accused of being involved in a hit-and-run accident and you say it's routine. Several people have already told me not to worry about it. Told me it would be taken care of? Now, I'm being asked to give a deposition. Routine? The hell it is! This thing was out of control."

But, he had no choice. He would have to comply with the directive.

When Conner arrived at the court-appointed attorney's office, he was ushered into a large conference room. Among the people in the room was a black couple seated near the door.

As he prepared to take a seat, the attorney asked the couple: "Is this the man who hit you?"

"No," the man replied, his voice traced with sarcasm..

"We told you the person who hit us was black!"

Apparently, the black couple had made an error in the license plate number they gave police. And Conner's car was mistakenly linked to the crime. When the court official dismissed him, Conner was relieved. At the same time, he was angry -- very angry! These people had subjected him to several weeks of mental anguish. And the whole thing was a result of carelessness and sloppy police work. He now realized the justice system was capable of ignoring the facts and blindly moving forward like some runaway team.

The more he thought about it, the angrier he became. What happened to the concept of innocence until proven guilty? What if the charges had been more serious? What if the person who had committed this crime had been white? He would still be trying to prove his innocence, he told himself.

Was the same thing happening to him again? Were those idiots at the sheriff's office trying to link him to that John Doe just to cover their asses? He could feel his anxiety level rising. "To hell with 'em! I haven't done anything wrong!"

Conner then grabbed his knapsack and left the cabin again. It was now noticeably brighter outdoors. The sun was making its presence felt. But with this thick cloud cover, there was no way the sunrise would be visible. Still, he might be able to get some interesting shots as the light levels increased.

As Conner looked out over the blanket of snow, his thoughts returned to his childhood. Smiling, he reached down into the snow and began forming a snowball, packing it repeatedly in his cupped hands. Then, with a look of fierce determination, he took aim and hurled the frozen mass toward the lifeless Beast sitting nearby. The missile hit the rear window with a thud. Conner chuckled to himself. This was the closest he could come to having a snowball fight. He tugged at his knapsack, turned and walked down the road into the trees.

Conner's house was virtually surrounded by the Nantahala National Forest, which was in the heart of the Smokies. Nantahala was an Indian term, meaning "land of the noon-day sun." In Conner's view, it was very appropriate, since the sun only penetrated the forest's thick canopy at noon.

The Nantahala consisted of more than half-a-million acres, making it one of the largest preserves in the federal land program. Across its mountainous slopes were more than 200 varieties of trees.

The forest also was home to a variety of wildlife, including bears, white-tailed deer, boars, wildcats, eagles, weasels, mink and turkeys. Conner liked to say, he lived in the middle of a wilderness that would never be commercialized.

Throughout the year, thousands of outdoor enthusiasts entered the Nantahala Forest to use its campsites, picnic areas, trout streams and man-made beaches. The Nantahala also contained hundreds of miles of well maintained paths and trails. One of the most heavily travelled was the Appalachian Trail, which wound through western Carolina on its way to New England.

Each time Conner entered the Nantahala, he was awed with its wonder. And this day was no exception. Over the next several hours, he followed his instincts, making his way up hills and down steep slopes. He was able to capture one compelling scene after another.

A female deer paused silently to survey nature's intrusion into her daily routine. Other creatures scurried about in the thick snow. They appeared to be enjoying the snow as much as he was. The more he walked, the greater the opportunities he saw. So far, he was delighted with the shots he'd taken. But when he looked at his watch, he could hardly believe his eyes. It was nearly four o'clock.

Conner estimated he was two -- maybe three miles -- from the cabin. He'd have to hustle to get back on time. Retracing his steps was not a problem. All he had to do was follow the footprints in the deep snow.

But, as he made his way through the trees, it began snowing again. So much for following his footprints. But, he knew where he was. The only problem was taking the shortest route.

When he reached the front of the cabin, the snow was coming down pretty hard. It was now a few minutes past four. But, there was no sign of the deputy. Just as Conner stepped onto the porch, he heard the sound of a vehicle making its way up the road. Funny, he thought. He had never been able to hear an approaching vehicle this easily before. Then it occurred to him the snow had improved the forest's acoustics and was amplifying the sound of the vehicle's engine. That made sense.

Conner entered the cabin, eased the knapsack from his back and placed it on the kitchen counter. He then stepped back onto the porch, just as the deputy's vehicle reached the crest of the hill.

Conner couldn't tell what kind of vehicle it was. They all looked alike these days. The only thing he knew was it was big and powerful -- one of those four-wheel-drive monsters.

It was all black, and it had a Macon County Sheriff's crest emblazoned on the side. The vehicle turned toward the cabin and pulled to a step. Deputy Eassel was behind the wheel. Conner wasn't sure who his companion was.

Just then, the passenger door opened, and Conner recognized the same tall, lanky deputy who had accompanied them on the helicopter flight. Bramley, was it? Conner moved to the edge of the porch.

As the two officers climbed from the vehicle, both looked at him and smiled. Conner acknowledged them with a nod.

"Afternoon, mister Conner."

Conner acknowledged the greeting with a nod and a forced smile.

"You remember my partner. Deputy Rife Bramley?"

"Yes sir."

The deputy acknowledged his introduction with a tip of his hat and a big grin. As the two men approached, Conner realized that the tall man was very homely. It hadn't occurred to him before. The thought triggered other images. The deputy was probably married to an obese, red-headed woman with no teeth, he thought.

But, that was unkind. The man seemed to be a nice person. Conner told himself that he was attacking him because he resented this continued intrusion into his life, and the suggestion that he knew something he wasn't telling.

Instinctively, Conner turned and opened his front door, motioning for the two men to step inside.

"Let's get outta' the cold."

As the two deputies entered the house, they removed their hats and stood awkwardly just inside the door. Conner motioned them toward the small table in the breakfast nook.

"Have a seat."

Deputy Eassel nodded and smiled. As the officers took seats, Conner retrieved a couple of logs from the hearth and placed them in the wood stove. He then removed his coat before turning back to his visitors.

"Would you like some coffee?"

"That'd be great, if it's no trouble," Eassel said.

"No problem. I'd like some myself."

Conner moved into the kitchen and went about brewing a fresh pot of coffee. From the other side of the counter, Deputy Bramley surveyed the living room area and turned to Conner.

"Nice little cabin ya' got here, Mister Conner."

"Thanks. It's small. But, it's enough for my needs."

"How long you lived here?" Eassel asked.

"Little over four months. Moved here from Atlanta."

Deputy Eassel looked pointedly at Conner, nodding his head to acknowledge what Conner had just said.

"Four months, you say?"

"Yes sir."

"And before that?"

Conner paused and returned the deputy's stare. He felt his muscles tighten. Why doesn't he just pull out a fucking interrogation light and cuff me to a chair? he asked himself. He looked quickly in the direction of deputy

Eassel without making eye contact. He then turned back to the coffee pot, purposely delaying his response to the question. But, he could not afford to come across as being uncooperative or antagonistic. It would only make matters worse. Conner took a deep breath, grabbed three coffee cups and walked back into the other room.

"I moved here from Atlanta. Got tired of big city life. The congestion and all that."

Conner forced a smile as he placed coffee cups in front of his visitors. He then returned to the kitchen and retrieved the pot of freshly brewed coffee. Back in the other room, he moved from one deputy to another -- carefully filling their cups. The familiar aroma of coffee filled the room. Finally, Conner poured a cup for himself and took a seat directly across from deputy Eassel. It was his turn to take the initiative.

"Tell me, deputy. How long have you been doin' this?"

Eassel responded with a chuckle.

"Sometimes, it seems like all my life. But, it's only been 12 years. Before that, I was in the service. Military police."

Conner responded with an approving smile. Before the deputy could resume, Conner continued.

"So. You haven't come up with much on that John Doe?"

Eassel nodded his agreement.

"Not very much at all. There was no identification. We know he was a Caucasian male. Probably in his late sixties to late-seventies. There were no apparent signs of violence. By that I mean no toxic substances, or trauma to the body. Our guess is that he probably died of natural causes. Possibly a heart attack or stroke."

"But, with what we had to work with, we can't be sure. The coroner estimated he'd been in the woods six to 12 months. Maybe more."

The deputy paused before continuing.

"You know, after a certain amount of time passes, it's tough to be specific with the forensic part of this kind of thing."

Conner looked at one deputy and then the other. Before he could respond, Eassel continued.

"You say you never saw this man before?"

"That's right. Not before I found him out there in the woods."

"Deputy, I'd like to remind you that I just moved up here about four months ago. And based on what you've said about the forensics, it appears this person has been dead for some time. Probably well beyond four months."

Eassel nodded his understanding, an intense look now on his face.

"Yessir. I remember your telling me that. But, you have to understand that we have to explore all the possibilities in an investigation of this sort."

The deputy pushed his coffee cup aside and leaned forward in his chair.

"You spend a lot of time up near those falls?"

"No. I'd never been there before. I've spent some time working the areas in and around Cashiers. Up by Whiteside Mountain, mostly. But, never anywhere near those falls."

"You ever hear of anyone living out there in the woods?"

"Nope! Maybe somebody in Cashiers might know something. But not me."

Again Eassel nodded. There was a pause before he continued.

"Mister Conner. The remains appeared to have been disturbed somewhat. Now, that's not unusual when we find a body in the woods. Animals and such. But, did you remove anything from the site? Or otherwise disturb anything at the site in any way?"

"No, I did not! I didn't get any closer than about 20 feet."

Eassel smiled a forced smile. But, Conner now had questions of his own.

"You think he lived there in the woods?"

"Yup. That would be our guess. He was dressed for the outdoors. But, he didn't have any of the gear you'd find on hikers or campers."

"Besides, he was pretty old to be out sightseeing by himself. Nah, I think he lived somewhere near those falls. And, if I were to guess, I'd say he went there a lot."

Conner was puzzled by the remark.

"Whatta' ya' mean?"

"There was a noticeable bare spot near that big boulder. Like a heavily travelled path. Somebody went there regularly. And I suspect it was him. Course, animals could have worn the area down. But, I doubt it."

"I assume you checked missing persons?"

"Yessir! That's the first thing we did. But there wasn't nuthin' there. We also checked census and tax records for that part of the county. No luck there either."

Conner looked at the two men and shrugged.

"Well. I wish I could give you some answers. But I don't have any. I'm as curious about this as you are."

Deputy Eassel smiled at the remark and rose from his chair. Bramley followed suit and stood awkwardly in the small room, holding his wide brimmed hat in front of him.

Eassel moved toward the door, paused and looked back.

"Mister Conner, I appreciate your help. And I hope we didn't inconvenience you too much."

"No problem. Just be careful going down the hill. It looks pretty nasty outside."

Eassel nodded and smiled. As he stepped outside, he carefully replaced his hat. The other deputy paused at the door and smiled, tugging at the brim of his hat.

"Much obliged."

Conner responded with a smile and a nod. The tall man closed the door behind him and the two men walked out into the falling snow. Dusk was beginning to settle over the mountains. Conner watched from his front door as the deputies sat briefly in the vehicle talking. Finally, the engine roared to life. Eassel then eased the van into a sweeping turn and headed back, driving carefully down the mountain. Conner continued watching until the vehicle disappeared into the trees.

CHAPTER TEN

For the rest of the evening, Conner replayed in his mind the conversation he had with Deputy Eassel. There were several things he found puzzling. If the mystery man had, indeed, lived somewhere near those falls, why weren't there IRS or Census Bureau records on him?

True, census takers didn't venture into the wilderness. But he was pretty sure the area where the remains were found was in the Nantahala Forest. If he lived there illegally, which was likely, chances were good no one knew he existed. Could it be he was a squatter? Nah, Conner didn't think so. And the man didn't appear to be a homeless person.

Just then, a thought occurred to him. It was triggered by something J.D. Stricker at the Fryemont had said.

There were a lot of people living in these mountains who didn't want their identities known. The bartender also guessed that some of them were in the witness protection program. Could it be this John Doe had been in the witness protection program? That might explain why there were no records on him.

As the name John Doe passed through his consciousness, it occurred to Conner the initials for John Doe were J.D. Suddenly, the frown on his face turned to a smile. Could it be that his friendly bartender -- J.D. -- had an alias? The thought caused him to chuckle. Maybe Stricker really was in the witness protection program. He dismissed the thought with a shrug.

"Nah. Too far fetched."

Conner's thoughts returned to the mystery man. There had to be a way to find out who he was. Just then, the dead man's image re-appeared to him.

He could clearly see the exposed skull, with the jaws partially open as if the man were trying to share his secret.

In all probability, the Macon County Sheriff's office was closing the book on this thing. But, Conner wasn't. There were too many unanswered questions. Maybe it was his newspaper background kicking in. But, there was a story there somewhere. And he convinced himself he was going to find out what it was.

The following morning, Conner rose early. After stoking the stove, he went to the rear window and gazed out. It was apparent the temperature had risen well above the freezing mark. The thick layers of snow covering the tree limbs were melting, cascading down to the ground in big chunks. Each limb danced briefly as it was relieved of its burden. And with the sun beginning to peek over the horizon, this process would only accelerate.

After eating breakfast, Conner showered and dressed. He spent a few minutes on the Internet, scanning the day's headlines from the New York Times site. NPR at this time of morning had the usual leftist drivel. Still, he listened. It was almost eight thirty when he tucked the 9-mm Browning in his belt, grabbed his coat, knapsack and thermos and left the cabin.

Outside, the old blue Bronco was still partially covered by snow. But its icy blanket, too, was beginning to melt. There was a mixture of snow and large beads of water on the flat surfaces. But all the windows were clear. Conner didn't bother pushing away the remaining snow. The bumpy ride down the mountain would take care of that, he told himself.

The main road into Bryson City was in good shape. County road crews had apparently plowed overnight. But there were still banks of mud-covered snow along both sides of the road. Once on the highway, Conner continued into Bryson City, where he stopped briefly to drop off a computer disc from the previous day's work. He then took route 19 to Sylva, before heading south.

When he reached Cashiers, Conner pulled into the old logging trail he had used before. It was the only way he knew how to reach the waterfall.

Entering the woods from any other point would simply be rolling the dice, he told himself.

Conner's pace through the woods was slowed considerably by the snow. There was still a thick covering on the forest floor. But, the warmer air was taking its toll. A few bare spots were beginning to appear in areas exposed to the sun. As he continued into the woods, an eerie light appeared over the landscape. Rays of sunshine reached down through the trees, illuminating vapors rising from the melting snow. Too bad he hadn't brought his cameras, he thought. But this was not a day for illusions.

It took over an hour to reach the falls. Once there, Conner climbed to the rocky ledge high above the falls and sat on a huge boulder.

For several moments, he avoided looking at the spot where the remains were found. Instead, he gazed up through the treetops.

Puffy white clouds partially obscured a clear blue sky. He guessed the temperature was already in the mid-forties. It was going to be a nice day, he told himself.

Finally, Conner turned and looked at the big boulder directly across from him. A chill swept over his body as he gazed at the spot near the big boulder. The area was still partially obscured by the snow. Some bare spots were evident around the base. But, there was no trace that a human life had ended there.

As Conner gazed at the site, his senses were dulled by the tumultuous roar of the cascading falls. Slowly, he looked around -- first at the water below, then the trees and the clouds overhead. This was, indeed, an incredibly beautiful setting. He could understand why the man had been drawn here. But, where had he come from? Conner forced himself to re-create the image he had captured that day.

Was there anything that would give him a clue? There were the faded old pants, khaki in color, he thought. And there were the tattered remains of a dark shirt -- possibly blue plaid.

Conner couldn't recall seeing any other garments. There was no coat nor jacket. Probably, the man had come to the falls in the spring or early summer. A coat would have been un-necessary. He continued to press his memory.

Just then, another image surfaced in his mind. It was that twisted and weathered old shoe laying off to one side. It was rather unusual, as Conner recalled, and rather large. It was not a dress or walking shoe. It had the appearance of a hiking or military boot. That was it! It was a military boot! If someone lived in these woods, wearing military boots made a lot of sense. They provided great support for the ankles along such uneven terrain. And they were good protection against snake bites.

Okay. Assuming he lived here in the woods, the question was where?

If Eassel was right -- that the man came here regularly -- what did that tell him? First, he was in good shape to walk through the woods. But, maybe he didn't have to walk too far. Maybe he purposely chose a site that was near the falls. That made sense. If he liked this spot, he would want to be nearby, wouldn't he?

At least that was a starting point. He'd start his search by looking in a half mile radius of the falls and work inward.

Conner grabbed his knapsack and walked directly to the spot where the remains were found. He paused briefly, silently paying homage to the deceased.

He then scanned the surrounding area, looking for a path or trail. There was none. If any kind of impression into the forest existed, it was now covered by snow.

There was something of an open corridor leading back into the woods, and Conner decided to follow that. The snow was now melting quickly, and his feet sunk deeply into the mush and to the blanket of wet leaves below. Conner was thankful his boots were waterproof. After walking for 20 minutes, Conner estimated he had gone at least a half a mile. Maybe more. He paused and looked in all directions. The only thing he could see was trees and underbrush.

He then decided to search to his left, and he turned and walked in that direction. He paused and looked up at the sun. It was now to his right. He'd use the sun as a makeshift compass. He also looked around for some sort of landmark. About 50 feet ahead was a big magnolia tree. It was an unusual sight in these woods. He'd be able to spot that. The last thing he needed was to get lost. And he wouldn't be able to follow his footprints in the snow much longer. In another couple of hours, much of the snow would be gone.

Conner continued walking, gradually moving to his left in his effort to search in an arching pattern. Nearly an hour passed. So far, he had nothing to show for his efforts. The uneven terrain was very forbidding. Certainly, it was not conducive to building a dwelling, he told himself.

Conner stopped and sat on the trunk of a fallen tree trunk. He then reached for his thermos and poured himself a cup of coffee. He sat sipping the hot liquid and looking up at the sunlight penetrating the heavy tree cover overhead. Just then, a sound invaded the quiet forest.

It was laughter. Instinctively, he turned and looked in that direction. Through the trees, he could make out the image of two men moving through the woods. They were walking toward him and not being very quiet about it.

Conner continued to watch as they drew closer. He wasn't particularly in the mood for conversation. Maybe they'd take a different path before reaching him, he told himself. But, one of the men spotted Conner and paused.

"Hey stranger. How's it goin'?"

Conner didn't answer. His eyes were fixed on the two shotguns they carried. As they drew closer, he continued sipping his coffee without saying anything. The two men stopped about 20 feet away. The first man placed his shotgun against a tree. The other one continued to cradle the gun over his right forearm.

The man who greeted him was short, had a puffy white face and a scraggly beard. His stocking cap was pulled down over his long dark hair and his big nose was red from the cold. The other man, the one holding the gun, had a mean look about him. He was taller than his companion, probably over six feet. He had a full beard of light brown hair and piercing green eyes. His faced was pockmarked, and he looked unkempt.

The shorter man moved toward Conner, an impish smile on his face. He paused and blew on his hands, which were partially protected by gray wool gloves. The tips of the gloves had been trimmed off, exposing the man's chubby fingers and dirty fingernails. As the short man massaged his hands, he looked back at his friend and chuckled. Slowly, he turned and looked back at Conner.

"What brings ya' out here, friend?"

Conner bristled at being called "friend" by this stranger. Who the hell were these people? He was beginning to feel a little flushed. He slowly unzipped his coat, looked straight at the shorter man and responded.

"Just doin' a little hiking."

"Pretty cold to be hiking, ain't it?"

"Yeah. Guess it is."

"That'd be coffee you got there?"

"Yep."

"Sure would like to have a little to warm me up. You got a little you could spare?"

"Not really. I plan to be out here a while longer, and I'll be lucky to make this last."

"Aw, that's too bad. I was hopin' you'd be a little more neighborly and share with a coupla' thirsty hunters."

As he spoke, the ugly little man continued to move closer to Conner, a fiendish smile now on his face. The second man flipped his shotgun up and eased his right hand back toward the trigger housing. Conner reached down and pushed his coat aside, revealing the black-handled 9-mm in his belt. At first, the short man did not see the weapon and continued moving toward him. Conner rose, and in one sweeping motion, he whipped the gun into firing position.

"You take one more step "friend" and I'll blow that fucking smile off your face."

Conner quickly glanced at the second man.

"And you, Slim! Drop that goddamn shotgun , or I'll put a few of these slugs in your ugly face.."

The short man froze in his tracks. The second man slowly bent his knees and placed his shotgun on the ground. The short man stepped backward ever so slowly, a nervous twitch now contorting his face.

"Wait a minute, mister. We didn't mean you no harm."

"Fuck you Charlie. Bust those shotguns open and drop the shells to the ground. You so much as quiver and your asses are history. Do it now!"

"Take it easy. Take it easy!"

As the taller man retrieved his gun and broke open the breach, Conner moved closer so he'd have clear sight of both. After throwing a shell to the ground, the tall man rested his weapon against a nearby tree. Conner then jerked his head toward the smaller man.

"Okay, asshole. Your turn."

Slowly, the man retrieved his shotgun and emptied the chamber.

"Now. Throw the rest of your ammunition on the ground."

"Com'on, friend! We ain't done you no harm."

"Do what I told you, goddammit!"

Slowly, both men reached inside their coats and dumped shell after shell onto the ground. Convinced they had emptied their pockets, Conner motioned for the short man to join his friend.

"Grab your shotgun and get over there."

The short man did as he was told, and the two men stood together, cradling their empty weapons. Both stared blankly at him.

"Now, turn around and get the hell outta' here. Your huntin' is over."

LYNN TERRELL

The short man shot a final glance at Conner, his eyes filled with hatred.

"Maybe we'll see you again, sometime."

"Don't tempt me, you ugly little sunuvabitch. Get the hell outta' here while you've got the chance!"

Reluctantly, the two men turned and began walking up a nearby knoll. Conner still had the two in his sight until they reached the top of the ravine and disappeared down the other side. He then lowered the weapon, put it on safety and slipped it back in his belt. He retrieved the shotgun shells from the snow and threw them as far as he could in different directions.

Although the confrontation had passed, he could still feel the adrenalin pumping through his body. But it would take a little while for his anger to subside. Conner returned to the tree trunk and sat down. He reached for his cup of coffee and took a long gulp. He sat for some time taking deep breaths.

"Thank God for the Second Amendment."

Clearly, he was still shaken by the incident. Conner removed his stocking cap and began running his fingers through his hair. It was a nervous reaction to what had just happened -- an outward expression of self examination. Could he have shot either of those men? he asked himself. He shrugged at the thought. He wasn't sure.

Other questions crept into his mind. Had he misinterpreted the men's intentions? Were they just being friendly in the only way they knew how? Hell no, he told himself. Those suns-a-bitches were animals.

If he hadn't called a halt to their little game, there was no telling what might have happened. Conner quickly convinced himself he had done the right thing.

Sometimes self doubt could begin eating away at you and twisting the facts. Conner had seen situations where victims had ultimately become perpetrators. It often happened because people let themselves be swayed by others, or by their own self doubt. Well, that wasn't the case here. There also was the matter of the veiled threat: "...maybe we'll see you again sometime." Conner thought about that, as well.

But, it wasn't something that concerned him. If and when that happened, he'd deal with it. After sitting for several more minutes, Conner stood and looked around. He didn't see any point in continuing his search in this same direction.

He grabbed his knapsack and headed back to the big magnolia tree. Once there, he walked in the opposite direction. This would take him back toward the creek that fed the waterfall. But it would be much farther upstream than the falls.

Conner was now walking to the west. The sun was over his left shoulder. After about 15 minutes, he reached a rise and looked down on the creek.

At that moment, it dawned on him. This was probably Boulder Creek. It was the same creek that crossed highway 107 up near Cashiers.

As he looked down, he could hear the rush of water making its way over shoals and exposed boulders. As he grew closer to the creek, the sound grew louder. Once there, he paused and looked up and down the stream. The mid-day sun shone brightly off the creek's bubbly surface.

According to locals, this stream was a haven for rainbow trout. As Conner looked out over the stream, he envisioned himself standing waist deep casting a line into the fast-moving water. He'd have to try trout fishing sometime, he told himself. Conner spotted a section of the creek to his left that was rather narrow. Several big boulders were spaced evenly across that section. They appeared to be stepping-stones from one bank to another. The water churned with foam as it pushed its way around these obstacles.

That was odd, he thought. Out of curiosity, he moved to have a closer look. The more he looked at the boulders, the more convinced he was they had been placed there, arranged to form a bridge across the creek. But, who had done this?

As if being called to the other side, Conner stepped onto the first boulder and then another, carefully making his way across the stream. After landing firmly on the opposite side, he smiled to himself with childish pride. This was the first time he could remember crossing a creek and not stepping ankle-deep in water or mud.

He then returned his gaze to surrounding terrain on this side of the creek. Just a few feet back from the water was a thick growth of fir trees -- each of them about 30 feet tall. They were evenly spaced and collectively they had the appearance of a privacy fence. Could these trees have been planted purposely by someone? He moved through the tree line and paused.

Right in front of him, the ground rose steeply to a small gorge that curved sharply around to his left. There was another line of firs that blocked the entrance to the gorge. In the distance were a steep rise and a thicket of hardwoods. Some of the trees appeared to be 50 to 60 feet tall.

Conner continued past the second row of trees and entered the gorge. At that moment, he was overcome with a strange sensation. He felt as though he had entered some mysterious place. It was eerie -- almost dreamlike. Straight ahead was a large opening, about 40 yards square. The entire area was void of trees and bathed in sunlight. Scattered across the field was a mixture of tall grass and wild flowers.

It was so unlike the rest of the forest. Conner stood for several moments, staring into the clearing.

Slowly, he moved forward. When he reached the center of the field, he stopped and looked around. Over to one side was what appeared to have been a garden. But, that couldn't be, could it? He continued examining the area. Just then, his eyes locked on to an unusually shaped mound to his right. It was right near the base of the steep cliffs. Whatever it was, was partially overgrown by underbrush and ground cover. Maybe it was an Indian burial site, he told himself. Instinctively, he began walking in that direction. As he grew nearer, he could see the mound was almost oval shaped. And it definitely was man-made.

Conner wasn't sure what he was looking at. But, it certainly blended in with the surroundings. But, the structure was at least 20 feet wide, 20 feet in depth and almost 10 feet high. The outer portions were covered with some type of mud or clay. This couldn't be a dwelling, he told himself. There were no openings.

Conner moved closer and continued examining the structure more closely. It had a crudely shaped cover, which was partially concealed by green moss. This further camouflaged the structure. Conner then moved to his left. This side was obscured by a row of bushes and shrubs. There were no openings here, either.

Finally, he went to the other wall. This side extended back into the hillside and the exposed areas were covered with ivy. As he examined the wall, something beneath the ivy caught his eye. He moved closer. The vines had overtaken it, but there clearly was a door here. And by the looks of things, it had not been opened for a while -- a long while.

Could this be where John Doe lived? That was a good possibility, he told himself. The thought caused his adrenalin to rush. As he stood on this precipice of discovery, he paused and asked himself: "What if this wasn't his home? What if someone else lives or lived here?

If I step through that door, he thought, I could be guilty of breaking and entering. Or, I could be getting involved with something that I'd just as soon avoid. Conner stood for several minutes. His gaze shifted from the door back to the big clearing behind him.

Clearly, he had misgivings about going any further. He was intruding into someone's personal life. Whoever it was had painstakingly created all of this. They had arranged those boulders into a bridge to forge the creek. They had cleared the gorge and planted a buffer line of trees for additional privacy.

And, they had built this dwelling, such as it was. Whoever did all of these things appeared to be one of those people Stricker had talked about. They had not wanted their identity or whereabouts known.

Conner looked back at the ivy-covered portal. His curiosity could not be denied. He took out a pocket knife and carefully trimmed the vines around the opening. Just then, a trivial thought occurred to him. What a clever way to tell if anyone had forced entry into your home -- plant vines over the door. He chuckled at the absurdity of the thought and continued cutting.

The door was made of small, hand-crafted logs. And it was secured with a carved wooden hasp. Carefully, Conner depressed the wooden latch and the door swung toward him. He paused and looked inside. His first reaction was one of shock. He was looking into a big room flooded in sunlight. How could that be?

Hesitatingly, he stepped inside. His attention was immediately drawn to the ceiling. Overhead was huge panels of glass or plastic -- which formed a gigantic skylight. All of this overhead light compensated for the lack of windows, he told himself. It brought sunshine into what would have been a dark cave.

The interior of the dwelling was surprisingly spacious. The rear portion extended into the side of the hill. It definitely was a case of being larger on the inside than on the outside. The interior walls were constructed of hewn timbers. But, they were covered with clay on the outside. Whoever built this thing certainly wanted privacy. Secrecy was a better term, he told himself. What would you call a dwelling such as this, he asked himself? In the traditional sense, it was more of a bunker than anything else.

Conner stood motionless for several seconds, letting his eyes absorb all the sights around him. The place was incredible. Scattered around the room were several pieces of hand-made furniture. At the center of the room was a large, square table, with two hand-made chairs on either side.

There was a glass, kerosene lamp on top. Conner had not seen one of those things in years. But, it appeared to be in good working order. Presumably, this table was where someone had his or her meals. Along the bunker's front wall were a small propane stove and several shelves stocked with canned goods.

A large galvanized tub leaned against the wall beneath the shelves. That tub could serve a variety of purposes, Conner told himself.

Everything Conner could see was very orderly and neatly arranged. But there was a thick accumulation of dust covering practically everything.

It was obvious no one had been in this place for a while. It had been abandoned. Whoever lived here had simply left one day and never returned.

Conner turned and walked to the back of the big room. Over in one corner was a small, wood-burning stove. That immediately piqued his curiosity.

There didn't appear to be a ventilating pipe on the stove. That would be deadly in this closed environment. But, as he stepped closer, he noticed a small flue leading from the back of the stove horizontally into the wall. No doubt, it was well disguised where it exited the bunker. Conner chuckled to himself. He should have given the man more credit.

About 20 feet away from the stove was a crudely made bed. The bed linens were tightly drawn, and there were extra blankets on top. Nearby, there was a free-standing clothes rack, which was pushed against the wall. An assortment of shirts, trousers and coats was neatly arranged on wooden pegs. As was the case with the other furniture, the rack was designed for functionality, not appearance. Nevertheless, it was sturdy, and it showed the craftsman knew how to use tools. He stepped closer to the clothes rack. There were a few women's garments as well. I can't believe this, he told himself.

On the floor next to the clothes rack was a wooden box, or storage chest. The box contained other items of clothing. Again, each piece was carefully folded and neatly arranged in the box. Conner leaned forward. The wooden chest had the smell of mothballs about it. There were women's clothes in this chest, as well.

Conner's gaze returned to the shirts hanging before him. They were plaid and similar in appearance to the one found on John Doe's remains. Conner's eyes then shifted to the bottom of the rack, where several pair of shoes were neatly arranged in rows. Again, there were a few pairs of ladies shoes.

Such orderliness had to have been learned in the military, he told himself. This person had to be a veteran. Conner's suspicions were reinforced by the presence of a well-worn pair of military boots. Right next to them was an obvious gap. One pair of shoes was missing. Conner looked again at the boots. They were identical to the shoe he remembered seeing with the man's remains. Conner was now convinced this was the house where John Doe lived.

For several seconds, Conner stared at the gap created by the missing pair of shoes. There was a symbolism here that he found compelling. But, if this, indeed, was John Doe's home, who the hell was this guy? And who was the woman that may have lived here with him?

Conner then turned and walked back to the front of the big room.

As he walked, his eyes were drawn to the flooring. It was black in color, and it was rather spongy. He guessed it to be a synthetic coating -- probably some kind of polymer. In any case, it provided protection from the moisture and dampness of the earthen floor. This guy thought of everything, he told himself.

In the front part of the bunker was a wooden cabinet containing several guns. There were two or three shotguns, a pump-action 22, and what appeared to a Winchester 30-30. In the bottom of the door-less cabinet were several boxes of shells.

Just then, something else caught his eye. To the right of the gun cabinet was a framed picture of an airliner in flight. It was the only decorative item hanging on the walls. He stepped closer. Why an airliner? he asked himself. Maybe the guy just liked the picture. Or, maybe he was a pilot at some point.

Conner shrugged and continued looking around. Another table, this one long and narrow, was placed against the far wall near the front of the place. Several books were stacked neatly on top, along with several writing instruments. A hand-made wooden chair was tucked beneath the table. This must have served as his desk, Conner thought.

Conner then walked to the table and picked up one of the books.

It was a collection of the works of T. S. Eliot. The person who lived in this cabin was no ordinary man, Conner told himself. He read poetry. Conner respected that. A piece of paper marked one of the poems -- presumably a favorite. Conner opened the book to that section and began reading. It was from Eliot's Choruses from "The Rock."

"The Eagle soars in the summit of Heaven.

The Hunter with his dogs pursues his circuit.

O perpetual revolution of configured stars,

O perpetual recurrence of determined seasons,

O world of spring and autumn, birth and dying!

The endless cycle of idea and action,

Endless invention, endless experiment,

Brings knowledge of motion, but not of stillness;

Knowledge of speech, but not of silence;

Knowledge of words, and ignorance of the Word.

All our knowledge brings us nearer to our ignorance,

All our ignorance brings us nearer to death,

But nearness to death no nearer to God.

Where is the life we have lost in living?

Where is the wisdom we have lost in knowledge?

Where is the knowledge we have lost in information?

The cycles of Heaven in twenty centuries

Bring us farther from God and nearer to the Dust...."

Conner was touched by the reflective meanings of the verse. He also was impressed with the former resident's interest in poetry. It said a lot about him. With the book resting loosely in his hands, Conner quickly scanned the bunker's interior once more. There probably were other vestiges of the man's personality and tastes hidden here. And somewhere in this room there had to be the answer to his identity and the identity of anyone else who might have lived here.

But, at that moment, a large cloud blotted out the sunlight streaming into the room from the overhead panels. The level of light in the bunker dropped noticeably.

In this diminished light, the structure no longer seemed as inviting, or as cheerful. Instead, it was now rather foreboding. Conner looked up through the big skylight. Was the former occupant of this place reaching out to him? Was he turning out the lights on this intrusion?

Conner returned his gaze to the dimly lit room, and his mind reeled in thought. If he stayed here for a while longer -- if he continued searching through these effects -- he could conceivably learn this man's identity. And he could possibly close the book on this whole mess.

Then, another thought occurred to him. Unraveling this mystery wasn't his responsibility. Shouldn't he just go back and get in touch with Deputy Eassel again? he asked himself.

Shouldn't he just dump this new information in his lap and let them figure it out? Somehow, the mere mention of the deputy raised his anxiety level a few notches. He didn't trust the guy. This might be police business, but he felt he was the best one to bring meaning to all of it.

Still, he had violated this man's private refuge. And he was now rummaging through his personal property. That wasn't right. What he really needed to do was talk with somebody about this dilemma. But, he had convinced himself the best thing for him to do was schedule another visit to this mysterious dwelling. Maybe even more than one.

Conner closed the book and replaced it on the desk. He then turned and walked to the door. Before stepping outside, he took one last look around the big room. After leaving the dwelling, he re-arranged the ivy strands around the door. Looking at the vines now, it was hard to see where he had cut them.

Just then, the sun re-appeared from behind the cloud and sunlight filled the small clearing again. Conner looked back at the bunker and a frown settled over his face. He then retraced his path through the fir trees, crossed over the creek and headed back to the Bronco.

It was not yet noon, and he felt exhausted. It was exhaustion brought on by growing uncertainty and frustration. But, there was one thing he had decided on this day. One way or another, he was going to find out what was going on here.

CHAPTER ELEVEN

It was another toss-and-turn night for Conner. At a few minutes before six o'clock, he climbed out of bed, threw a blanket over his shoulders and stepped onto the deck and into the early morning cold. Understandably, there were no lights on at houses in the valley.

Most of the leaves had fallen from the trees, and some neighboring houses were now visible farther down the mountain. Conner could now see Pete Musser's place – his closest neighbor. But there were no lights on yet in Musser's home.

Musser was the first person Conner had met in the area. It went all the way back to move-in day. Conner was driving slowly up the mountain road in a rented truck filled with all of his earthly possessions. Musser was on foot with his dog after a long walk, and he had stopped to observe this intrusion into the idyllic spring day.. When the truck reached Musser, Conner jammed on the breaks, fearing the heavily loaded vehicle might begin drifting backward because of its heavy load and the road's uncertain conditions. Conner rolled down the window and smiled at this man, whom he assumed was one of his new neighbors.

"Howdy friend. My name's Mitch Conner, and I'm moving into the cabin at the top of the mountain.," Conner said, flashing his best smile.

"Howdy yourself, Mitch. I'm Pete Musser, and welcome to the neighborhood, such as it is!"

Conner chuckled.

"Great to meet you Pete. But, I don't trust this truck's breaks. So, when I get settled in, we'll have to get together for a beer."

"Sounds good. Lemme' know if I can be of help. I'm home most of the time."

Conner waved, smiled and gunned the old truck, which creaked as it resumed the slow climb up the mountain. Conner remembered that first meeting vividly, and since that time he and Pete had met a few times.

Conner had only been in his cabin a couple of days when Musser appeared out of the woods one afternoon. He was carrying a very long walking stick and a peach pie. The pie was a thoughtful gesture of neighborliness, Conner felt.

That had been a few months earlier. But, on this morning, Conner braced at the cold air outside the cabin, taking several deep breaths. Though it was still early, he had a busy schedule planed. And nothing he planned on doing this day involved the police. He smiled at the thought.

When Conner returned to the cabin after his day of chores, it was already dark. He looked down at Pete Musser's place, and there was smoke coming from the chimney.

"Good. The old man's home," Conner said to himself.

Conner grabbed his coat, a bottle of Dewar's Scotch and made his way down the hill. He had taken a flashlight to help navigate through the trees in this darkness. The temperature was dropping, and each breath he took was clearly visible in the chilled night air. He guessed it was below freezing.

As he stepped onto Musser's front porch, the boards creaked beneath his weight. Conner paused briefly at the door. From inside the house, came the deep, muffled bark of Musser's German Shepherd, Blitzen. The sound was violent and intimidating. Conner heard Musser approaching the door, admonishing his dog as he did. When the door opened, Musser gazed squarely at his neighbor, his face void of expression. It was as if he'd just seen Conner five minutes earlier. Truth was, the two men had not seen each other in a several days. But, Musser seldom showed signs of emotion. It was his way.

Before speaking, Musser turned again to chide his dog. He then looked back at Conner.

"Evenin' Mitch. Don't pay no attention to him. He knows you, but that's just instinct barking."

Conner nodded, but he kept his eyes glued on the big dog.

"Evenin' Pete. Thought I'd drop in for a visit. That is if you're not busy."

"Not busy a'tall. Com'on in. But, whatcha' carryin' that bottle of whiskey for? It's too late in the year for snake bites."

Conner laughed as he moved past Musser into the front room. It was the first time he had laughed in several days. And it felt good.

"Nah. Nothin' like that. I'm doin' a little celebrating tonight, and I thought you might want to help me drink a little of this Scotch ."

"Drink a little? Why don't we just drink a lot? And if you want, you can tell me why you're celebratin.'"

Conner chuckled without responding. He remained just inside the door and looked at the animal hovering nearby. Blitzen was watching his every move.

This was only the second time Conner had been in Musser's house. And that was not enough time to have ingratiated himself with the dog. The German Shepherd had the classic black and tan markings of his breed. But, what set him apart was his size.

He was very powerfully built, which was un-nerving to Conner. This dog was one mean looking sunuvabitch. The trick was to have him as a friend, not an enemy.

There was a hearty fire in the big fireplace. The warmth of the small house felt good. As Conner took a seat in a wooden rocker near the door, the big dog continued to stare at him. After several more minutes of sizing him up, the dog returned to a throw rug near the hearth and plopped down in front of the fire. But, his big brown eyes continued to be locked onto Conner.

On the surface, Musser was rather surly looking. He was tall and wiry -- probably a shade over six feet. And he didn't appear to weigh much more than 180 pounds. His dark brown eyes were hawkish. And the unkempt strands of long hair dotting his head were mostly white. Deep furrows in his brow, and wrinkles around the eyes, added to his irascible appearance. But unlike many people who lived in these woods, Musser was always clean shaven. It was difficult to tell exactly how old Musser was. Conner guessed him to be in his late 50s. Maybe less, maybe more.

To most people, Musser was unfriendly -- maybe even cantankerous. But In Conner's mind, he just seemed to be a private person who was selective of the people with whom he associated. Conner also had seen evidence of someone who could be decent and caring. Conner also felt he never wanted to get on Musser's wrong side.

But, there was no question about Musser's outspokenness. One of his more endearing mannerisms was an insistence on calling people "crazy bastards." He used the term indiscriminately for both friends and enemies. The only way people could distinguish which category they were in was by his tone of voice.

Musser emerged from his kitchen with two water glasses, half filled with ice. As he entered the living room, he retrieved the big bottle of Scotch, which Conner had placed on a nearby table.

"Now, how about we drink some of this whiskey, you crazy bastard?"

Conner laughed as Musser poured a man-sized amount in both glasses. Musser handed one glass to Conner, clinked them together and took a healthy sip of the amber liquid.

There was a smile on his face as he spoke.

"Now, that's good whiskey! Some of my cheap friends try to convince me their bargain Scotch is the same as the well-aged stuff. Hell, those crazy bastards can't tell the difference between horse radish and horse shit."

Conner chuckled and raised his glass in agreement. He then took a long sip of Scotch and savored the rushing sensation of alcohol making its presence felt in his body. There was something invigorating about the first taste of a stiff drink. After that, it was just more of the same. But, a lot of things were like that, he reminded himself.

Musser walked across the room and slumped into an oversized, red velvet chair near the fire. He turned and looked directly at his guest.

"You know what gives Scotch its smoky taste?"

"No, not really."

"They dry the barley malt over peat fires. That gives the contents its bitterness."

Conner pursed his lips and nodded. His neighbor had told him something he didn't know. Conner took another sip of Scotch before responding.

"Peat's just another form of mold isn't it?"

"Yeah, I guess you could say that."

"And penicillin is made from mold."

Musser nodded his agreement.

"Stands to reason, then, when you drink Scotch, you're building up your immune system."

Musser chuckled and raised his glass.

"Here's to good health," you crazy bastard!"

Musser took another sip from the tall glass. Conner used the momentary silence to gaze around the comfortable little house. Musser's home reminded him of a tourist lodge out of the 1940s. All the furniture was dated. Most of it looked as though it had been purchased at garage sales.

The lampshades were accented with faded white fringe. And there were gaudy, braided throw rugs on the hardwood floors. But, it was all very functional, and Musser kept the place clean. Conner felt welcome here. Musser took another sip of whiskey and let out a long sigh before speaking.

"Haven't seen you around lately. You been takin' a lot of pictures out in the woods?"

"Not really. I've been busy with other things."

"Izzat so?"

Musser looked curiously at his visitor.

"Yeah. A few weeks ago, I had a little encounter with the police."

"Naww!"

"Yeah. I didn't break the law or anything. I was workin' up near Cashiers one day, and I came across a dead body."

Musser leaned forward in his chair. He did not respond. Instead, he merely squinted his eyes at Conner, waiting for additional information.

"The next thing I know, I'm in a helicopter with Macon County deputies, identifying the site where I found the guy. Then, they start comin' around asking me questions."

Musser looked down at his drink before re-establishing eye contact with Conner.

"I saw that sheriff's vehicle up by your house a few days back. It was right when we had all that snow. I thought it was curious. But I figured you'd tell me about it if you wanted to."

"Yeah. One of the deputies was a guy by the name of Eassel. He thought I mighta' known somethin' about the guy I found. Pissed me off, really. I did what I thought was the right thing. Called them about finding the remains. Then they came up here and started askin' questions and puttin' me on the spot."

"You say it was Eassel?"

"Yeah. Deputy John Eassel."

"I know that crazy bastard. Slipperier than eel shit. Don't trust the sunuvabitch."

"Whoa!"

"Believe me. You can't trust the guy!"

"Yeah. Well, I'd just as soon forget the whole thing. But, you know this guy Eassel? You had dealings with him before?"

As soon as he asked the question, Conner knew he had stepped over the line. He was prying. And, you didn't do that with friends. Not up here. Musser returned Conner's stare without responding. Then, after a deliberate pause, he continued.

"Let's just say that me and Eassel have crossed paths."

Conner nodded his understanding. There was an awkward pause before Musser continued.

"Then, you haven't heard any more about it?"

"Nope. And I don't care to."

"I assume the law didn't find out who that guy was?"

"You got it. Another example of the competence of Western Carolina's finest."

Musser chuckled and took another sip of Scotch. Conner purposely turned his gaze away. He was uneasy talking about this anymore. Conner liked Musser and he trusted him. But, Conner felt there were aspects of his activities over the past few days he preferred not to discuss. It was time to change the subject. Conner took another sip of whiskey before looking back at his host.

"Hey Muss. You been up here a long time."

"Yep. Goin' on 19 years."

"You ever run into strange people out there in the woods?"

"All the time! That's why I seldom go out there without one of those."

Musser nodded his head toward a gun cabinet tucked away in one corner of the room. Conner turned and looked at the cabinet. Funny, he thought, that he had not noticed the gun rack before. Maybe that was because it blended in with the rest of the room. And guns were commonplace up here. Musser's large cabinet contained several guns, including shotguns, rifles and what appeared to be an automatic weapon. On a shelf at the top of the cabinet were several handguns. One of the high powered rifles was equipped with a scope.

Conner turned and smiled nervously at his friend.

"That's quite a collection."

"Some people got a different pair of shoes for every day of the week. I've got a different gun for every day of the week."

Musser flashed a proud smile and looked into his near empty glass. He held it up and drained the contents, then wiped his mouth with the back of his hand. Without asking, he walked across the room and poured himself a refill.

"You ready?"

"No. I'm fine."

Musser returned to his big chair, and looked back at his guest.

"You run into some crazies out there recently?"

"Yeah. That's exactly what they were. Crazies!"

"Well, you spend enough time in these woods, and you're bound to come across some weirdoes who don't play by the rules. Funny thing about the wilderness. It can bring out the best in people. And it can bring out the worst. The trick is to treat them all the same. That way, you don't get caught by surprise."

Conner thought about the statement. Musser was right. He was still pondering the thought when Musser continued.

"One time, I came up on a bunch of young punks in the woods all hopped up on drugs. When they saw me, they started shoutin' obscenities."

"They surrounded me and began taunting me like I was some kind of goddamn animal. I gotta' tell you it was scary. Fortunately, I had that 44 magnum tucked into my belt. I pulled out that beauty and fired a couple of rounds in the air.

Caught their attention real quick. Those little piss ants ran like it was rainin' skunk piss."

Musser rolled his head back in laughter. Then the look on his face turned serious.

"Out there, you shoot first and ask questions later."

"Yeah. I know what you mean."

Conner then told Musser about his encounter with the two men in the woods. He recounted every detail, including the self-doubts that swept over him after it was all over.

"Sounds to me like them sumbitches were up to no good! Believe me, you did the right thing! Like I said, in situations like that, you shoot first and ask questions later!"

Conner nodded. And Musser sipped from his glass and continued.

"I tell you what, Mitch. You ever get into a pinch like that, you yell for old Musser. I'm a good man to have around when a fight breaks out."

Conner smiled a nervous smile. He knew Musser was right. And he knew anyone who took Musser lightly would be making a big mistake. He suspected that his lanky neighbor could be meaner than his dog, Blitzen. At the same time, Conner took comfort in Musser's offer of assistance, if the situation ever called for it. That might come in handy one day, he told himself. Musser had become reflective and he gazed at his drink for several moments before continuing.

"Ya' know. Those Jehovah Witness people could take a page from your book. If more of 'em showed up at front doors with a bottle of Scotch, they'd get a lot better receptions. Probably get a lot more converts, too."

Conner laughed before looking inquisitively at Musser.

"Those are the ones who keep several wives, aren't they?" Conner asked.

"Naw. I think that's the Mormons. But, that's somethin' old Musser could get behind. Havin' more'n one woman in the house. Havin' them do whatever you want. Old Brigham Young had about 15 wives, as I recall. Whooeee! Just imagine the possibilities."

Both of the men laughed. Before Conner could comment, Musser continued.

"These days, you'd play hell trying to get a bunch of women under one roof -- all catering to the wants and desires of the same man. Nawsir. That'll never happen again. Feminists have seen to that."

Musser chuckled. Before Conner could respond, Musser continued.

"Course, when you come right down to it, livin' with more than one woman would be disastrous anyway. Hell, it's tough enough just livin' with one."

Conner laughed and nodded his agreement. Musser hesitated, then continued with an afterthought.

"I couldn't do it."

"You were married?"

"Yeah. Got married while I was in the Navy. But, it didn't last. Only about five years. And most of that time, I was at sea."

"After that, there was a series of live-ins. But, I got tired of comin' home and finding my goddamn clothes out in the front yard. Didn't need that shit! Naw, sir!"

Again Conner laughed. He took another long sip of Scotch and listened intently as his friend continued.

"You know, I don't think there's anybody alive who's figured out why women do what they do. I mean, when my ex-wife and I broke up, she looked at me and said she never loved me. We were married for 5 years, and she never loved me? Shit."

Musser looked intently at Conner, then continued with an after-thought.

"'Course, when I gave some thought to what she said, something occurred to me. That poor woman never loved anybody. Oh, she got married again, real quick. Never met the sap, but I can tell you one thing. She never loved him, either. I think maybe it was somethin' in the way she was raised. She was one of those pessimists. Never remembered the good times. Only the bad times. Glass was half empty, and all that. Actually, I feel sorry for her. People like her will never be happy."

"You happy, Muss?"

"Hell yeah, I'm happy."

Musser's glass was empty again, and the tall man headed for the kitchen counter and the bottle of Scotch.

"You ready for another drink, you crazy bastard?"

"Sure." But make it a small one. I'm driving."

With one last sip, Conner emptied his glass.

Musser poured him another small drink, then replenished his own. As he walked back to his chair, Musser resumed the conversation.

"So. What is it that we're celebrating?"

Conner had come here with the thought of sharing his concerns about finding John Doe's possible residence. But he had changed his mind about that.

If he was going to dig further into this thing, the fewer people who knew about it, the better. Conner delayed his answer before responding.

"Well, today's my anniversary of being here in BC. It's been five months exactly when I ran into you on the road out there. And it's gone well since then. There have been a coupla' bumps in the road, but for the most part, it's been a good ride?"

Conner looked at Musser and continued.

"My new business is going well. And I have a couple of other things I'm looking at. But, I'm happy with my decision. When I moved here, I didn't know what to expect. But things are good."

Conner paused, then continued.

"One of the things I'm thinking about is getting a job at WCU teaching writing, advertising….maybe even journalism."

"The hell you say!"

"Yep. I made a pretty good life for myself and family through writing, and I think I could teach young minds something about it."

"I'm sure you're a good writer. But teaching journalism?"

Conner shrugged. He was now on the defensive

"It's really just another skill. But, there are tricks to it. Rules to follow. Ideas to be considered. But, it's not as easy as it may seem. Not everybody can write well."

Conner paused and sipped his drink before continuing.

"When I was still writing speeches, I kept a folder in my desk; I labeled it gobbledygook. It was filled with memos and letters I had received from colleagues, bosses and peers. I've still got that folder. I pull it out sometimes. And it's a stitch reading some of it."

He paused briefly and then continued.

"The samples in that folder were written by college graduates, smart people and successful people – some very successful. But they had one thing in common. They couldn't express themselves on a piece of paper. It was funny, but sad. And IBM over the years had hired the best of the best."

"But from my point of view, I was lucky they couldn't write. If they had been good writers, I wouldn't have had a job."

Musser chuckled and nodded.

"You're right."

Conner paused briefly before continuing.

"I remember a professor I had at Northwestern. He told me one thing that had a major impact on my writing."

Musser leaned forward in his chair, awaiting Conner's point.

"Before becoming a professor, he was a big time writer and editor at a major New York magazine. It was called Look Magazine." Conner said.

Musser interrupted with a side comment

"Yeah, I remember Look."

"Well," Conner added, "The professor told me when he wrote, he let it sit for a while then read it again to see if that was really what he wanted to say. More often than not, it wasn't" Conner said.

"And my taking his advice made me a better writer, particularly when I worked as a speechwriter for executives. That's one of the most difficult kinds of writing there is," in my view. "You're putting thoughts on paper for someone who often has no idea what they want to say. It's tough as hell, and you often have to go through draft after draft after draft.... Sometimes I went through so many drafts, it seemed like I had come full circle and had returned to the original draft." Conner said, smiling.

Conner took a deep breath before continuing.

"I liked how one former speechwriter put it; "writing speeches for another person was like chewing a string coming out of your butt."

Musser laughed at the analogy.

Musser held his glass up, raised it to his lips and took another long sip.

"Now, I don't want cha' to take this wrong, Mitch. But, I never had much use for journalists. They don't make anything. They don't solve anything. And they don't cure anything.

"Now, I don't want cha' to take this wrong, Mitch. But, I never had much use for journalists. They don't make anything. They don't solve anything. And they don't cure anything. All they do is sit on the sidelines writing about the things other people do. Kinda' second guessing everybody else. I put 'em in the same category as those movie actors who play out stories that other people live."

"They're all the same. When they're not playin' make-believe, or makin' up stories, they're tryin' to tell us how to live our lives. Hell, they can't even handle their own lives." Conner nodded before responding.

"I couldn't agree with you more, Muss. I don't much like journalists either. In fact, when I was graduated from college, I chose not to work in the media for those same reasons. I went into business communications instead."

"But my training as a journalist sharpened my creative skills and helped substantially in my career. I don't have any regrets about the choice I made."

Musser nodded his understanding.

"I thought you said you worked for newspapers."

"I did. But only while I was in college. For most of my career, I worked for big companies, doing everything from speechwriting to advertising."

Musser leaned forward in his chair.

"Now that sounds interesting. I think I cudda' been good in advertising."

Again Conner laughed.

"And why's that?"

"Cause, I'm a good ideas man."

Again, Conner chuckled.

"Good ideas about what?"

"About a lotta' things."

"Give me an example."

"Okaay, the CIA!"

Conner sensed Musser had really mellowed out, and he really seemed to be in a playful mood. It also was obvious to Conner this was the real Muss talking, and he was less likely to be selective in answering personal questions.

So, it was not a time to exploit this new friendship. But, Musser was not the kind to let down his guard unwittingly. Conner continued with a question.

"What about it?"

"I'd replace it with the maff-e-ah."

Conner shook his head in mock disbelief.

"You'd replace the CIA with the mafia?"

"Yuup."

"Why?"

"Well, let's look at it this way. Today, those fuck-ups at the CIA can't find their asses with both hands. It used to be an effective, hard-hitting operation. Covert and vicious. The operatives were like surgeons."

"But, over the years, they had their nuts cut off and handed to 'em. Today, they're nothing more than political hacks. Useless! Ineffective!"

"That would appear to be the case."

"It is the case! Believe me!"

"Not only are they worthless, they costing us billions of dollars a year, and we're getting nothin' for it."

Conner nodded his agreement as Musser continued.

"So, this is where the maff-ee-ah comes in. Those Sicilians have their fingers on the pulse of everything that goes on. They know who's cheatin.' Who's stealin.' Who's outta' line."

"In fact, not too many people know this, but the U.S. government used the maff-ee-ah on some secret assignments during world war II. And I can tell you they did one helluva' job."

Musser took another long sip of whiskey.

"Sooooo! Here's my idea."

"We close down the CIA and replace 'em with the maff-ee-ah. Save a whole bundle of cash. And when some Middle East dictator pulls some shit, we turn our Italian friends loose on 'em. Zaap. The guy's history. No pussy-footin' around. And no questions asked."

Musser turned and looked at his dog.

"It's like turning old Blitzen here loose on some varmint in the woods. He'd get the job done real quick."

Musser stroked his dog affectionately and laughed. The big dog looked up and tilted his head sideways -- a confused look on his face. Blitzen knew he was being talked about. But, he didn't understand what his master expected.

"All I'd have to do is give old Blitzen the word. Hell, maybe I should change his name to Guido."

Again, Musser laughed out loud. The whiskey had taken its toll, and he now seemed totally uninhibited.

"Hey, Muss. That's not a bad idea. But, you seem to be pretty well versed on the CIA. You ever work over there?"

Musser looked directly at his guest, his eyes blinking repeatedly.

"I can't say. It's still classified."

Again Musser laughed at his own humor. Conner smiled nervously.

"Hey, you crazy bastard. How about another drink?"

"Naw, Pete. I think I better head back home. If I stayed much longer, I'd have to crawl up that damn hill. But, I'll leave the bottle here. You help yourself."

"Don't mind if you do."

Conner rose from his chair and returned his empty glass to the kitchen. The big dog stood erect and closely following Conner's movements. When Conner returned to the living room, he slipped his coat on and approached his host, who was still seated. With noticeable effort, Musser pushed himself up from the big chair and stood motionless, an openly friendly smile on his face. Conner returned his neighbor's smile and patted him on the back.

"Thanks for the hospitality."

"No thanks necessary, you crazy bastard! You drop by anytime, you heah. Old Blitzen and me are most always home."

"You take care, Muss."

Musser smiled and nodded. Before leaving the house, Conner looked back at Musser and then glanced one last time at the big dog.

Blitzen acknowledged the look with a wave of his tail.

CHAPTER TWELVE

Conner was trying to run, but his legs wouldn't move. He was unable to get away from this troubling threat. He began to call out for help…but the calls went unanswered. Suddenly, he heard a noise that gave him hope. It was a familiar sound, but he couldn't tell what it was. The noise got louder and it stirred him into action. Conner opened his eyes and snapped to a sitting position. Looking around the room, he realized he was in bed and the familiar sound was that of a helicopter flying pretty low over the cabin.

He had just awakened from a bad dream…Conner rubbed his eyes and fell back on the pillow, relieved. He had no idea what time it was, but with the angle of the sun shining in the window, he guessed it to be mid-morning. He hadn't slept this late for quite a while.

The dream indeed had been just that - a dream, he told himself. He swiveled himself out of bed and looked around the room.

"It's time to go out and see what the world's got for me today." he told himself.

In his mind, Conner replayed the elements of the dream, to see if he could make sense of it…draw any conclusions about the symbolism. But even psychologists seldom succeeded in interpreting dream symbols, he reminded himself. And it could have something to do with the peanut butter sandwich he had right before bedtime.

Conner pulled on a pair of pants and headed for the deck, plugging in the coffee pot along the way. The sun was just climbing over the treetops, and with a light cloud cover, the skies had all the elements of a magnificent red and amber painting. It occurred to him that it was a Sunday sunrise…a religious sign.

It had been quite a while since Conner last attended a church service. When he was still in Atlanta, he was a regular at a Presbyterian Church just a stone's throw from his home. He had been a regular at that church for a number of years and he missed those Sunday services.

Over the years, friends and acquaintances had often asked him what he expected from attending church regularly. His reply was as truthful and meaningful as he could make it: "It begins with a belief in God."

"And I think if I go to church and hang out with righteous and compassionate people, just maybe some of it will rub off on me."

Conner then remembered what a friend had once said about attending church. Some years back, he had called that friend, to see if he wanted to go for a beer.

"I can't do it tonight. I've got choir practice.," the friend had said.

"Choir practice?" Conner asked. "Bob, I've heard you sing, and I know you can't sing a lick. So why'd you join the choir?"

"'Cause it gives me a reason to go to church," came the reply.

"Then why do you go to church?" Conner persisted.

"So, I can sing in the choir," came the response.

That rhetorical exchange always made Conner laugh at the reasoning of his friend.

But, there was a more telling commentary in Conner's personal life that related to the loss of his mother at an early age and the time he spent in the military. Losing his mother when he was 11 resulted in his growing up with feelings of loneliness and uncertainty about the future. As a result, he tended to hang onto temporary friendships, and he was often deeply affected when those friendships were terminated, usually as a result of his or his family's relocation.

The military, in particular, tended to build such temporary friendships among young men who likely would not have been friends otherwise. They became friends because recruits spent so much time together. And such friendships were typically strong and meaningful. But after recruits completed their "basic training," most were sent off for specialized training in far-flung places, which meant the friendships ended and were replaced by new ones.

Conner found himself involved in such a situation as a 19-year old soldier. He was on his way – alone - to what seemed like a third-world country, some 7,000 miles from home. He had travelled by bus, by plane, by troopship, by train and finally in the back of an oversized U.S. Army truck to his permanent assignment at a military compound in Seoul, South Korea. Within a matter of two weeks, he had left his home, family, friends and all he had cherished.

At the time, it appeared to be one of the most devastating upheavals in his life. And without pre-thought, Conner shouldered his duffel bag and began walking, with no destination in mind.

There was a small Quonset hut straight ahead, and he paused and propped his bag against the small building. On the door was a Cross, and Conner realized it was a chapel.

The door was unlocked, and he stepped inside, walking slowly to the front row of the chapel where he took a seat. There was another Cross attached to the front wall, this one much bigger than the one on the door. Conner remembered sitting in the tiny chapel for some time. He was alone with just his thoughts and total silence.. As he sat there, Conner began to feel a sense of tranquility and peace settling over his body. And then it came to him. The anxiety was gone. The loneliness was gone. And in his mind and soul, he was never alone again.

After a few more moments of silent meditation, Conner had stood and left the chapel reassured. It was time for him to re-engage, by reporting for duty and signing in with the Officer of the Day in the orderly room. It was time for him to get on with his life.

Conner's recollection of that past experience had a noticeable effect on his emotions as an adult. Just thinking about it now brought moisture to his eyes. And it occurred to him this was a Sunday. He told himself it was time for him to re-engage in Bryson City.

Conner had driven past the Bryson City Presbyterian Church on many occasions since moving to BC, and that would be his choice on this day even though he knew very little about the little church. On the plus side, it was the same denomination he was. But, it was much smaller than the churches he had attended in the past.

It was shortly after 10:30 when he pulled into the church parking lot and made the short walk to the sanctuary. He hesitated at the front door, stepping to the side briefly to gather his thoughts. As he entered the church he was greeted by an elderly couple, welcoming him to the service.

Conner had arrived early in an effort to avoid meeting a large number of members welcoming him to their midst. He was not being antisocial; he just didn't like becoming a spectacle in situations such as this. And in Conner's mind, there were not many things that stuck out more than a visitor at a small church service. If he felt at home among these congregants, he wanted to allow the process to develop naturally and not be forced.

The interior of the church clearly had been remodeled many times over the years. It was a good combination of old and new. There were rows of plain wooden pews with the glow and smell of fresh cleaning.

An attractive young woman was seated at a table Just inside the sanctuary, preparing name tags for all attendees, members and visitors alike. Conner liked that idea because he wouldn't have to remember names, just glance down at nametags.

The greeters at the door also had given Conner a copy of the bulletin for this day's service. And according to the bulletin, today's sermon would be delivered by the senior pastor, whose name was Sidney Chamblis.

There was a picture of the pastor, and he had the appearance of an academic, in Conner's mind. He was bald, and he wore wire-rimmed glasses.

What little hair he had was largely white, and he kept it closely cropped. He also had a very pleasant smile, Conner thought.

After taking a seat, Conner spotted a small pamphlet in the hymnal rack in front of him. It was a history of the old church, and it basically confirmed the little he'd known about it. The quaint little church had very deep roots, dating back to its founding in 1880, making it one of the oldest public structures in town. It was formed by a handful of worshipers just 15 years after the U.S. Civil War ended.

And its classic steeple with its calling bell had helped the little mountain church become a beacon for worshipers over multiple generations. Conner guessed it probably had about 400 active members.

But during that terrible conflict between North and South, the whole Western Carolina area was pretty much torn apart by the war, both physically and emotionally. Some of Western Carolina's young men joined the Union troops in the conflict and others joined the Confederacy. And a corresponding conflict in loyalties also occurred among the general population. But after the war ended, the BC Presbyterian Church had become something of a mediator and coalescing force in bringing the two divergent groups back together again, Conner read.

The service began pretty much as Conner had expected. It was a mixture of Bible references and readings and announcements involving upcoming activities.. Conner was quickly impressed with the pastor's verbal skills. He had a deep voice and his delivery was compelling.

But as the service progressed, Conner immediately recognized several major difference between this church and others he had attended. The church had replaced the traditional organist and choir combinations commonplace in most churches with four baroque style musicians whose voices and largely string instrumentation added a softness and reverence to the service.

The selections included traditional religious hymns as well as original hymns composed and performed by the group. And the lyrics for the music was projected professionally on two large screens mounted up-front high enough for all to see. The projection system also eliminated the need for hymnals and other printed materials that oftentimes were difficult for some people – particularly older worshipers - to read.

Pastor Chamblis' sermon on this morning was entitled "Leave it to the Children," and it focused on the importance Jesus had placed on children and the need to cultivate in them a respect for the Ten Commandments and the promotion of Peace among Men. And Biblical references supporting this parable were projected on the overhead screens and read aloud by worshipers.

And as the pastor continued his sermon, he also changed the flow of the service, first urging attendees to huddle together in groups of 4 or 5 and share how this teaching may have influenced or effected their lives. And then as the sermon neared its end, the pastor urged members and visitors alike to turn and greet their seated neighbors and wish them well. Conner approved of this additional gesture as well. It came across as legitimate and sincere in his mind.

Conner was impressed by the personal nature of the whole program and the way the pastor involved today's worshipers in the service. And the use of technology had played a key role. It wasn't like technology had taken over this little mountain chapel. It had helped the church staff make the services more personal and meaningful, he thought.

As Conner left the small sanctuary, he was upbeat and spiritually motivated. And he did something he seldom had done before. He stood in line to tell the minister how much he enjoyed his message and the service overall. He then smiled at the Reverend Chamblis and added: "This was my first visit, and I'm looking forward to my next."

CHAPTER THIRTEEN

Conner rose early the next morning. He didn't know what all the day had in store for him, but he guessed it would be interesting. As he left the cabin, he grabbed a computer disc containing a few days' work. He'd drop that off at The Scarlet Letters for processing. It had been a coupla' weeks since he'd talked to the store's owner, Gretchen Dunner, or her husband Camden. Gretchen and Camden had married sometime after she opened the store. And any rights to ownership on his part were subtle and openly subordinate to hers.

Camden was a smallish man in his mid-fifties. He had receding brown hair -- which he kept combed straight back, and he had average features. He also sported a well-trimmed mustache, and his standard dress always included a bow tie and a white shirt, the sleeves of which were rolled up to his elbows. There was the trace of an eastern accent in his voice, and he spoke in quick, short bursts. . Still, he was a hard worker, good-natured, and he had a good sense of humor, punctuated with a hearty laugh.

Gretchen was a matronly woman of generous proportions, robust and rather boisterous. She had deep blue eyes and rosy cheeks highlighted by dimples. Her hair was mostly all white, and she typically wrapped it in a bun. She was a kind-hearted woman, sharing her husband's trusting and generous nature. The couple had four step-children and several grandchildren, all of whom lived back east. When Conner first met Gretchen, he liked her immediately

Conner got the impression Camden knew just about everything that went on in Bryson City. But, when Camden didn't know something, Gretchen could be counted on to supply the answer. The couple lived in an apartment just above the store.

As Conner entered the busy store on this morning, Gretchen was arranging greeting cards near the front of the store.

"Mornin' Mitch. What brings you out so early?"

"Mornin' Gretchen. Haven't you heard. Early-rising's the sign of a guilty conscience."

The heavyset woman laughed. Conner continued to the rear of the store where Camden was working. The storekeeper paused and wiped his hands on a towel hanging over one shoulder.

"Hey Mitch!"

"Mornin' Camden."

"Up kinda' early aren't cha?"

"What's the deal here? You and the missus asked me the same question. You know what they say? Live with somebody long enough and you start lookin' like 'em. Next, you start thinkin' alike. One of these days I'm gonna' come in here and find you wearin' panty hose."

Camden laughed; his eyes gleaming.

"I don't like 'em. They make my feet sweat."

Camden laughed at his own humor. Conner laughed and shook his head in disbelief. There was still a smile on his face as he scooped into the knapsack and retrieved the computer disc from within.

"Well, I'd like to stand around here and swap lies, but I got places to go."

Camden smiled as he pulled an order sheet from beneath a counter and looked expectantly at Conner. .

"With all this weather we've had, I imagine you've been busy?"

"Yeah. Yesterday was great with the snow everywhere. I got an early start before the melting started. I think I got some pretty good stuff."

"I'll bet."

Camden paused momentarily, then continued.

"You want special processing on any of these?"

"Nope. Just standard. Lighting was pretty good."

"Contacts?"

"Right."

Camden continued writing on the order sheet.

"Where you headed?" Camden asked.

"Cashiers. Probably spend most of the day there."

Camden nodded and paused briefly before continuing.

"Anything else I can do for ya?"

"Naw. That'll do it."

Before Camden could reply, Conner had an afterthought.

"Say…Is Carolyn working today?"

Camden appeared surprised by the question, and Conner continued before Camden could reply.

"I don't know whether she mentioned it to you or Gretchen, but I ran into her a couple of weeks ago at the Universal Joint. I was there to see the Georgia football game, and she was there with a friend…that cute little Oriental girl."

"Carolyn was at the Universal Joint watching a football game?"

Before Conner could answer, Camden had a follow-on question.

"I didn't know she liked football."

"Well, I don't think she went there for the football. She and her friend had just finished running a few miles, and they dropped in to cool off with a cold beer or two."

"Well, I can't picture Carolyn watching football. Drinking beer I can see, but not watching football."

"Holy cow, Camden, I don't know the lady that well, but, seems like you should get to know your employees a little better. I can tell you somethin' else about her. She and her friend were in running shorts and tennis shoes when they came into the Universal Joint. And so far as I can tell, she didn't have any tattoos!" Conner added.

The little man laughed.

"Well, that's good to know. And to answer your question yes, she is here today. I think she's over in the book section."

"Thanks, Cam"

Conner smiled and nodded to the storekeeper as he walked away.

When Conner spotted Carolyn, she was seated on the carpeted floor, rearranging and adding to the inventory of books. She was intent on her work and didn't see Conner approaching.

"If you're on commission," I'll buy ten of everything in stock," Conner said with a big smile.

Carolyn was caught by surprise, and she had something of an embarrassed look as she eased quickly and gracefully from a sitting position to standing, rising with all the grace and control of a ballet dancer. Conner was mesmerized by her agility and didn't realize she was talking. Her tone was a mixture of warmth and enthusiasm.

"What are you doing here?"

Conner laughed before replying.

"Seems you said that exact thing the last time I saw you."

Carolyn laughed a happy laugh and blushed.

"Well, you know what I mean."

"Yes, I know what you mean."

Conner then blushed as well.

"I had to drop off some new photos, and I thought I'd see if you were in today."

Before Carolyn could reply, Conner continued.

"I'm here to collect on your offer to buy me a beer.

Carolyn looked at him with a false sense of disbelief.

"Now?"

"No, not now. At some time in the foreseeable future."

Carolyn giggled at the statement.

"Are you thinking when it's light outside or dark outside?" she asked.

Conner chuckled at her response, a quizzical look on his face. Before he could respond, Carolyn continued.

"When it's light outside," Carolyn explained, "the proper beverage is beer. But when it's dark outside the proper beverage is wine. Which do you prefer?" Carolyn asked.

"Why don't we start with beer," Conner said smilingly.

"Suits me fine," Carolyn replied.

Carolyn then pulled a pen from her pocket and began writing.

"Here's my phone number. Let's talk."

Conner smiled as he shook the small note in front of her and left the store.

Conner's conversation with Carolyn was still on his mind as he left the city limits and headed for Cashiers. But what he was about to do quickly took over his thoughts, and he could feel the anxiety rapidly building in his body.

The basis for his anxiety was his decision to re-visit the old bunker and get more of the materials the old man had produced and gathered over the years. He was not looking forward to re-entering that old structure again, but he knew it was necessary.

After 30 minutes of walking, Conner stopped and leaned against a large boulder near the water. The big rock was covered with a bright green algae, the result of many years of exposure in this misty setting. Conner then retrieved his thermos and poured a cup of steaming coffee. As he downed the hot liquid, it radiated warmth throughout his body.

Conner lingered for several more minutes, savoring both the coffee and his frigid surroundings. At one point, he exhaled several times to watch his breath vaporize in the frigid air. He guessed the temperature was somewhere in the mid-to-low twenties -- maybe even colder. But, despite the cold, it was a pretty day -- bright and sunny.

In Conner's experience, there were certain telltale signs that indicated the cold was taking its toll on the body. The signs included a slurring of speech, watery eyes, a runny nose and a numbness of exposed skin -- particularly around the face. Conner could feel all of those things now.

But, he was dressed for the weather, and he took comfort in the fact that all of those symptoms were temporary. Still, in the outdoors there was always a concern about frostbite. But, it was not cold enough for that, he told himself. After sipping the last of the coffee in his thermos top, he tugged at his stocking cap and resumed his journey.

His path was taking him in a northeasterly direction. Once he reached the falls, he should have no trouble finding the bunker again. At least, that was his guess. After another 15 minutes of walking, Conner stopped and leaned against a large boulder near the water.

He couldn't see the falls yet, but, he could hear the sound of the water as it dashed onto the rocks below. And he could see the soft mist that hung above the creek as it spilled over the rocky precipice.

Conner continued toward the rim. After a couple of minutes, he spotted the stepping stone crossover about 50 feet ahead. The arranged boulders spanning was still visible, though not as prominently as before. Rushing water lapped at each stone, causing them to glisten in the bright sunlight. That meant the surfaces would be wet and slippery. He'd have to be careful as he made the crossing. The last thing he wanted was to fall in this frigid water. Hypothermia was a definite possibility under these conditions.

Conner approached the crossover and paused to secure the knapsack on his back. Carefully, then, he stepped onto the first boulder. Fortunately, the stones were spaced close together, and he was able to plant each foot securely before shifting his weight. When he finally reached the last stone, he leaped to the safety of the bank. Then he turned and looked back at the makeshift bridge and shrugged. He had passed the first test.

Conner now shifted his attention to the row of big fir trees looming nearby. The trees were dark green in color. But, in this light, they appeared almost black. First-time visitors to the area would simply have looked on the trees as magnificent examples of the many species found in Nantahala.

But, these trees were more than that. They stood there like giant sentries, guarding the secrets of that canyon just beyond. Clearly, the former resident had purposely added them as his first line of defense against intruders. Conner smiled at the foresight the man had shown. But what was it he had wanted to hide?

As Conner stared at the tall trees, a sudden gust caused their big limbs to dance violently in the wind. The sight was chilling -- almost foreboding. It was as if the trees were admonishing him not to go any farther.

Conner took a deep breath of the cold air and deliberately pushed his way through the low-hanging limbs. He continued across a small clearing to the second line of firs. These, too, had been planted by the former resident. Conner made his way through the second row, then stepped into the hidden gorge just beyond. As he moved into the clearing, he felt as if he were an airline passenger whose jet had just climbed through the clouds and emerged into a bright blue sky.

Conner stood for several moments looking out over the sprawling meadow. Everything appeared to be the same as it was the first time he saw it.

Only now, the tall brush and wild flowers were gone, replaced by a thick layer of snow. Conner also spotted the unmistakable impressions of animal footprints in the snow. The wind and additional snowfall had partially obscured the prints. But clearly, they were animal footprints.

He then looked to his right, toward the canyon walls rising steeply from the meadow. His eyes followed the base of the canyon until he spotted the mound-shaped structure. It was at least 200 yards ahead. With the heavy blanket of snow covering everything, the structure was more difficult than ever to identify.

From this distance it could easily be mistaken as just another rise in the canyon's uneven terrain. But, he knew what he was looking for. Before proceeding, Conner cautiously looked around him. But, he saw no sign of movement. He then held his breath and listened. But the only sound was the rush of wind through the big fir trees.

Finally, he returned his gaze to the snow-covered mound. It didn't seem that far away. But, walking straight through the open meadow was out of the question.

That would leave telltale footprints. It would be the same as drawing a red line straight to the bunker's location.

And it could prove that he had been here. Once again, Conner looked around nervously. It was important for him to play it safe -- to choose a path that was not so conspicuous.

Just then, his eyes locked onto the thin line of trees separating the meadow from the canyon walls. He turned and quickly made his way into the trees. Once there, he proceeded on an irregular path -- as if he had no particular destination in mind. He also walked in shaded areas, where his footprints would be less noticeable. If someone wanted to follow him, they certainly could. But, he wouldn't make it easy for them.

As he neared the bunker, he paused once more. There were no movements or sounds. He then followed the base of the cabin wall to the entrance.

The ivy-covered door was pretty much as he'd left it. He could still see where he clipped the shoots to gain entry. But, the cold weather had taken its toll. The vine's dark green color had faded, and the leaves were noticeably withered. Still, it was alive. With the return of warm weather, the ivy would flourish again and obscure the doorway.

Before entering the bunker, Conner used his foot to clear away the mound of snow blocking the door. He then depressed the wooden latch, and the door swung freely toward him. Once inside, he stood for several minutes looking around the big room. So far, winter had done little to change its appearance. In fact, in this cold mountain air, the dwelling's interior had a crisp look about it.

Conner turned his gaze to the small wood-burning stove at the rear of the place. It would be nice to crank that baby up and add a little warmth to the room, he told himself. But that was not a good idea. A fire would generate smoke that could be seen for miles. Besides, he could already feel the sun radiating heat through the large glass panels overhead.

After a few moments, Conner felt warm enough to remove his gloves, slip the wool cap from his head and unbutton his coat. Finally, he removed his coat altogether and placed it on a peg extending from the wall. The makeshift coat hook was another example of John Doe's attention to detail. Conner stood for several more minutes, refreshing his memory of the bunker's interior. There were so many things that had escaped his notice during his previous visit.

But his eyes kept coming back to the rectangular table in front of him. As he gazed at the table, he told himself this was where John Doe had done his reading and writing. This was the centerpiece of the man's life in this isolated place -- his primitive link with the outside world.

At that moment, beams of sunlight burst through the overhead glass panels and flooded the table in light again. Conner was moved by the symbolism here. He looked nervously around the room. Had he seen some sort of aberration? he asked himself. He immediately dismissed the thought. All he'd seen was the sun reappearing from behind a cloud, for Chrissake! Nothing more than that.

Conner then walked deliberately across the room and stood over the table. The collection of books was just as he remembered them -- neatly arranged along the top. Off to one side was a small Campbell's soup can containing pens and pencils. That also had escaped his notice before.

As he examined the table, he was struck with the light color of the wood. He guessed it to be either pine or poplar. Both types of wood were abundant in these mountains. Instinctively, he moved his hand along the surface. It was very smooth to the touch. Great pains had been taken to plane this top. He imagined a sharp axe or knife had been used for that purpose.

Conner then pulled out the hand-made wooden chair and took a seat. He sat for several moments, then ran his fingers gently across the back of the T.S. Eliot book of poetry. But, he did not remove the volume from its place. Instead, he tilted his head and read the titles of other books arranged neatly along the row. Many of the books were familiar. Some were not. The former resident of this dwelling appeared to have been well-read.

Just then, Conner's eyes settled on a white envelope that was tucked between the pen and pencil soup can and several books lying face down in the desk. He had previously overlooked this, too, in his earlier visit. He pulled the envelope from its lodging and laid it flat on the top of the desk. There was a piece of paper also next to the envelope, and it fell on the desktop when the envelope was removed.

He placed that with the envelope, which he'd open when he was back in the security and privacy of his home. ...his own home.

At that moment, Conner's eyes settled on a thick journal, which was nestled among the others. It was slightly larger than the rest. He hesitated, then pulled the journal from its place. The cover was a tapestry of mottled, black-and-white patterns.

The book's spine was covered with a course, black material. Conner opened the journal and flipped through the pages. He expected to find the columnar rules of a financial ledger. But there was none. Instead, the journal had the widely spaced lines of an elementary school tablet. This imagery from his past brought a smile to his face.

Conner then turned his attention to the journal's contents. Each page contained handwritten entries in ballpoint pen. And each one was dated. Some entries were a quarter to a half-page in length. Others went on for several pages. Conner hurriedly thumbed through the rest of the journal.

About two-thirds of the way back, the handwriting ended. After that, the pages were blank. Conner guessed that handwriting appeared on at least

40 to 50 pages. He turned back to the first few pages. His eyes focused on one of the entries.

At first, the words were meaningless. Then, one by one, they started to resonate -- even echo -- in his mind. Suddenly, his mind recoiled in discovery.

This was John Doe's Diary, he told himself. This was the man's record of personal thoughts and experiences here in the mountains. Conner looked up from the journal and his hands dropped to the table. Slowly, he looked around the little dwelling. He could almost feel another presence in the room with him. But, no one else was there. He was alone.

Conner returned his attention to the diary, and he sat staring blankly at the page before him. At that moment, his mind drifted back in time -- back to his childhood. He was a boy of ten. And his family lived in a big house in a middle-class section of Atlanta.

Early one evening, when his older sister was out, he had deliberately entered her room. He knew this was wrong. But he was driven by a child's curiosity. Standing just inside the door, he slowly looked around the room with all the curiosity of an anthropologist exploring an Egyptian tomb.

At that moment, his thoughts returned to his childhood, and he had walked into his older sister's bedroom. His eyes settled on the small red book resting on his sister's dressing table. It was her diary. He knew the little book was sacrosanct. And he had been told that it was wrong to invade the privacy of others.

But the temptation was too great. He picked up the small red book and began to read. But, his venture into the unknown was short-lived. He remembered feeling his mother's presence in the room -- even before he turned and discovered her behind him. After seizing the diary, his mother made her displeasure very clear to him. What he had done was wrong, she told him. A diary was a very personal thing. And his reading it without permission was a terrible invasion of privacy!

Even to this day, Conner could recall his mother's words. And he could vividly remember the humiliation he felt at the time. He looked up from the journal now in his hands. He was doing what his mother had told him was wrong.

The thought of his mother brought a smile to his face. But, that same sense of guilt he felt as a boy was sweeping over him now. In fact, his mother's message was just as applicable now as it was then.

But, Conner reminded himself that the circumstances were different. The person who had written the things in this journal was no longer alive. This was more of a historical document than anything else. And it just might tell him who this man was.

Conner dismissed any misgivings he had, turned back to the final entry and began reading again:

July 4th:

I rose before dawn this morning. For some reason, I was filled with an extraordinary sense of enthusiasm. I haven't felt this way in some time. It would seem my biorhythms -- my physical, emotional and intellectual phases -- were all perfectly aligned. More and more, I'm convinced of the legitimacy of biorhythms. There are many instances of people -- including myself -- feeling down on certain days and high on others -- all for no apparent reason. And on some days, everything seems to fall into place. While on others, it all falls apart. To my way of thinking, biorhythms explain such phenomena as well as anything. Still, it's possible my euphoria was a result of it being a holiday! I've always loved holidays -- particularly as a child. In our family, holidays were festive and fun-filled occasions. And the Fourth was one of my favorites. For me, it has come to represent cookouts, picnics, parades and fireworks – all the good things of summer! And as I've grown older, I've come to appreciate the Fourth of July as a time to honor our military heroes. As a veteran, I take that responsibility seriously. It seems the older I get, the more patriotic I feel.

Conner looked up from his reading and made a mental note about the writer being a veteran. After a brief pause, he continued:

Early in the day, I gave serious thought to venturing into town. I'm sure there were many special activities planned. And the idea of mingling with the tourists was appealing.

Again, Conner looked up from his reading. He assumed the writer was referring to the town of Highlands. Maybe he meant Cashiers. even though it's a village and not a town.

At that moment, the image of the White Swan restaurant appeared in his mind. Was it possible the old man sometimes dropped in at the White Swan for a meal? Conner shrugged at the thought and returned to the diary.

But, it turned out to be a glorious day here. The meadow was spectacular. There was a slight breeze in the morning, and the windflowers seemed to be dancing ever so gently in the early morning sun. The animals also came for their feeding. And we spent a friendly morning and afternoon together. I cherish the time I share with my trusting little friends. Before I knew it, the day was practically gone. It was too late for my journey. But, it was just as well. As the evening wore on, I remained outdoors, and I was able to hear the sounds of fireworks. I even saw an occasional sky burst overhead. When I made the decision to move to the mountains, I was prepared for a life of loneliness and solitude. But, my life has been anything but that. Just as a blind man sharpens his remaining senses to compensate for a lack of sight, I've adjusted to my way of life by appreciating the serenity and beauty of my surroundings. I've also had the blessing of loving two wonderful women in my journey, and I thank the almighty for enriching my existence with the lives of each, albeit too briefly in both cases. I'm reminded of my childhood when I was enthralled with the adventure of radio. The visual reality of television cannot begin to match the imagination that radio so cleverly tapped. Seeing those fireworks from this distance was much more exciting than seeing them up-close. As I looked into the darkened sky, I enhanced them in my mind. They could not have been more spectacular! More colorful. My thoughts also were with the young men and women who -- down through the years -- gave their lives in faraway wars and made possible the life we enjoy on this day. I can think of no better way to have celebrated the Fourth of July! I do not miss everyday contact with the outside world. An occasional venture into society is enough to remind me why I made the decisions I did. I also remind myself that being alone is not a curse...it's a blessing.

Conner looked up briefly from the handwritten passage. He then returned to the page and reread the final words:

"An occasional venture into society is enough to remind me why I made the decisions I did. I also remind myself that being alone is not a curse...it's a blessing."

Conner repeated the words over and over in his mind. What were the decisions the man had made? And he had mentioned two women, who apparently had died before he did. More new information to chew on, Conner told himself.

Once more, he glanced around the little bunker. In some ways, he could understand how the old man could be happy here. In fact, he could identify with many of the man's thoughts on living alone.

As he continued to gaze around the room, he asked himself if there were other surprises hidden within these walls? He then returned to the final passage, and his eyes locked onto the date of July 4th.

As he stared at the date, his thoughts drifted back to one of his conversations with Deputy Eassel.

The deputy had told him the remains he found were in the woods for a good four months -- maybe more. And he had found them in early October. Conner used his fingers to move backward three months from October. He quickly arrived at the month of June. Eagerly, he turned back to the front of the journal and read the dates above a number of other entries. All the dates were sequential. It appeared that John Doe made some kind of entry each day.

And the fact that the entries ended abruptly on July 4th meant only one thing: The man had died sometime around July 5th, or sometime soon thereafter. These were his last words. This was the final chapter of his life!

Suddenly, Conner felt a rush of adrenalin, and his heart began pounding. He carefully placed the journal back on the table and, once more, he gazed wistfully around the structure. After a few moments, his glance returned to the diary. His focus was now on the man's handwriting. From outward appearances, the style appeared almost classical. All of the letters were deliberate and well-defined. Capitals were done with a flourish. It all was very legible. Conner guessed the man had been schooled in penmanship during his early years. They didn't teach that anymore, he told himself.

Conner then reminded himself he didn't know anything about handwriting analysis. But, from the looks of things, these passages had been written by a man with a rather flamboyant personality -- a man of strong convictions.

Again, Conner eased back in the chair, trying to make sense of what he'd read. He had gained a little more insight into the man's style and personality. But, he still didn't have a clue about who John Doe was. As he repeated the name John Doe, it seemed so impersonal -- even clinical. That had been Deputy Eassel's term. Conner decided he would no longer refer to this man as John Doe.

He'd choose something else -- something a little more personal. But what? Again, he looked around the room. He'd have to give that some more thought. Just then, Conner was overcome with a feeling of concern. Sitting in this bunker reading this man's diary was neither practical nor wise. That was something that also could be done in the privacy and comfort of his home.

Conner closed the journal, placed it back on the table and sat motionless for several moments. There were so many thoughts rushing through his mind -- so many questions.

As he looked at the journal, another thought occurred to him. At best, the diary contained several weeks' worth of entries. Maybe more. Maybe less. And it appeared the writer seemed dedicated to making entries each day where possible.

Certainly, this was not the only journal. There had to be others, he told himself. But, where were they? Again, he picked up the diary.

Out of curiosity, he turned to the inside cover. There, in the bottom left corner was the number "28." The figure could mean anything. Or, it could mean this was number "28" in a series of journals. Also, written with a flourish next to what appeared to be the journal number were the letters HGM in that same classical style as the other entries.

What was HGM. Did that stand for some well-known phrase or saying, such as TGIF for Thank God It's Friday. Conner spent several moments trying to match popular sayings with that three-letter combination. Then it occurred to him HGM could simply be the guy's initials. He repeated the letters to himself and finally shook his head in frustration. Another puzzle to solve. But the more he thought about it, the more convinced he became the three letters were the man's initials. Instinctively, Conner rose from the chair and walked to the rear of the bunker. His eyes focused on the small door just to the right of the neatly made bed.

The doorway was no more than five feet in height, and it was secured with a simple wooden latch. Conner depressed the latch, and the door responded to his touch. He was immediately greeted by a musty smell emanating from the darkened cave just beyond.

Conner peered inside, to no avail. He then walked back to the front of the bunker and removed the glass shade from the kerosene lamp. The wick appeared to be in good condition. And the lamp's kerosene reservoir was nearly half full. Conner looked around the room. There was a box of matches on a small shelf near the wood burning stove. It took several tries to light the lamp. But the flame finally rose from the kerosene-soaked wick. Conner adjusted the flame, replaced the glass cover and headed toward the rear of the cabin.

Beyond the small doorway was what appeared to be a modest storage area. But, from where he was standing, he could not see inside. Holding the kerosene lamp out front, he ducked his head and cautiously entered the darkened room.

The lamp immediately bathed the small room in light, creating contrasting black and white images. Conner slowly looked around. He felt as though he had entered the storage room of an antique shop. The entire room was filled with boxes, old tools, utensils and keepsakes. He guessed the area to be no more than 20 feet square.

But the former resident had maximized every inch of available space. And considerable effort had been made to protect the contents from its damp, earthen surroundings. The room's walls and ceiling were reinforced with sapling logs. Cracks and open spaces were filled with a synthetic material.

And a protective coating had been applied to the logs, giving them a shiny look. The flooring was of the same black epoxy that covered the main room of the bunker.

Conner placed the lamp on a stack of old magazines and began looking through boxes. Some were filled with old clothes.

Others contained miscellaneous items of memorabilia. Finally, he opened a box that was just behind the door, and a feeling of satisfaction swept over him. The old journals were arranged in rows and stacked two-deep. Slowly, he began to remove them. As he did, he thumbed through each one to verify its contents. He also checked the inside front covers and his earlier suspicions were confirmed.

Each journal contained a hand-written number -- beginning with one and continuing through 28. The man who lived here was very thorough -- maybe even predictable, Conner told himself.

Conner selected about a dozen journals -- ranging from the older ones to the most recent ones -- and placed the others back in the box. Finally, he returned the box to the spot where he'd found it. With the lamp in front of him, he moved back to the doorway. He paused and took one final look around the darkened room. Was this the sum total of the man's life? he asked himself.

Conner dismissed the thought and moved back into the bright sunlight of the structure. He then carefully placed each of the journals in his knapsack. Finally, he reached for the journal on the table and placed it with the others. He then walked through the interior to make sure everything was just as he'd found it.

He made a point to eliminate the gap in the row of books -- the spot formerly occupied by the last of the journals.

With this done, he began preparing himself for the outdoors. He was not looking forward to the walk back to the Bronco. But, he was anxious to get home and examine the contents of these diaries. He was convinced they held new information on this man and his life in the mountains.

CHAPTER FOURTEEN

Residents of western Carolina were in for a cold evening. The sun had just slipped below the horizon, and temperatures were falling quickly toward a predicted overnight low in the teens. A biting wind out of the north added to the deteriorating weather. It was just after six-thirty when Conner pulled the Beast into the parking lot at Mean Willie's. Just within the past few minutes, snowflakes had begun to swirl through the headlight beams. Conner grabbed an empty spot in front of the bar, killed the engine and looked over to his right.

Mean Willie's was a classic, hole-in-the-wall saloon on the north end of Bryson City. It was one of the few places in town that served alcohol by the drink. The others included the Mountaineer Lodge and the Fryemont Inn. But Willie's was not in the same league with either of those places. Both the Fryemont and the Mountaineer catered to business travelers and tourists. Willie's was strictly for locals. It was the bar of choice for town folks who wanted to tie on a cheap drunk, or have a few beers and forget about their meager lifestyles.

Seldom did the passenger seat of the Bronco hold anything other than bags of groceries. But on this evening, it was occupied by Pete Musser. Conner peered up through the windshield at the swirling snowflakes, then turned back toward his neighbor.

"This weather could turn ugly!" Conner said, looking into the darkness.

"All the more reason to ride it out in a bar. Worst case, we can sleep on the floor!"

Conner chuckled. The two men climbed from the Bronco and braced at the frigid evening air. Conner reached the entrance first and looked back at his companion. On this evening, Musser actually looked presentable. He was wearing jeans and black cowboy boots, and his tall frame was concealed under a three-quarter-length, black leather coat. A black, ten-gallon hat sat snugly on his head. Strands of his long gray hair were tied into a pony tail in back.

Conner opened the door. And as he waited for his friend to enter, he gazed around the parking lot. Flashing neon beer signs from inside the bar cast an eerie red glow over the mixture of old cars and muddy pickup trucks. To the right of the doorway, two black Harley Davidsons leaned heavily on their kickstands.

The sight of the tired and battered old vehicles in the parking lot brought a smile to Conner's face. The gasoline in their tanks was probably worth more than the vehicles themselves, he told himself. Conner included his vehicle in that assessment. He was still smiling when he followed Musser into the musty smelling bar.

Most of the patrons at Mean Willie's were men, though an occasional female dropped in alone or was accompanied by an escort. If one of the bar's regulars had too much to drink, a volunteer would usually see that he or she got home safely. Course, those looking for trouble could find that here, too.

The most striking feature at Willie's were the oversized booths on each side of the room. They were covered in tattered red vinyl and bore the scars of many years of hard use. At the center of the room was a smattering of cheap tables and chairs. The bar, itself, took up most of the rear wall. And scattered along the top were several video games. At the far end of the bar was an antiquated juke box that offered customers an extensive selection of country western songs, most of them dating back at least 25 years. The walls of the place were cluttered with pictures of race car drivers, country singers and other notables photographed with the owner, Larson Tyler. Just beneath the front windows were several pinball machines and a shuffleboard.

Bar drinks at Willie's were three-seventy-five, and beer was three bucks. Customers could choose from three well-brand whiskeys -- Wild Turkey, Echo Springs or Four Roses -- and half dozen domestic beers, including

Budweiser, Pabst Blue Ribbon and Miller's. Anyone interested in Scotch --
and there were few -- had one choice: Old Forester, which tasted as though
it had been aged for about two days. Willie's had two choices in wine, bottles
of which had-screw off tops. And there wasn't much call for light beer. The
closest thing to food were pretzels, bags of pork rinds and pickled eggs.

During the winter months, Willie's was heated by a large oil heater that
was situated off in one corner. This accounted for the pungent smell of fuel
oil in the place. In hot weather, the closest thing to air conditioning were the
big overhead fans that did little more than agitate the smoke and stale air
hanging over the room.

Pete Musser frequently referred to Willie's as the "dump." He liked to say
it was about two degrees short of an eye-sore and that he'd seen abandoned
buildings that were in better shape. The building's rough-cut siding had never
been painted. And the wood was badly weathered. The tin roof was noticeably
rusted. But it kept the rain out. There was a lone, ventilating pipe protruding
from the back. Four narrow, horizontal windows were spaced across the front
-- about six feet from the ground. It was obvious that Mean Willie's customers
weren't interested in looking out.

And they didn't want passers-by looking in. Willie's clearly had its own
personality -- shaped largely by neglect and customer indifference.

On this evening, Musser walked straight to the bar and took a seat.
Conner slipped onto a stool just to his right. No one bothered looking up
as the two entered. From across the room, the jukebox was playing Conway
Twitty's "There She Goes." Conner followed his friend's lead and ordered a
Budweiser beer.

He then turned and casually looked around the place. Just to the left of
the door, two men wearing short-sleeved T-shirts and dirty blue jeans were
playing pinball.

Their arms were covered with garish tattoos, and their partially consumed
beers rested on the games' sloping glass tops. Both men were totally engrossed
in their activities, banging their hands and bodies violently against the

machines to assist the steel balls bouncing around inside. The result was an incessant cacophony of pings and bells coming from that side of the room. As Conner watched, he guessed these two probably owned the Harleys out front. Then again, they could be surgeons, he told himself, smiling at the thought.

When the beer arrived, Conner raised his bottle in a toast.

"Here's to crazy bastards!"

"To crazy bastards!"

The bartender glared at the two. He then turned and walked slovenly back to his perch at the far end of the bar, where he was watching the small TV mounted on an overhead ledge. Musser smiled and shook his head.

The bartender at Willie's was a balding, beady-eyed man by the name of Lamar Underwood. On this evening, he wore black jeans and a black T-shirt. What remained of his dark brown hair was combed straight back, revealing two receding bald spots on top. As was the case on most evenings, Underwood's head was covered with beads of sweat. Underwood was of average height -- no more than five-ten -- and stockily built. Adding to his considerable presence was a bulbous girth -- probably from bad eating habits, Conner guessed. Because of his powerful forearms, regulars had given him the nickname "Popeye."

Underwood typically acknowledged customer requests or comments with a grunt. Musser overlooked such rudeness, reminding his companions that Willie's was not the place to go to chat with a Nobel Prize winner. Underwood also had the strange habit of seldom blinking his eyes.

This gave the impression he was constantly staring. Musser dismissed the quirk, saying that Underwood was just stupid and couldn't remember how to blink.

"Anytime you say hello to that crazy bastard, he's stumped for an answer," Musser often joked.

But, the thing that bothered Conner most about Underwood was his long, yellowish fingernails. Conner considered them repulsive. The first time he saw those fingernails, he asked himself what the man did to make them turn yellow. He decided he didn't want to know. Conner was just thankful those hands were not involved in the preparation of his drinks, or anything else, for that matter.

As a precaution, Conner was careful not to order anything other than bottled beer. Both Musser and Conner took lusty gulps of the cold beer placed before them. Not more than a couple of minutes had passed when Musser motioned for the bartender to fetch him another beer.

At the same time, he looked expectantly at Conner, who hadn't made much of a dent in his drink yet. In Musser's view, Conner was coasting. But Conner reminded his companion he was driving and needed to pace himself. Conner continued to gaze around the place, savoring the atmosphere. Finally, he placed his beer on the bar and turned toward his companion.

"Glad I caught you at home tonight."

"Hell, I'm at home every night."

Conner laughed.

"What I meant was I'm glad you could join me for a drink. I just didn't feel like hangin' around the cabin."

"Lemme' tell ya,' Mitch. I'm always lookin' for opportunities to get out and talk to somebody other'n the dog. Besides. Drinkin' with you's better'n drinkin' alone!"

Again Conner laughed. He knew the comment was the closest thing to an expression of friendship he'd get from Musser. It was fun to be around this old man, Conner told himself. It wasn't that everything Musser said was funny. It was the way he said it. Both men sat silently for several moments, casually sipping their beer. Conner felt comfortable with Musser. He didn't feel pressured to make conversation or to entertain him. That was a sign of friendship, he told himself. Conner drained the remaining contents of his bottle and ordered another beer. It was Musser who broke the brief silence.

"I came damn close to fightin' old Freddie this mornin.'"

Musser's comment was aimed at his mailman, Freddie Preston.

"What? I thought you and Freddie were friends."

"We go fishin' sometimes. That don't make us friends. But, this mornin', he had a bug up his ass about somethin.' Maybe he and Elba tangled again."

Conner smiled.

"What'd he do that was so bad?"

"He was late. Real late!"

"And you got pissed off at him for that?"

"Hell yes! I got other things to do other than wait around for that skinny little bastard to deliver my damn mail! I told him so! How come, I sez, you're always late during the week and always early on Saturdays?"

Conner looked at his companion expectantly.

"You know what? He shrugged me off! Gave me some mumbo jumbo answer about workload."

"Can you believe it? A postal employee complaining about workload? Every time I go to the damn post office, those crazy bastards are hidin' in back -- doing God knows what! And it doesn't matter how many people are waitin' in line! As I see it, postal clerks are like that goddamn groundhog, Punxsutawney Pete. They peek out, see their shadow and disappear for six weeks! That's what they are. Just a bunch of fuckin' groundhogs!"

Conner laughed. Then Musser leaned close to his companion, as if to share some very personal information.

"And you know they throw half our goddamn mail away! Rest of the time, they're standin' around scratchin' their fat asses! Some workload that is!"

Conner laughed out loud, causing Musser to turn and glare at him.

"Hey, I'm serious here! I walk all the way down the hill this mornin' and wait for that crazy little bastard in his fairy mail truck. I end up coolin' my heels for about 45 minutes. Can you believe it? I mean, he's supposed to be working for me, goddammit! It's my money that pays his salary!"

"Sounds to me like it was your fault for going down there and waitin' around."

Musser shook his head and glared at his companion.

"My fault? Shiiit! It wasn't my fault!"

"Anyway, I came damn close to kicking his skinny little ass!"

"What stopped you?"

"I didn't want to go to jail, that's what! Postal workers are federal officers. Hit one of them, and the government will put your ass in the slammer, real quick. Naw. I'll find some other way to get even with the little piss-ant!"

Conner rolled his head back in laughter.

"Man, I don't wanna' get on your bad side."

"You got that right!"

Conner looked pensively at his beer and shook his head.

"Why don't you and Freddie work out a signal? Maybe he could blow his horn when he delivers your mail."

"I thought about that. He told me it was against regulations. I got his regulations! Right here!"

Conner chuckled and took another swig of beer. After a momentary silence, he looked back at his companion, before turning his gaze back to his empty beer bottle. Conner previously had decided not to tell anybody about his finding John Doe's place in the woods. But, he had changed his mind about telling Musser, who Conner now believed could keep things to himself. And he seemed to be the kinda' guy who was very loyal to his friends.

"Speakin' of going to jail. You ever purposely do something that you knew was against the law?"

"Hell yeah! Lots of things! Runnin' a red light's against the law."

"I'm not talking about traffic violations. I'm talking about somethin' that could send you to jail. Like punching out your mailman!"

Musser turned and looked at Conner without responding. The look on his face was now dead serious.

"Why you askin'?"

"Well, I'm not trying to pry, if that's what you mean. I'm asking for my own benefit."

"You tryin' to tell me you've done somethin' wrong?"

Conner shrugged his shoulders without responding.

"If there's somethin' you wanna' discuss, it won't go any farther than this room."

Conner looked at his friend and nodded.

"Yeah, I know."

Conner stared straight ahead for several moments before turning back to Musser.

"Remember what I told you about that body I found in the woods?"

"Yeah."

"Well, that whole mess started preying on my mind. So, I went back up there lookin' for anything that might tell me who the guy was. Lord knows, old Deputy Eassel wasn't goin' to do anything."

"You got that right!"

"Anyway, I stumbled on this structure in a little canyon. And I'm pretty sure it was his."

Musser raised his eyebrows in a look of surprise.

"What makes you think so?"

"Lots of things. For one, it hadn't been occupied for a while. Looked like somebody just walked away and never returned."

"Maybe somebody just pulled up stakes and left."

"Naw. Too many personal effects. Too many provisions left behind. No, the person who lived in that structure planned on returning."

Musser nodded his head and pursed his lips.

"I also found some of his diaries."

Musser quickly turned and looked at his companion.

"Diaries?"

"Yeah. From what I saw, the guy made entries in his journals just about every day."

Slowly, Musser turned away in thought. He took another sip of beer and then looked back at Conner.

"I assume you read 'em?"

"Just a few passages. But there were lots of 'em. Lots of stuff written down. In fact, I took several of the journals, and I'm hopeful I can find out who he was."

"Any clues yet?"

"No. But, I think I'll find somethin.' And there was one other thing that convinced me that place was his."

"What's that?"

"The last entry in his diary comes within the range of dates the coroner listed for his death.."

Musser nodded without responding.

"The point is, I broke the law when I entered that dwelling. I could probably be charged with trespassing. Possibly even breaking and entering. I also took some of the guy's personal effects."

"You mean his diaries."

"Yeah. I took quite a few of them."

Musser gazed straight ahead. He then lifted the beer bottle to his lips and swallowed deeply. Before speaking, he wiped his mouth with the back of his hand.

"Well, son. If you ask me, you got nothin' to worry about. What you just described is a tort. And that's no big deal."

"Whatta' ya' mean tort?"

"It's a violation of civil law, as opposed to criminal law. In most cases, charges must be brought before any action is taken. And if no charges are filed, then nothing happens. It's like the old basketball rule: no harm, no foul."

Conner looked intently at his friend and nodded. Musser smiled and continued.

"Besides, the man's dead. So, it's unlikely anybody will file charges against you. And based on what you've told me, he didn't appear to have next of kin that he cared about, or would admit to."

"Otherwise, he wouldn't be livin' out in the goddamn woods by himself. But, it's not unusual for people who live up here to cut all ties with their previous lives. Believe me!"

Conner turned and looked at Musser without speaking. His friend took another sip of beer and continued.

"Sounds to me like you just stumbled on the man's abandoned domicile. Who knows. You just may turn out to be some kind of hero, you crazy bastard!"

Conner chuckled. It felt good to laugh. And discussing his concerns with Musser helped ease his conscience. He didn't know if Musser knew what he was talking about. But the statements sounded logical. In any case, Conner was glad he brought it up. He raised the bottle to his lips and drained what remained of his second beer.

At that moment, blurred movement in Conner's peripheral vision caused him to turn his head to the left. His eyes focused on two approaching figures, and he felt an immediate rush of adrenalin. Musser sensed his friend's uneasiness, and he, too, swiveled around in his chair.

Standing just a few feet away were two men, both wearing faded blue jeans and plaid wool shirts. The two reeked of beer and body odor. The nearer of the two was short and stocky. His pudgy white face was partially obscured by an unkempt beard and long, disheveled brown hair. He had a large nose, and his face was transformed by a sinister grin. At that moment, Conner realized it was the two idiots who had accosted him in the woods a couple of weeks earlier.

The man behind him was more than six feet tall, and his pock-marked cheeks and unruly hair gave him a menacing look. The shorter man moved closer to Conner and spoke in a sarcastic tone:

"Well, well, well. If it ain't our coffee-drinkin' friend from Cashiers."

Musser shot a quick glance at Conner, but never fully removed his eyes from the two strangers.

"Who the hell are these people, Mitch?"

"They're the ones I ran into in the woods."

Musser nodded his understanding, as the shorter man turned toward him and snarled.

"Hey, old man! You stay outta' this! It ain't none of your concern."

"Oh, but it is! This is my friend, and whatever concerns him, concerns me!"

"Have it your way! But your buddy and I have a little unfinished business!"

Without speaking, Musser rose from his chair and stared down at the shorter of the two men.

"Listen Poncho. I'm gonna' give you some free advice. Take your lap dog over there and get the hell outta' here before you get hurt!"

The man's head rolled back in drunken laughter. Musser looked at Conner and shrugged. Suddenly, the man's laughter turned to a growl, and his face contorted in rage. With one swift motion, he snatched an object from his pocket and assumed a crouching position in front of Musser. There was a noticeable click, and Conner's eyes locked onto the silvery blade of a large switchblade knife.

Musser's reaction was instantaneous.

His right foot shot forward with piston force and smashed into the side of the attacker's left knee. Conner heard the crunching sound of tearing muscle. The man's knee buckled against his body weight, sending him sprawling on the floor. Dazed by the suddenness of the attack, the second man lunged forward. Musser spun to his right. His clenched fist smashed into the charging man's throat, causing him to fall to the floor, gasping for breath.

Conner darted a stunned look at his friend before looking down at the two men lying helplessly on the floor. He then looked quickly around the big room. All of the bar's patrons were standing silently, their eyes locked on the two men on the floor. The only sound now was the jukebox playing in the background and the attacker gasping for breath.

Musser looked down at the short man, who was writhing in pain at his feet. The man's knife, no longer a threat, lay abandoned on the floor some six feet away. Carefully, Musser knelt and whispered something into the man's ear. He then climbed back to his feet and tugged at the lapels of his leather coat. Finally, he eased back onto his bar stool and smiled at his companion. Conner continued to stare at his friend in disbelief.

"Holy Shit, Musser! Who the hell are you, anyway?"

"I'm just a citizen who doesn't like bullies."

Conner considered the response and sat silently for several moments. When he spoke, he motioned toward the short man lying on the floor.

"What did you whisper in that guy's ear?"

"I told him it would be best if he didn't come around here anymore."

Musser then leaned forward and motioned for Underwood, who was standing at the far end of the bar. The look on the bartender's face was one of total shock. Conner knew immediately that Underwood was shaken by what he saw. His eyes were blinking rapidly. As the bartender approached, Musser looked at him and smiled.

"Hey Popeye! You better call 911."

CHAPTER FIFTEEN

After a restless night, Conner awakened early the next morning. As he laid motionless in bed, he was suddenly aware of an eerie silence hanging over the cabin. But, he was still too groggy to make sense of it. Whatever it was could wait. He lingered for several minutes, savoring the warmth of the bed and allowing his head to clear. The secret to draining the last drop of comfort from sleep, Conner felt, was to delay opening the eyes as long as possible. Once the eyes were open, it was time to get up.

Finally, he turned his head on the pillow and peered through the window. The panes were frosted, and he couldn't see anything. But there was sufficient light filtering through to tell him the sun was making its presence felt.

With great effort, he swung his feet around and sat on the edge of the bed. It was cold, very cold! He'd have to stoke the fire. Just then, thoughts from the previous evening rushed into his mind. He vividly recalled Musser attacking the two men in the bar. The images were as frightening now as they were then. But, he was thankful his friend had been there. Otherwise, there was no telling what might have happened.

Conner also recalled the conversation he and Musser had had. And he remembered the paramedics arriving and removing the two strangers from the bar. But, that part of the evening was something of a blur. Finally, he recalled dropping Musser off and then making the trip up his own driveway in the drifting snow. But, he didn't remember how many beers he had consumed during the evening. It must not have been too bad, he told himself. He didn't have a hangover!

Conner lifted himself from the bed, nestled into his bathrobe and made his way down the hall. As soon as he reached the living room, he turned and gazed through the big picture window to his right.

His reaction was immediate.

"Whoa!"

Overnight, a blizzard had dumped about a foot of snow across the nearby mountains. Suddenly the eerie silence made sense. All the sounds that normally echoed across the hills were now muted by the heavy blanket of snow. There were no cries or chattering sounds from the forest's winged and furry creatures.

There was not the occasional muffled hum of traffic rising from the roads down below. That probably meant the highways were snow covered -- maybe even closed. Even the shrilling cry of trains snaking through the valley had been silenced.

To some people, being isolated by such weather could bring on a sense of futility -- even helplessness. But, Conner felt neither of those things. Instead, he was instilled with a sense of well-being. Everything he needed to survive the ordeal was right here in the cabin. And, he knew that if he really needed to get out he could. The Beast would see to that. Winter storms, he told himself, were nature's gift to working people. The thought brought a smile to his face.

Conner continued to look out over the wintery landscape just outside his window. Strong winds overnight had whipped the snow into sharp-edged drifts, some of them three to four feet deep. And the normally colorful forest had now been transformed into contrasting shades of black and white. It was a magnificent picture without sound.

Just then, his photographic instincts kicked in, and he visualized capturing those images with his camera. But, that was out of the question. Just nego-tiating the deep snow drifts would be difficult -- even risky. No, there would be no venturing out on this day. Instead, he'd spend this as a forced day of relaxing and enjoying the comfort of his home.

From the hearth, Conner retrieved several logs and banked the smoldering embers in the stove. He then adjusted the flue and waited for the fire to catch. Before leaving the room, he flipped on the stereo and turned up the volume. Since there was no sound outside the cabin, he'd create his own sound inside. Suddenly, the room reverberated with Bach's Brandenburg Concerto No. 3, courtesy of National Public Radio.

The first order of business in the bedroom was making the bed. This was an inviolate part of Conner's daily routine. In his view, there was nothing worse than entering a bedroom that had disheveled bed linen. It was true of his own home, as well as for hotel rooms when he travelled. He knew numerous people who simply didn't place much importance on making their beds in the mornings, or hanging up their clothes, for that matter.

To Conner, making the bed was every bit as important as mowing the lawn, washing the dishes, throwing away old newspapers and folding and storing clean laundry. To do otherwise was slovenliness and the sign of a cluttered mind, in his view.

Conner traced his neat and orderly lifestyle to his years in the military. It was not something he learned as a child.

After brushing his teeth, Conner stood briefly before the mirror rubbing his chin and assessing the length of his beard. It would have to be trimmed soon, but not today. This was a day of rest. Before stepping into the shower, he adjusted the temperature a little higher than normal and eased into the stream of hot water. This would help take the chill off, he told himself.

Back in the bedroom, Conner retrieved a clean pair of jeans and a warm shirt. He then pulled on a pair of wool socks and slipped into his house slippers.

Finally, he made his way to the kitchen and selected the appropriate utensils for preparing breakfast. Soon, the kitchen was filled with the aromas of blueberry pancakes, grits and ham -- all mixed with the pungent smell of freshly brewing coffee.

As he sat down to eat, Conner heard the familiar NPR radio jingle from the other room. That told him it was the top of the hour and time for the local and national news.

"Good morning. It's nine o'clock and this is National Public Radio in Asheville. I'm Karl Hopkins. And I'm Judy Wharton. Our top story this morning...Western Carolina paralyzed by a winter storm."

The male announcer gave details on the storm. A large number of residents had lost power overnight. At the mention of power outages, Conner looked up from his meal. He was thankful he still had electricity. But, if it went out, he was prepared. He had flashlights, candles and a battery powered radio. And, if necessary, he could cook on the wood-burning stove.

The announcer then switched to comments from a state transportation official. Roadways were ice-covered and hazardous, the man said. The official appealed to residents to remain off the roads. A brief weather forecast then followed. Scattered snow squalls were predicted over the next 24 hours. As the newscast continued, Conner looked toward the radio when something caught his attention.

The female announcer was next, providing a lengthy list of school closings and meeting cancellations. Classes at Western Carolina University also had been suspended, she said. Again Conner paused. The mention of Western Carolina brought Cynthia Henchel to mind. In all probability, she also was stranded. The weather front that produced this snowstorm extended eastward almost 75 miles. That would certainly include the Cashiers area, he told himself.

Conner found himself staring through the kitchen window in thought. He imagined the young woman alone in her lake house, casually dressed and reading a book in front of a fire. He was fantasizing about this woman, he told himself. In reality, she probably was painting a bedroom and covered with paint. Or maybe she was doing laundry. He chuckled at the thought. Just then, a heavy clump of snow cascaded from a pine limb just outside his window, dashing his thoughts and returning his attention to the radio. The news had just ended and the cabin was once again filled with the strains of classical music.

Conner lingered at the kitchen over one last cup of coffee. Then, with the kitchen back in order, he returned to the living room and sought the comfort of the big leather chair. He sat motionless for several minutes, surrendering his senses to the crackling of burning logs and sounds of the Chicago symphony. It was a pleasurable mixture of woodwinds, percussion, brass and violins. This was total contentment -- total relaxation, he told himself.

At that moment, the effects of the hearty meal and the warmth of the fire began to take their toll. He felt his eyelids growing heavy. It would be easy to doze off, he thought. But, he forced his eyes open and looked around the room. Once again, images from the previous night's activities drifted into his mind. He dismissed the thoughts, and his gaze settled on the knapsack resting on the floor to his right. He had not touched the bag since returning from Cashiers. With considerable effort, he climbed to his feet, retrieved the knapsack and returned to the chair.

As he unbuckled the straps, his nostrils were filled with the musty smell that permeated the bag's contents. The old journals had absorbed more than memories over the years.

Conner shuffled through the ledgers, casually inspecting their covers. Each, in varying degrees, bore the evidence of time. The older ones were noticeably discolored, their once white pages now a faded shade of yellow. Here and there were traces of water stains. But, overall, the diaries were in remarkably good shape, considering that several dated back more than 20 years.

Conner then randomly selected one of the old ledgers and set the others aside. On the inside front cover of the journal was the number three, circled and underlined for emphasis. That identified it as one of the earlier ones. After a brief pause, he turned to the first page and began reading. Above that first entry was the date, February 2nd.

February 2nd:

Three months have passed since I came to the mountains. Last night I was finally able to move into the dwelling. Much remains to be done. But, the walls are in place and the roof is secure. Overall, I'm very pleased with the way things are shaping up. This modest little place is everything I had hoped for. At least, it soon will be! It's amazing what can be done when you set your mind to it. I hope to have this in good shape for Amy. She seems to be fully recovered and willing to travel now. I'm sure Roebie has no interest. He would consider this place a hovel. But, I'm sure Amy can turn it into a home. She's so talented at everything she does. Looking back over the past two months, bringing the materials back here was probably the worst part of the whole ordeal. At times, I felt as though I were a worker ant, taking morsels of food back to the colony. But, it's nice to be out of the cold. It's nice to have a roof over my head. Living in that tent was not a very pleasant experience. It brought back many memories of the past. But, I survived! The boys of 82nd would be proud of me!

Conner looked up from the page. He was momentarily stymied by the mention of the 82nd. It was ambiguous. He knew that the writer was a military veteran -- but a veteran of what branch? Without further thought, the answer popped into his mind. The guy was referring to the 82nd Airborne Division! That had to be it!

Conner smiled to himself, and his mind was now filled with images of men in full combat gear tumbling into space through the gaping hole of a transport plane. The old man had been a paratrooper at some point. As he reflected on this new piece of information, one other thought occurred to him. He still didn't know the man's name. In fact, he might never know. That would be unfortunate.

At that point, a totally whimsical idea entered his mind. Why not call the old man "Jump?" he asked himself.

It was an irreverent name but totally appropriate for a former paratrooper. Certainly, it was a sight better than John Doe. In fact, the old man probably would have liked it. Conner found himself saying the name out loud several times. Somehow, it just sounded right. The notion brought a smile to his face. From now on, the mystery man would be known to him as "Jump."

Conner returned his attention to the journal, and his mind re-focused. Over the next few minutes, he read of additional work being done on the dwelling. Jump had described his efforts in considerable detail.

He told of improving the facility's creature comforts, and doing several things to further disguise its exterior. Clearly, concealing his existence in the woods had been a high priority.

Again Conner looked up from the diary. One question, above all, nagged at his consciousness. What the hell had this guy done? What had happened four months before he wrote this passage? Some 20 or 25 years had passed since then. But whatever it was, Jump seemed proud of it. And what was the evidence he still had? It probably was still right there in the dwelling, Conner told himself. And who the hell was Amy?

The answer to those questions were probably somewhere in these journals, Conner guessed as he looked down at the diaries. It was too bad the contents were not on a computer. Then, he could do a subject matter search and sort this thing out. But, that wasn't possible. He'd just have to keep wading through this stuff. Conner shrugged at the thought and continued. There were additional references to Jump's building different pieces of furniture -- including the table and chairs and the bed. After more than an hour of reading, Conner reached another passage that caught his attention. It was dated March 15th.

March 15th:

I spent most of today in town, purchasing supplies and mingling with the locals. I've taken a liking to the people in Cashiers. They're friendly and helpful. I try to be as civil as possible without encouraging familiarity. And I try not to go to the same store a lot. I don't want my presence to become routine with any of the shopkeepers. But, I've become particularly fond of that quaint little restaurant along the creek. The wait staff there is very nice. I've come to know many of them by name. And they don't ask a lot of questions. There's so much turnover in restaurants these days, that I don't feel my exposure there represents a real threat. But of course, I don't give them my real name.

Again, Conner looked up. Jump could be referring to the White Swan restaurant. It could have been around that long.

The restaurant certainly looked as though it had been there for at least 25 years -- maybe longer. It also was possible the Swan had operated under a different name at the time. Longevity wasn't exactly commonplace in the restaurant business. So, the old guy liked the White Swan restaurant. They had that much in common. Conner kinda' liked the place, himself. He smiled and continued reading.

I also bought a newspaper in town. It was the first I'd seen since coming up here. I guess I'm not surprised, but my little escapade is still making news. It's been four months, and the authorities are still searching -- still advancing their outrageous theories.

Conner looked up in thought. It would have been nice if Jump had been a little more descriptive of his "…little escapade." But that might come up again in writings elsewhere in these diaries, Conner guessed. After another moment of reflecting, he returned to the diary accounts.

Others seem convinced that I'm dead! That suits me just fine. As I read the accounts, it all seems so unreal now. But, it was real enough. I've got the evidence to prove it. I can't believe I actually pulled it off. I've gotten my revenge -- my little pound of flesh. But, I won't feel totally safe until a little more time passes. If I ever get caught, possibly I can take comfort in selling the movie rights to my story. Even Roebie might be interested in that!

The reference to movie rights caught Conner's attention. And the name Roebie had popped up again. Conner laid the ledger aside. Whatever it was that Jump had done, it must have been spectacular! He repeated the reference under his breath: Movie rights? Conner then gazed thoughtfully through the big picture window, and his mind wandered. How much had he learned about this man? he asked himself. It was obvious that Jump had come to the mountains to elude his past. But, in that regard, he was in good company. A lot of people had come here to get away from something, he now felt.

Conner also knew that Jump had been a paratrooper. And authorities had searched relentlessly for him shortly after he did what he did. Clearly, they had not found him. For one thing, they had searched in the wrong place!

The idea of Jump eluding police triggered thoughts of the young man who was suspected of bombings at the 1996 Olympics and at several abortion clinics. He, too, had disappeared in these mountains. After combing these hills for months, the FBI had thrown in the towel and appealed to the public for help. But, the response had been predictable. No one came forward! Conner chuckled to himself.

"Damn, I love these people!"

There was still a smile on his face as he returned to the diary. He continued reading, and another passage caught his eye. The entry was dated *June 17th*:

I think I'm becoming paranoid and overly suspicious of everything around me. When I go outdoors, I get the feeling I'm being watched or followed. Maybe I have these feelings because I fear being caught. This is not Oregon, but I've become very attached to my little hideaway here in the mountains.

Conner now paused at the mention of Oregon. He tucked that piece of information away in his memory, then returned to the page before him.

I'd hate to give it up. But, over the past few weeks, I've dreamed about being locked up in a small jail cell, and I awake with cold sweats. The dream is very frightening. On my way back to the dwelling this morning, I stopped several times and looked around. There was no-one there. It was all in my mind. I hope this feeling passes soon. I don't like it!

Conner paused and laid the book aside. Suddenly, he was overcome with feelings of compassion. He was beginning to feel sorry for the man, even though he had never met him and didn't know who he was.

But, from what he'd read, Jump was not a violent person. He didn't seem to be the type to inflict harm on others. Certainly, he was not a coward, which was the case with terrorists who left bombs in public places. The more Conner was learning about Jump, the more he liked about him. It was as if Jump was becoming something of a friend.

Conner rose from the chair, yawned and stretched his arms high over his head. All that reading had made him drowsy. He added a couple of logs to the fire, then turned and walked to the window. At that moment, rays of sun burst through a small opening in the clouds, flooding a nearby area in light. Exposed snow crystals now took on the appearance of sparkling diamonds. Conner was fascinated with this brilliant display. But, just as quickly, the sunlight disappeared and the snowflakes once again revealed themselves for what they were -- particles of frozen water.

Conner chuckled at the imagery. It was a classic case of objects appearing to be something they weren't -- a case of some things looking totally different under different circumstances. Light had a way of changing the appearance of many things -- even people. From his high school chemistry classes, Conner also recalled several examples of the effects that light had on many different objects.

It certainly had a big impact on photography. There were other agents of change, as well. Different environments could even change the total appearance of some animals. The chameleon was a perfect example. There were other things that influenced perceptions, as well. Included were personal beliefs and biases.

A family with the ugliest child in the world looks on their offspring as beautiful -- perfect in every way. Some people created their own blind spots.

Alcohol was another agent of change and misconception. How many times had he met women in a bar who become more attractive with each drink he took.

The thought brought a smile to his face. Alcohol could definitely affect the way a person looked at things -- even the way they perceived themselves. The thought of alcohol caused Conner's stomach to churn, a delayed reaction to the incident that had taken place at the Mean Willie's bar, Conner told himself.

Pete Musser also popped into his thoughts. Conner smiled. Instinctively, he went to the phone and dialed the number of his next door neighbor. The phone rang several times before being answered.

"Yeah."

Conner was taken back by the abrupt response.

"What kind of greeting is that?"

"Whatta"ya expect? Musser res-i-dence?"

Conner chuckled.

"Well, I never know what to expect when I call you. But, I'm just glad you answered. I wanted to make sure you weren't dead."

"If I was dead, I wouldn'ta answered the phone, you crazy bastard! It's one of the conditions set forth by the phone company. Signed a contract and promised not to answer the phone if I was dead."

Again, Conner chuckled.

"I'm glad you're not dead."

There was a brief pause. before Conner continued

"You got everything you need? Coffee? Milk? Bread?"

"Is this Mitch Conner, or the Red Cross?"

Conner chuckled.

"Naw. I got everything I need. Unless you got a woman over there with big old tits."

Conner laughed. There was a brief silence before he continued.

"No. Nothing like that. If I did, I wouldn't have called you. Hey, the real reason I called was to thank you again for what you did at Mean Willie's."

"Well, no thanks necessary. I'll tell you what. That crazy bastard had his eye on taking a piece of both of us. I just reacted quicker than you did."

"Anyway, I was pretty impressed. You move pretty good for an old man."

"My dog taught me if you don't move quick in life, you get pissed on.."

Conner chuckled at his friend, before responding.

"I don't know about that. I do know that I owe you one."

"You don't owe me nothin.'"

There was a brief silence on the phone Before Musser continued.

"Well, I'm deeply touched you were concerned about my safety," Musser added somewhat satirically.

"Why else do you think I called? Cause I miss you?" Conner shot back.

Musser chuckled.

"Well, since you asked if I need anything, I am running kinda' low on Scotch."

Conner chuckled and responded.

"I think I can solve that problem."

CHAPTER SIXTEEN

I t wasn't often that Conner called on friends for favors. But the circumstances in this request were unusual. First, Conner needed legal advice. And whether it was a casual request or a formal inquiry about legal representation, he needed someone he knew who could give him counsel - maybe even represent him in court - and would honor his request for anonymity.

And Conner knew immediately the person he needed to see. It was his Atlanta lawyer friend Chad Greenlee. Conner had known Greenlee for nearly 20 years, primarily through their association at Conner's place of worship, the Presbyterian Church in Atlanta. And Conner considered Chad a good friend, in addition to being a good lawyer.

A number of days had passed since Conner visited Jump's place for the second time. And Conner had spent considerable time reading the journals he removed from that remote little bunker. Conner had discovered some additional clues in those telling documents, but they were only clues. So far, trying to decipher these journals were like assembling a 1,000-piece puzzle, Conner thought.

And this man must have been a consummate gambler, Conner guessed of the deceased. The old man trusted that whomever discovered his little secret would understand his story and not be punitive about its contents.

But the most compelling issue in this whole affair was the letter Conner found among the deceased's records, giving him Power of Attorney over any investigation of who the deceased really was and bequeathing ownership of all documents, materials, and possessions to the discoverer. It was a letter addressed "To whom it may concern." The strangest thing about this whole issue was the more Conner read about the man, the more he felt he'd known him for quite some time. And the guy seemed to know this would happen, Conner concluded. He certainly was no dummy, Conner told himself.

When Conner reached Greenlee on the phone, the two exchanged pleasantries before Conner told his friend about the reason for the call. When Conner finished his explanation, Greenlee's response was total silence. When he did reply, his response was cautious and caring.

"Mitch, I'm at a loss for words. And if there's some way I can help, you know you can count on me."

"Thanks Chad. I appreciate that."

There was a momentary silence before Conner spoke again.

"I'd really like to hear your thoughts on what I should do," Conner added. And for that reason, I'd like to see you in person. But before we proceed, I'm saying I'm on the clock with you," he added, referring to Chad's fee."

Greenlee quickly responded.

"Hey, you're talking to a friend here."

"I know Chad. I know." Conner added.

Greenlee suggested they meet somewhere about halfway between Atlanta and Bryson City. But Conner had insisted on going to Atlanta, and Greenlee finally recommended they meet at his office.

When Conner finished the call, he felt relieved. And he felt good about having someone he could rely on to watch his back during everything that was likely to come.

As Conner made the unexpected drive to Atlanta, he was travelling through familiar surroundings. He could never have anticipated having to make this unexpected trip back to Atlanta, despite his own estimates it wouldn't happen anytime soon. But, having visited Greenlee's office before, he had no problem finding it.

Chad Greenlee had the appearance of a West Point cadet. He was about six feet tall, had closely cropped brown hair and green eyes. And his cleft chin further added to his military cadet resemblance. In fact, he had served in the military as an infantry officer prior to attending law school. He and Conner were about the same age.

Greenlee was expecting him and when Conner arrived, his secretary immediately led him into the lawyer's office.

"Whatta' ya' say big fella," Greenlee said, grabbing Conner in a bear hug.

"Hey, Chad. It's nice to see you again."

The two men stood momentarily smiling at each other before Conner took a seat right in front of Chad's desk.

"Okay, where do we start," Conner asked after making smalltalk for several moments. Conner then proceeded to answer his own question, by discussing in greater detail his discovery of John Doe's remains. He told of taking photos of the remains, as well as the surrounding area. And he mentioned his calling the police to report his discovery. Finally he described revisiting the site by police helicopter and the accusatory nature of the subsequent police interrogationist.

Then he discussed finding the deceased's residence and his taking materials from that residence, neither of which the police knew. Conner also discussed finding the legal document that gave him the "Power of Attorney."

Conner also brought the bequeathing document and the transmittal letter, both of which he surrendered to Greenlee, who took several minutes to scan both without comment. But, it was the accompanying letter that quickly became the center of attention for the two.

That document - bequeathing to some yet unknown person at the time of its writing – was a quintessential expression of pure trust by the deceased. It was a trust this unknown person would not simply dump the material in the hands of law enforcement, thus ignoring the legal rights term "without prejudice."

Greenlee mostly listened to his friend without asking more than one or two questions. When Conner finished his thumbnail review, he fell silent.

Greenlee swiveled around in his desk chair and gazed out at the skyline of the City of Atlanta just outside his windows. He remained silent in thought before swiveling back around to face his friend.

"I've never seen or heard of anything like this in my life," Greenlee told his friend. "But, my first reaction is to share a few general thoughts on where we are," Greenlee continued.

Conner liked his friend's use of the word "we" because it made it sound like he was no longer by himself.

Before Conner could respond, Greenlee posed a question.

"I have to ask you, why didn't you just walk away from this whole thing and turn it over to the police?"

Conner thought about the question for several moments, grasping his hands together before him on the desk.

"That's a good question, Chad. That would have been the smart thing to do. And I've certainly given it a lot of thought. You probably are going to think what I'm about to say as crazy. But in a few words, I don't think he would have wanted me to do that."

Before his friend could respond, Conner continued.

"From the beginning, I've had something of a sixth sense about what's happened here. I don't know who this guy is, or was. But, I think he wanted to have his story told…even after death. It's highly probable he had something to hide. Probably, he did something he wasn't proud of."

"Or he could have been wronged in some way. But, from the beginning, I've not had a good feeling about how the police would handle the information. And it would appear the deceased had the same concerns."

"Don't get me wrong." Conner continued. "I have the utmost respect for law enforcement. But, it seems to be their nature to be suspicious. To prosecute wherever there's a hint of wrong-doing. To look at issues with skepticism instead of objectivity. And maybe that's because they live in an environment of evil and bad people who do evil and bad things. Am I making sense here?" Conner asked his friend.

"Well, you've certainly answered my question," Greenlee responded smilingly.

This was a prolonged pause between the two before Greenlee spoke again.

"Let's get back to the issues here. Several items seem to fall into the category of Precedent, which is a basic legal term for court decisions that are used as standards for deciding subsequent cases that appear similar or identical to cases under review. There's another legal term, stare decisis, that requires courts to apply these precedent cases to ensure individuals in similar situations are treated alike, instead of based on a particular judge's personal views."

"Now, law enforcement could probably challenge your entering another person's domicile without permission, and certainly your removing contents from said domicile without permission. But you essentially do have a document, albeit Ex Post Facto – or after the fact – that gives you permission to remove such material. Essentially it's a "get out of jail free card." So, I doubt if you'd be charged for any of these things."

"There's also the issue the deceased did not put his name on the will, nor sign his signature, and you might think that invalidates it.

But the justice system is pretty tolerant on this whole issue. In fact I had a case once where this came up and the will was still declared valid. It was not exactly like this, but very similar.

Greenlee swiveled around to his computer and made a connection on the internet. After a brief delay, he made several other entries, before pausing to read information displayed on his screen.

"I'm reading here from a site I use a lot," he explained to Conner. On the subject of the Testator's name on the will it says:

"As long as the testator signs his or her name with the intent of making a will, knowing what she was doing and understanding its significance, the will is valid regardless of whether she used her given middle name or her maiden name or middle name…in some cases even initials."

Or if the testator's will was handled by an attorney and the testator's name is on file with that attorney, that should be acceptable, Greenlee explained.

"Does all of that make sense?" a smiling Greenlee now asked.

"Yes it does…particularly the part about my not being charged with unlawful entry," Conner added with a chuckle

"As for the police trying to connect you to a death when there's no way of telling how the deceased died and the fact you were living in another city when the death occurred, you can sweep that under the rug, as well."

The two friends smiled nervously.

"Now, since you've already had contact with a police agency, you may get some flak if they find out you're doing your own investigation of this man. But, you'll have to see how that plays out."

"If that happens, we'll just have to deal with it, "Greenlee said. "Otherwise, I don't see any additional exposures at present. If something else comes up, you know where I am."

As Conner stood to leave the office, he walked around the desk and hugged his friend.

"I can't tell you how much I appreciate this, Chad. But I want to pay you for your time."

"Nawww…. Just remember what the Godfather sez: "Fo get ah-baa-dit."

"Now, get outta' here," Greenlee added with a big smile. "Maybe the next time you're in town, you can buy me lunch," he said to his friend as Conner turned to leave.

Conner's drive back to Bryson City took about two and a half hours. But to him, the trip seemed to have taken about 15 minutes. It all was a matter of attitude, Conner felt. And right now, he was in a great mood.

It was shortly after noon when Conner pulled into BC. The temperature was in the thirties but a brisk wind made it feel colder. It was pretty much a raw day. Conner stopped at The Scarlet Letters to drop off another computer disc for processing. He scanned the store briefly and didn't see Carolyn. But he didn't want to bother her. He did linger for a bit, chatting with Camden before leaving the store and heading home. It had been a very eventful day, and it wasn't over yet.

Conner had just about reached the Bronco out front when he noticed a man walking very slowly toward him on crutches. The man clearly was having great difficulty, with one leg partially suspended above the sidewalk, either in a cast or just heavily wrapped.

As the subject moved closer, Conner recognized the face immediately. It was the short little man who had pulled a knife on him at Mean Willie's Bar. At that point, Conner was perplexed.

Should he just continue on his way to the Bronco or should he confront him. Without hesitation, Conner chose the latter. He turned and walked deliberately in the path of the man and stopped, thereby blocking the man's passage.

"Do you remember me?" Conner asked, his voice laced with hostility.

"Yesir,' I remember you," the little man said, struggling to maintain his equilibrium on the wobbly crutches. Before Conner could continue, the man launched into something of a lecture:

"I've gotten myself ina' lot of trouble because ah you. And I'm lookin' at lotsa' jail time…got out on bail and have to wear this here ankle bracelet. Yeah, I rememba' you," he said, his voice trembling with emotion.

"Listen, you crazy little sunuvabitch. I didn't cause the trouble you're in. You caused the trouble you're in! And I'm gonna' tell you somethin' else. "

"If you ever threaten me again, or pull that knife on me again, it's going to be worse than sitting in a damn prison cell. A few months ago, I got one of these."

As Conner talked he pulled out his wallet and retrieved a small card, holding it up for the little man to see.

"This is a concealed weapons carry card for my 9 millimeter handgun. And you can count on my having that weapon on my person if you ever try that stunt again. Do you understand what I'm telling you?"

"Yessir" the man said sheepishly. "I hear you, but there ain't gonna' be no next time, I can promise you that."

"What did you just say?"

"I said there ain't gonna' be no next time. I can promise you that."

Conner was taken back by the man's quick change of attitude and his apparent willingness to admit and atone for his past transgressions.

"What's your name," Conner barked, reflecting his distrust of the man's sudden reversal of intensions.

"How's that?" the little man asked rather sheepishly.

"I said, what's your name."

"My name is Willard Posey," he replied in something of an embarrassed tone.

"Lemme' see your driver's license. ""Yessir," came the reply, as Posey adjusted one of the crutches to reach the wallet in his back pocket. Without hesitation, Posey handed Conner his wallet. It appeared to Conner as an act of total submission.

"My driver's license is in here," he said.

Conner opened the wallet and immediately spotted the license under a clear plastic protector. With a quick glance, he was able to verify that Posey was telling him the truth, and he handed the wallet back to his would-be attacker.

The two men quietly stared at each other without comment, before Posey spoke again.

"I dunno' what to say about what happened between us. I know I'm going to' go to jail for what I did. All I can say to you is I'm sorry."

"You're sorry? You accosted me on two different occasions and now you're sorry?"

"Yes sir. I'm truly sorry."

Conner was surprised at Posey's admission and humility. It made him feel awkward and exposed. Still, he decided not to reciprocate to Posey's apology. But he did not want this change of attitude to go without acknowledgement. The words did not come easily.

"Listen, I appreciate what you're trying to do. And if you mean what you just said, maybe I can help. Don't know if it'd make any difference, but if you'd like, I could appear at your trial and ask for clemency on your behalf. It's up to you."

"Thank you sir," Posey replied. "That'd be mighty kind of you."

Before leaving, the little man nervously fumbled with the grips on his crutches.

Conner caught his attention one more time: "By the way, my name is Mitch Conner."

Posey nodded his head. Conner lingered for several more moments, watching the little man hobble toward his destination. At that point he asked himself if this guy had just scammed him? He admitted to himself it was a possibility.

But Posey had too much hanging over his head to have lied to him. He was right when he said he was facing some hard time in prison for his actions. And not accepting this opportunity for a helping hand would be totally stupid on his part.

Conner considered that thought and finally told himself, he'd give the guy the benefit of a doubt and accept his apology, and his promise for a change in behavior. He climbed into the Beast and headed home

CHAPTER SEVENTEEN

It was almost four thirty in the afternoon and Conner was headed to the Universal Joint to meet Carolyn Briggs. The last time he had talked to her, she offered to pick up the tab for a return to the popular little bar where Conner had graciously paid for her and her friend Susan's drinks a few weeks earlier. There were few opportunities in life that could match that offer, Conner told himself.

To his surprise, Carolyn was already there. She was seated at the L-shaped bar by herself, talking to one of the young female bartenders. She immediately swiveled around from her barstool perch and smiled as he approached. Carolyn was dressed casually and colorfully, but not overdone. She wore a dark blue wool skirt, a white turtle-neck sweater, with an oversized scarf tucked under a tan, all-weather, suede coat. Conner, on the other hand, wore jeans and a large-nit winter sweater beneath his distressed, black leather jacket.

"Hey there, Mitch. I was beginning to think you forgot."

"Who me? I don't forget when a lady offers to buy the drinks. In fact, I'm a little early. That ought to get me a hello hug."

Carolyn chuckled and smiled, her blue eyes sparkling as she reached out with both arms to fulfill his request.

"You look great." Conner said, smiling at her. "Makes me wanna' go back home and change."

"Don't be silly. You look fine."

Conner smiled at his friend and turned to bartender Jill, who was standing before them, waiting for their order. After acknowledging Jill, Conner turned to his friend with a question.

"Well, this is a "light outside" gathering, and you said when it's light outside, you drink beer. Is that your preference?"

Carolyn paused in thought.

"You know, I'm really not thirsty for beer right now. I think I'll have a glass of white wine."

"I'll have the same," Conner told the playful young bartender.

There was a brief silence as the two watched Jill pour wine into oversized glasses normally reserved for red wine. Conner touched his glass to Carolyn's and took a small sip of wine.

"The last time we were here, I didn't get to talk to you much about you. Tell me, who is Carolyn Briggs?"

"Wow. That's some question. This is not a job interview, is it?"

"No. No. I'm just interested in your background. I wanna' know who you are. I guess it's my training as a journalist coming back to haunt me."

There was a brief silence as Carolyn gently and carefully swiveled her wine glass around, watching the contents rotate and sparkle under the overhead lights. When she spoke, it was at a staccato pace.

"I'm from a big family. I have a sister and four brothers. Born in Clayton, Georgia, grew up playing baseball, basketball, football and throwing horseshoes. My father worked for a furniture manufacturer in Franklin. And my mother was a school teacher."

Carolyn paused and nodded playfully before continuing.

"And if I have another glass of wine, I'll end up telling you about the real Carolyn Briggs."

Conner laughed at the frankness of her statement and quickly changed the conversation back to himself.

"Okay. Let's talk about me, then."

Conner took another sip of wine and continued.

"I came from an even bigger family. There were eight of us, four brothers and three sisters. I was born in Savannah, Georgia. And my father owned a dairy farm. When I was eleven years old, my mother died and my father never married again. For a lotta' years my dad was both a mother and father to me. But he ended up selling the dairy farm, and we moved a lot. In 12 years of schooling, I went to 13 different schools. I ended up hating school."

"That's terrible," Carolyn said, her face in something of a frown. "I can't imagine what it was like not having a mother at that age."

Conner looked reflectively at his glass sitting on the bar.

"Well, it worked out okay. For one thing, I grew up to be very independent…a survivor, if you will. That was the good news. On the other hand, I think I became rather selfish as a result, something I had to deal with later in life."

"That's sad, too," Carolyn added.

Before Conner could reply, Carolyn continued.

"But, if you hated school so much, how did you end up going to college? Who influenced you to get an education?"

Conner hesitated before responding.

"Friends I made in the military. I was in military units that were composed of mostly college students or college graduates, and they urged me on. They sold me on the benefits of getting a degree, or degrees, as it turned out. In fact, I'm in the process right now of registering at WCU to get a PhD."

"Well, your story started out on a sad note. But it seems now it's heading for a happy ending," Carolyn added, smiling. Before Conner could reply, she continued.

"I don't remember, but did you tell me you were married for several years and have two children?"

"That's correct. I've got a son and a daughter, and I've been single for about six years," Conner replied.

"Okay. Okay. I guess it's my turn again. I got married when I was 19 years old. Married my high school sweetheart. But it turns out, he was not that much of a "sweetheart," and I divorced him after two years. That was 15 years ago. Got no kids, and I'm currently 12 credit hours away from getting my masters at WCU."

"Is that where you received your undergraduate degree?" Conner asked.

"No, I got a degree in education from the University of Georgia, with a minor in American history. And for eight years I taught fifth graders at an elementary school in Franklin. My goal is to get a job at the college level, but that'll probably require a PhD."

Conner nodded his understanding. He then saw her wine glass was empty, as was his.

"Are we having another wine?" Conner asked pensively.

"Why not," she replied. "It's late afternoon and that means it's "dark outside." So it's appropriate to drink wine when it's "dark outside." "And besides," she added. "It's Friday!"

Both Carolyn and Conner watched as Jill refreshed their drinks. Conner noticed the young bartender was being very generous with her wine pours.

"With your background in American history, does that mean you're a trivia person?" Conner asked her.

"Maybe yes. Of sorts," she responded. "I like trivia. And I have a good memory for dates and things. And I know a lot of stuff," she said."

"I also remember jokes. I had a friend who used to tell me all the new jokes she heard so she could retrieve them later for retelling."

"You know a lot of stuff?" Conner asked leaning away from her in mock disbelief.

Carolyn slowly shook her head in the affirmative.

"Yup," she added. "But why do you ask?"

"I ask because one never knows when they'll need an expert to settle disputes or be their partner in trivia games. And if you know a lot of stuff, you gotta' have a lot of answers."

Carolyn laughed and smiled as Conner continued his questioning.

"By the way, my goal is to get a PhD in American history. Is it okay if I call on you sometimes as an additional source," Conner asked.

"That would be fine, assuming I'm still around these parts."

"Oh? Does that mean you may be leaving us here in the mountains?" He asked.

"Not necessarily. But I might just come down with a case of wanderlust and exercise my options."

The conversation continued for the better part of three hours, during which a total of three glasses of wine each were consumed. Neither of them had eaten, and Conner noticed Carolyn was showing signs of her wine more than he was. There was compassion in his voice as he spoke.

"Hey, I don't know exactly where you live, but I'm only about six or seven minutes from here. It might be a good idea if we got a little fresh air and a cup of hot coffee. I've also got some leftover bar snacks at home, if you'd like. Whatta' ya say?"

"Sounds like a good idea," she replied with a smile.

As the two walked to the Beast, somewhat apologetically Conner shared the Bronco story with his friend. He told her about the flashy sports car he used to drive. And he also told her about his modest cabin and his million dollar view of the world. This drew something of a playful chuckle from her.

It was completely dark as they climbed from the Bronco outside the cabin. Carolyn was immediately awestruck with the resplendent view before her, a cornucopia of lights from homes across the valley below, creating sufficient illumination to see smoke plumes rising from chimneys here and there.

She made an unintentional gasp, covering her mouth with both hands

"Mitch, this is beautiful. You were right, this is a million dollar view!" she said, excitedly.

"I felt exactly the same the first time I saw this place," Conner told her, smiling.

"Come on," he said. "Let's get outta' the cold."

As they stepped inside, Conner paused and made a sweeping motion with his hand.

"This is my humble residence," he said. "Have a seat I'll have the coffee on in a sec."

Carolyn stood momentarily, her eyes eagerly scanning the modest but inviting home. As Conner busied himself stoking the stove and preparing the coffee, she eased onto the living room couch and ran her hand across the smooth surface of dark brown leather. She kept her eyes on Conner who was consumed with his tasks in the kitchen.

Instinctively, she stood and walked to the large window that opened onto the deck outside. Without asking, she opened the sliding door and stepped out onto the deck, looking down again in awe at the sight below. When Conner joined her, he had two cups of steaming coffee and handed one to her.

"I forgot to ask. Would you like cream or sugar?"

"Nope." she shot back. "Coffee's not coffee if you muck it up with milk and sugar."

Conner laughed, as she carefully eased a small sip of coffee to gauge how hot it was. The temperature was to her liking and she took another full sip.

Without speaking, both Mitch and Carolyn leaned against the railing and stood silently gazing into the night. The conversation continued for several minutes before Carolyn headed for the warmth of the cabin's interior. Conner followed her inside and stood behind her. Unexpectedly, she turned and kissed him softly. He then pulled her toward him and kissed her a little more assertively.

"It seems I've succeeded in my goal to get you drive worthy," he said, caressing her cheek with his non coffee hand.

"Are you telling me it's time for me to leave?" she asked looking up at him playfully.

"No, that was the "light outside" Mitch talking," he said, gazing affectionately at her. "The "dark outside" Mitch wants to know if you prefer white or whole wheat toast?"

Conner put his coffee cup down and kissed her again.

It was only 6:00 a.m, when Carolyn awakened, wrapped herself in a blanket and quietly went to the kitchen. It was her turn to make the coffee, she told herself.

Embers in the wood stove were still radiating warmth, making the area more comfortable than the chilly bedroom. She snuggled onto Conner's chair and began sipping coffee.

About 10 minutes later, Conner appeared in the living room and smiled at her. He had slipped into a pair of jeans and was standing before her bare-chested. His hair was disheveled, and he did not appear to be totally awake yet.

He tried to speak, but his voice cracked and hesitatingly, he cleared his throat to jump start his vocal chords. Carolyn began to chuckle and almost spilled her coffee. When Conner spoke this time, his voice was near normal.

"Hey."

"Hey yourself," she said, smiling at him.

"Nice to see you're making yourself at home."

She acknowledged him with a nod of her head and another smile. Before she could respond, Conner continued.

"I get the feeling you look great even when you're not supposed to. You certainly do more for that chair than I do."

"Thank you kind sir. You don't look bad yourself."

Conner moved toward her and kissed her gently on her forehead. He then stepped back as he spoke.

"I'll stoke the fire a bit, and then we can discuss breakfast. I don't know about you, but I'm starving," he said.

CHAPTER EIGHTEEN

For motorists travelling through the area for the first time, Western Carolina University seemed to appear out of nowhere. The school was located along a stretch of state route 107, seven miles south of Sylva and 15 miles north of Cashiers. It was surrounded by farmland in the little hamlet of Cullowhee. Cows in adjacent fields routinely looked up from grazing to observe the sights and sounds emanating from the busy campus nearby.

From outward appearances, Western Carolina could have passed for one of the scores of community colleges that were hastily constructed during the 1970s and 1980s. Most of the school's dormitories and classrooms were of modern design -- amber-colored brick buildings accented with large, sweeping windows. It was an architectural style of clean and simple lines -- a style that was widely copied during that period of rapid educational expansion.

But, WCU was far from a community college. It was a full-fledged university -- a constituent member of the North Carolina system of colleges and universities. The school was granted full university status in 1972. Its charter, at the time, was to serve residents of the western portion of the state. Eastern and central Carolina were already well-served by numerous prestigious educational institutions, both private and State supported.

But, in a relatively short period of time, WCU far exceeded its original objectives -- growing significantly in both stature and drawing power. By the mid-1980s, it was offering degrees in more than 80 disciplines and attracting students from around the world. The school now had an enrollment of some 13,000 students, and nearly 90 percent of its 400-plus faculty members held doctorate degrees. Indeed, it was a university with impressive credentials, in Conner's view.

There were other things about WCU that Conner found impressive, as well. But, one thing -- above all -- set the school apart. And it had nothing to do with academics or scholarship. It was the school's setting. Students and faculty were blessed with a magnificent view of the blue-hazed, Smoky Mountains -- looming majestically to the east and setting a magnificent backdrop for this dynamic institution.

As Conner pulled the Bronco onto the campus on this morning, he suddenly felt a sense of belonging, although there was no basis for that yet. He had first toured the campus shortly after moving to BC.

And it was strictly as a visitor getting the lay of the land. But WCU administrators now had the opportunity to recruit the sizeable talents of Mitchell Bradley Conner and enhance their academic profile. He chuckled at the thought..

It was a beautiful day. An early-day haze partially diffused the bright sunlight, adding a softened hue to the morning air. Conner continued his careful drive through the narrow streets winding through the campus. It was now apparent classes had just changed. Sidewalks and crosswalks were crowded with students making their way to other classes, to the library or to other campus locations. Still other students lounged casually in grassy areas -- reading books, scribbling in notebooks or engaging in small talk with friends and classmates.

This snapshot of university life caused Conner's mind to drift back in time -- back to his first visit to Northwestern University a while back. As he stepped onto the Northwestern campus on that first day, he was taken with the images before him. First, there was a distinct international flavor of the students who moved quickly past him, carrying their books and knapsacks. Many of them wore the dress of their native countries.

But the thing that had impressed him the most was the stately architecture of the buildings -- including the imposing library that was a centerpiece of the Northwestern campus. That weathered stone structure resembled an old gothic cathedral. Then graduate student Conner lingered for several minutes, allowing his mind to digest these interesting new surroundings.

Clearly, Northwestern looked like a university should look, he told himself. It had the same mystical quality about it as one of the old European universities. It had the look of history and tradition -- a look that clearly identified this as an institution of higher learning. He remembered thinking that inside these walls, the emphasis would be on the classics and on scholarship. This was the big leagues of higher education. Here, students would succeed or fail strictly on their own. He found the thought un-nerving.

But, much had changed since then, in Conner's view. Today, politically correct educators in too many institutions had reshaped the curricula to level the playing field -- making educational instruction more "relevant." It was all very disturbing to him -- another example of the dumbing down of America; it was another example of the one-size-fits-all mentality that was too prevalent in society. He shrugged at the thought and returned his focus to the Western Carolina campus.

It was about nine-thirty when Conner pulled the Bronco to a stop in front of the Fine Arts building. His appointment was not until 10 o'clock.

But, he didn't want to be late. He gazed up at the five-story structure. It was relatively new -- probably no more than 10 years old. And it had the same architectural style as many of the other buildings on campus -- a functional blending of brick and glass.

Conner turned his gaze from the building to the nearby mountains, and his mind drifted again. Here he was, on the verge of accepting another challenge in his life. On one hand, the possibilities were exciting. On the other hand, he was stepping into the unknown -- the unfamiliar. Quietly, he asked himself if he were up to it? Could he cut it in the classroom?

Just then, the old chestnut about teaching an old dog new tricks came to mind. There was an element of truth in that, he told himself. He found that the older he got, the less likely he was to accept change. Change represented a deviation from the norm. It involved setting aside those things that were familiar and comfortable. And that never came easy.

Conner reminded himself he had always handled change well -- particularly when it was thrust upon him. But, in this case, he was the one who was initiating the change. He convinced himself he'd handle this the way he'd handled it in the past.

As he climbed from the Beast and headed for his appointment, he felt as if he were a schoolboy again, and this was the first day of school. There weren't too many experiences in life that were more frightening than that. He shrugged and continued toward the building.

When he reached the entrance, several students were leaving the building. All of them were neatly dressed and well groomed. One of the young women looked at him and smiled. Conner returned her smile and nodded. At that point, he felt more relaxed.

Once inside, Conner found himself in a huge atrium that clearly was the focal point of the facility. At the center of the big atrium was a large, circular reflecting pool, fed by an ornate, black fountain. From overhead, a massive skylight washed the entire area in light, creating interesting patterns and shadows on the slate floor. Along the walls of the atrium were large tropical plants in oversized ceramic pods.

Conner was immediately consumed by the flurry of activity before him. Students flowed into and out of the atrium through corridors connecting the adjoining wings of the building. Other students sat around the reflecting pool, sprawled cross-legged on the floor or leaned against the walls, talking to friends .

At the rear of the atrium was a floor-to-ceiling, glass wall that provided a spectacular view of the looming Smoky Mountains in the near distance.

Conner approached the big wall and stood for several moments, admiring the view. The chatter of voices brought his focus back to the reason for his visit. He quickly glanced at his watch. The meeting was in 15 minutes. From the large directory on the wall, he searched for the dean's office number. Conner then shared the elevator with several students and exited on the third floor. The dean's office was to his left -- about half way down the hall.

As he walked, he passed a large classroom. Curious, he paused and peeked through the narrow glass window on the door. The room appeared to be empty. Conner eased the door open and looked cautiously inside. Satisfied that he was alone, he entered. As the door closed behind him, all sounds from the hallway faded. An eerie silence now hung over the empty room. Conner stood for several seconds, looking around. The big classroom had raked seating, with multiple rows of narrow tables arranged on descending levels from back to front.

The hall would probably accommodate 100 students -- maybe more. Large white chalk boards dominated the entire front wall. Conner guessed the hall was used for introductory or compulsory courses for broad segments of the student body.

Just then, the door opened and Conner was somewhat embarrassed at his unannounced presence in the empty room. It was as if he had been caught looking through someone else's house.

"Are you Mister Conner?"

"Dean Frees?"

The educator smiled and nodded as he entered the room. He reached out and shook Conner's hand with a firm grip.

"Yes…It's nice to see you," Frees said, trying to make his visitor feel at ease.

"Nice to see you, too!"

Conner smiled.

"I was just on my way to your office. Thought I'd just take a look at the classroom… take a look at the playing field."

"No problem. I was just passing by and I mistook you for an instructor."

"Well, I have to admit I couldn't be mistaken for a student - these bright young faces I've seen so far this morning."

Frees chuckled at the remark.

In Conner's mind, Harrison Frees looked more like a former drill instructor than a college professor. He appeared to be just under six feet tall and was barrel-chested. His salt-and-pepper hair was combed straight back, revealing his receding hairline. He had long arms and big hands that hung loosely at his side. And there was a swagger to his walk. Frees' ruddy complexion was not that of a man who spent most of his time indoors. But, he had friendly green eyes and dimples that punctuated a robust smile.

Without commenting, Frees turned and made his way slowly down toward the front of the room. He walked with a confidence that said he was moving in familiar territory. Conner hesitated momentarily, then instinctively followed the dean down to the lower level of the room. Frees slid onto the top of the large desk at the front of the big classroom. He leaned forward, his hands anchored on either side of the desk and his feet dangling some 12 inches above the floor. The dean looked very much at home on his classroom perch.

Somewhat hesitatingly, Conner took a seat at one of the tables on the front row, directly in front of the professor. Frees looked around the room reflectively, waving his hand in a sweeping motion as he spoke.

"I used to spend a lot of time in this room."

He paused, a wistful look in his eyes.

"Not anymore."

Conner looked intently at his host.

"What did you teach?"

"Mostly mass communications. Some broadcast journalism."

"You ever work in radio or TV?" Conner asked.

"No. Not really. Not in any major markets. Just small time stuff. I guess you could say I've built a career teaching subjects in which I've had very little practical experience."

Conner chuckled.

"I'm sure that's not the case," he said.

"It's absolutely the case! In fact, very few people who stand in front of students these days have practical experience in the disciplines they're teaching.

There's a lot of truth in that old cliche: 'those who can, do; those who can't, teach!' That's why I envy people such as yourself. You've been out there! You've done it!"

Conner leaned back and crossed his arms.

"Maybe so."

"Don't be so modest. Just remember what Dizzy Dean said: 'if you've done it, that ain't braggin.'" Conner smiled and leaned forward on his desk, his hands clasped together. He turned and gazed through one of the sun-soaked windows before looking back at Frees.

"In the back of my mind, I guess I always wanted to teach. That's one of the reasons I got my master's. I only wish I hadn't waited so long to do it."

"Maybe you weren't ready."

"That's probably true."

Frees nodded his agreement.

"Just remember, if you'd gone into teaching earlier, you'd be just like the rest of us. All hat and no cattle. Don't sell your credentials short. You have a lot of valuable information and experience tucked away up there. A lot of knowledge to share."

Conner looked squarely at his host and smiled, a look of intensity in his eyes.

"I'm not worried about the subject matter. I can handle that. What scares me is getting through the first 30 minutes of my first class."

"Trust me! You'd be fine. Just tell is like it is. I remember the first time I stood before a group of students. I was nervous as hell. But, after about five minutes, I felt like I'd done it all my life."

Conner smiled.

"I guess it's rather like diving into a cold mountain stream. The thought of taking the plunge is intimidating. But, once you get in the water, it's not so bad."

"Exactly!"

Before Conner could respond, Frees continued.

"If it makes you feel any better, I got a rather late start in life, myself. I spent eight years in the military before deciding to become a teacher.

When I finally entered college, I was 26 years old. And when I got my doctorate, I was 32. Course, I got some breaks along the way."

Again, Conner smiled. Frees looked pointedly at him as he continued.

"In my mind, there are definite advantages to getting a later start in life. If you begin too early, you make too many wrong turns. You stumble. But, as you get older, you become more confident. More decisive. You speak from experience, and people listen to what you have to say. As I see it, that's about where you are now."

Conner nodded and Frees continued.

"I'm reminded of my wife's late father --God bless his soul. He spent most of his life talking about opportunities that got away. Truth was, he never chased any of his dreams. He always found an excuse for not taking the first step."

Frees paused and took a deep breath.

"I remember his telling me one time that if he were only 10 years younger, he'd start his own business. At the time, he was 45. Then when he was 55, he said that if he were only 45, things would be different. And when he reached 65, the magic number had moved to 55. The point is, he could have grasped the brass ring at any time. But, he didn't. He never was serious about taking the first step. As a result, he never really achieved his dream."

Conner nodded, and smiled a knowing smile.

"I can understand that. Can't identify with it, but I can understand it. I have to tell you that when I pulled up in front of the building this morning, I asked myself if I was too old for this? Too old to deal with kids about half my age?"

Frees nodded without responding.

"It just seems that the older I get, the more reluctant I am to accept change in my life. The more reluctant I am to accept new challenges. Is that just me?"

"Absolutely not. I know exactly what you mean. Believe me, there are a lot of people -- including myself-- who share those feelings. But, at certain points in our lives, we have to be willing to embrace new ideas and adopt new ways of thinking. Here in the classroom, that's particularly important. We have to stay on our toes. If we don't, these kids will eat us alive. They force us to stay out front and set the pace. And we do it without thinking."

Still, you gotta' be committed to doing it."

Conner smiled and nodded.

"There's a lot of truth in that."

Without responding, Frees eased himself from the tabletop and stood momentarily, smiling down at his guest.

"Whatta' ya' say we head over to my office?"

Conner nodded and eased from behind the desk. He followed his host through the big door and down the hallway to the office of the dean. For the next 45 minutes, he provided the dean with additional information on his educational background, his job history and a thorough tutorial on specifics of his communications experience and skills. He also was asked to provide certain documents and information, including copies of his degrees and reference sources.

There were other administrative details to be handled. But he and the dean had reached an agreement. Conner was offered a job as a senior instructor and would begin teaching Writing for Business in the Continuing Education program in roughly 60 days, when the new semester began. Background checks and other employment requirements had to be met, including taking a physical. He would be under contract to teach two days a week and his contract would be renewable in six months.

There also were papers to be signed, most of them details about terms of employment and other issues associated with becoming an employee of the State of North Carolina. When he left the Fine Arts building he was both elated and proud. He and Dean Frees had struck up a good relationship, in his assessment. The dean appeared to be a good man, and he liked him. Conner also was proud about achieving yet another goal in his life.

It was almost noon when Conner left the building. The temperature had climbed into the low-fifties, and the sun felt good on his face. Conner was on an emotional high when he reached the Beast.

He threw his things inside and looked around. Without thinking, he began walking toward the center of the campus. He had missed this area of the campus on earlier visits. This was where the school's original buildings were located.

As he walked, he encountered various historical markers that chronicled the school's evolution. From these markers, he read about the transitional years at Western Carolina. The University's roots dated back to August of 1889 when the facilities of nearby Cullowhee High school were designated for use as a chartered higher education instruction facility.

And in 1893, the North Carolina legislature designated it as a publicly funded normal school, which meant it would began training high school graduates to become teachers in the western part of the State.

During the next several years, the school continued to expand its reach and its curriculum, and in 1929 it was designated by the State as a Junior College. In 1953, it was chartered as a four-year college, under the name of Western Carolina Teacher's College. The school was elevated to university status in 1967.

Today, Western Carolina had become a modern and respected member of the State's academic population, joining such prestigious other schools including the University of North Carolina, Duke, Wake Forest, North Carolina State and Davidson. And WCU's enrollment had reached some 13,000 students from countries around the world.

As he continued to walk, he read of other facets of the school's history. One of the older buildings now on campus was Robertson Hall, a student residence built in 1932. Other historical structures included Hoey auditorium, built in 1939 and the Bird Alumni House, dating back to 1940. The Robinson Administrative building -- which housed the president's office -- was a relative newcomer, built in 1979.

It was about 12:30 when Conner turned and headed back toward the Fine Arts building. As he proceeded, his eyes locked onto a woman approaching him from the opposite direction. She had long dark hair, a confident walk and she was strikingly attractive. The woman was carrying a briefcase, and she wore a tan all-weather coat. Hers was a familiar face, but Conner didn't immediately place her. As she drew nearer, it occurred to him who she was.

This was the woman he'd met at the Fryemont bar a few weeks earlier -- the professor who had recently relocated from Baltimore. She was taller than he remembered, probably about five feet seven. Conner reminded himself the first time they met, she was seated. As she drew nearer, Conner stopped and waited for her to approach. At first, she looked at him somewhat cautiously. Then, a smile of recognition transformed her face. It was Conner who spoke first.

"Hi. It's Cynthia, right?"

"Yes."

" Mitch Conner. From the Fryemont."

"Yes, Mitch, I remember."

"It's nice to see you again."

"It's nice to see you, too."

He reached out and shook her gloved hand. The two stood paused momentarily, smiling at each other. Conner had forgotten how green her eyes were. They were beautiful. And in this early morning light, she was every bit as pretty as she appeared that night in the bar. The woman grasped her briefcase with both hands and held it in front of her, somewhat nervously. She appeared rather child-like standing in front of him. There was a trace of color now in her cheeks.

"What brings you here, Mitch?"

"Well, I finally got my appointment to teach, and I've just completed my first meeting with the Dean of Fine Arts."

"That's great! Congratulations!"

Conner shrugged his shoulders and tilted his head in a sign of modesty.

"Well, it's only part-time. And it's in the Continuing Education area. But, at least it's a start. I'm really excited about it."

"I'm sure you'll do a great job."

"Thanks."

Conner looked intently at her.

"Did you ever find a place to live?"

"Actually, I did. It's a small creekside house south of here. About half way between here and Cashiers."

"That's great!"

"Yes. I like it a lot. But, I've still got a lot of work to do there."

"That's always the case with a new home. I've got several things I really want to do at my place, too."

The young woman nodded and smiled.

"Say, have you had lunch yet?" Conner asked.

"Well, no. But I have two counseling sessions scheduled with students. I'm afraid I'll be having lunch at my desk."

Conner's face showed his disappointment.

"But, I'd love a raincheck," she said, smiling

A smile quickly appeared on Conner's face.

"A raincheck it is!"

Without responding, the young woman took a piece of paper from her briefcase and hurriedly wrote down her phone number. As she wrote, she balanced the large briefcase awkwardly on her upper thigh. Conner couldn't help noticing the scent of her perfume. Finally, she handed him the paper and smiled.

"Give me a call. Maybe we could meet for lunch or a drink."

"Sounds great."

She acknowledged the comment with a smile.

"Well, Mitch, it was good seeing you again."

"Good seeing you, too."

She reached out and shook his hand. Then she turned and walked away, looking back briefly and smiling. Conner returned her smile. He continued watching as she walked briskly toward a nearby building. Finally, he turned and walked back toward the Fine Arts building and the Beast.

CHAPTER NINETEEN

As Conner drove into Bryson City on this late afternoon, he gazed at roadside vendors selling a variety of seasonal treats, including freshly harvested fruits and vegetables that were a prelude to the approaching holidays. With Thanksgiving only days away, the most popular items were the pumpkins that would soon decorate residential displays throughout the area. Other favorites ranged from jams, jellies and locally harvested honey to boiled peanuts, maple syrup and fresh baked pies and pastries.

Over the next few days, Conner told himself, he'd have to stop and take advantage of these roadside delights. Such seasonal offerings seldom lasted throughout the year. And generally, they were more likely found in rural and mountainous areas and not so much in metropolitan settings. The prospect of someone selling boiled peanuts along Peachtree Street in Atlanta brought a smile to his face. Conner loved this time of year, and the fast approaching holidays were only a few weeks away. November and December were such festive months, in his view.

And although most of the area's hardwood trees had lost their foliage, there were scores of different species of pine trees in the Nantahala Forest that still provided seasonal color across the areas' rolling landscapes. And one of the most popular pines – the Fraser Fir - was widely grown hereabouts and harvested as Christmas trees. Some 1,600 growers in Western Carolina annually cultivated 25,000 acres of the Christmas Firs for consumption throughout the southeast.

The Georgia and Carolina mountains also were well known for their apple and peach festivals that attracted visitors by the thousands during the fall and early winter months.

One of Conner's personal fall attractions were the pancake breakfasts held in local fire stations to raise money for volunteer public services. The breakfasts were really fun, and a great opportunity to meet other members of the community, he felt.

And just across the Georgia State line was another seasonal favorite that was very popular with locals, luring visitors from as far away as Atlanta and beyond. It was a pumpkin farm, and it was particularly appealing to parents with young children, who brought their youngsters to frolic among hundreds of different types and sizes of pumpkins. It also was an easy drive from BC.

Some of the pumpkins at the farm were so large –- weighing up to 500 pounds or more -- they could only be moved by a forklift. And with so many children exploring the grounds, it was a photographer's delight. Conner made a mental note to take advantage of that opportunity over the next few days.

Conner also enjoyed seeing the colorful yard displays and decorations that were an integral part of the holiday season.. And he never tired of hearing the Christmas music that already was beginning to appear on the radio. All these things were well underway on this day, and they seemed to be adding to Conner's holiday spirit.

Nearly a week had passed since Conner talked to Carolyn. On this night, he had chosen the Fryemont Inn to meet her. It was a dark and cold evening, and the fire in the main dining room at the Fryemont was invitingly appealing. Conner had arrived early and proceeded straight to the bar, where he ordered a Dewar's Scotch and waited for his guest to arrive.

Conner had just begun a conversation with bartender, J. D. Stricker, when he noticed Carolyn stepping inside the lobby. He quickly settled with Stricker and met her at the entrance.

"Good evening Ms. Briggs. Don't you look great?"

As he spoke, he reached out to lightly squeeze her hand in greeting. Before she could respond, Conner continued.

"But, I don't ever recall seeing you when you didn't look great, even in running shorts."

She laughed subtly at his compliment and responded.

"I'm a sucker for flattery," she said with a smile and a hug.

Conner ushered his guest to the maître'd, an older gentleman by the name of Phillip Wilson. Wilson was a tall and accommodating man who was well groomed and pleasant in nature. Conner asked for a table near the fire, and Wilson complied. Conner had been at the Fryemont often enough to know most of the wait staff by name. And they all seemed to know him, as well. This was a result of Conner's easy-going personality and his generosity, most would say.

As Carolyn took a seat, Conner assisted with her coat. Beneath her knee-length white topcoat, she wore a low-cut black dress, accented with a choker strand of pearls and matching earrings. But once again, Conner felt under clothed, though he appeared appropriately dressed in a gray plaid sports coat and complimentary beige slacks.

Carolyn was close enough to the oversized hearth to feel the comforting glow of the fire. Yet, her cheeks were still flushed from her exposure to the weather outside. It was a healthy look, and it seemed to make her blue eyes sparkle even more than normal.

Conner found himself noticeably taken with her appearance in a way it hadn't done before. He wondered if his perception of her had changed, or if she was trying to impress him. Probably a little of both, he concluded.

Just then, he realized he was staring at her, and he tried to cover his embarrassment with a smile. She seemed to recognize his uneasiness and returned his smile.

On the drive to the Fryemont, Conner had decided to tell the young woman about the mystery man, though he didn't want to get into the complications and complexities involved with the whole thing. He would tell her if the opportunity presented itself. But he wouldn't press the issue. After all, at this point there were more things he didn't know about the deceased than what he did know.

After ordering a glass of wine, the couple spent several minutes discussing the incidental things that had happened to each other since being together last. Otherwise, Carolyn seemed to be in a quiet mood, almost transfixed with the warmth and appeal of the crackling fire. Finally, she returned her gaze to Conner and spoke softly.

"We were really busy at the store today. In fact, it was rather frantic. And it's nice just to sit here and relax."

Before Conner could reply, she shared an afterthought.

"I'm glad you called."

Conner acknowledged her comment with a nod and smile. And he, too, turned his gaze to the fire. There was a brief silence before he spoke.

"For some reason, I'm in very much of a Christmas mood this evening, though we've got a couple of weeks to go yet. But, I've always been a Christmas kind of person."

"I like the Christmas season, too," she replied. Conner paused before continuing.

"The other day, I was driving into town and I noticed quite a few people who were getting ready for the holidays. Maybe that helped trigger my Christmas spirit."

Carolyn held up her wine glass for a toast.

"Here's to Christmas," she said with her bright smile.

"You know, someone once told me that people who like Christmas typically had good experiences as a child. And I certainly believe that's true."

"I was the eighth and youngest child in a large family. And I was spoiled not only by my mother and father, but by my older siblings. I remember one Christmas, my dad gave me a goat and wagon. We lived on a dairy farm, and having a goat was not out of character." Conner explained.

"But to a seven-year-old, it was like getting my own horse and buggy. I was not only ecstatic, I was a little overwhelmed. It was quite a rig.".

"The goat had a little harness so it could pull the wagon, and there was a "buggy" seat on the wagon, just like the grown up version. It was fantastic."

"But, looking back on it now, I think it was a gift the adult members of my family appreciated more than the recipient. And, I don't remember having it at my disposal very long," Conner recalled.

"I think my father realized taking care of a goat was more work than he estimated. And he already had a lot of work to do with the dairy. Then one day, it all just disappeared. The goat, the wagon – everything. But I don't remember losing it as much as I remember getting it."

"That's a great story," she said. "It's story to remember," she added.

Carolyn paused before continuing.

"I can't match that. But growing up with four brothers, at Christmas time I felt like one of the boys. I always seemed to get Christmas presents that were more suited for a boy than a girl. Like, baseball gloves…soccer balls…or new tennis shoes."

"I did get a girl's bicycle one Christmas, and I loved that. I felt like I could now travel anywhere on my bike, though my parents were pretty restrictive on how far from home I could venture. I have to blame myself for some of that. I was something of a tomboy growing up. But, I guess that's to be expected with four brothers."

There was something mesmerizing about watching flames dancing in a fireplace on a cold and windy night, Conner felt. And this night was no exception.

With each pause in the conversation, each of the two turned their thoughts and attention to the oversized hearth.

Carolyn broke the brief silence with a question.

"I haven't seen you at the store as much this week." she stated rhetorically.

Conner paused before responding.

"Well, I've been pretty busy lately. Haven't been going out in the forest as much. I've started class work for my PhD. I'm also spending quite a bit of time getting ready for my role in the classroom… not only gathering and organizing material for the course – which begins in January - I'm also trying to corral a few of the butterflies associated with this major career change."

Carolyn squeezed his arm and looked directly at him with a smile.

"I have one piece of advice. Just be yourself," she said softly.

Without speaking, Conner silently mouthed the words "thank you."

There was a prolonged silence before Conner changed subjects.

"One of the reasons I wanted to have dinner tonight was to tell you how much I enjoy your company. I also enjoy talking to you."

"That's nice of you to say," she replied. "I enjoy your company, too."

The comment drew smiles from each, and Conner reached across to her and squeezed her hand.

"There's something I was looking forward to saying to you, as well," Carolyn added.

Conner nodded and looked at her expectantly.

"It's about the other night. I don't know exactly how I feel about what happened. I don't know whether it was a good idea or a bad idea," she said softly.

"Well, it did happen kinda' spontaneously," Conner said.

Carolyn paused momentarily before responding.

"That doesn't make it right. I guess that's what I'm trying to say. The left side of my brain said it was a bad idea. The right side said it was a good idea. Right now, I think I'm siding with the left side. If we didn't have this working relationship, and if there weren't so many things going on in each of our lives, it might be different," she said.

Carolyn paused before continuing.

"You know, since my divorce, I've had very few personal relationships with men. I have mostly female friends. I do have one or two men friends and I enjoy their company. But, they're just that, friends. I guess what I'm trying to say is I don't want to lose sight of my goals right now. Do you know what I'm trying to say?" she asked.

"I know exactly what you're trying to say, and I agree with you totally."

Again Conner reached across the table and squeezed her hand. He picked up his glass and held it up to her glass.

"Here's to friends. Good friends."

Conner did indeed know how Carolyn felt. In his mind, she was telling him she didn't want to get involved in a serious relationship at this point in her life. He rather agreed with her and pretty much felt the same way. But, he was not ready to totally write her off. He sincerely liked to be with her.

They truly could become good friends, if they weren't there already. And who knows what would happen down the road? And he was about ready to test that friendship. After a brief pause, his voice took on a more serious tone.

"I've been meaning to tell you about something that happened to me a couple of months ago. It was very disruptive, and I really have not felt comfortable enough to discuss it openly with many others."

Conner paused again and looked directly at her before continuing. There was a noticeable change in Carolyn's expression, with the appearance of furrows on her brow that reflected her expectancy.

Somewhat hesitatingly, Conner continued.

"In late October, I was out in the woods on a shoot. It was up near Cashiers. An area that I had not explored before. I was doing my usual job of point-and-shoot when I came upon something that totally blew me out of the water. I discovered human remains in one of those canyons. I won't get into all the details, but I quickly got the police involved," he said as he nervously recalled the incident.

"Looking back, my initial reaction was somewhere between disorientation and panic."

Carolyn leaned forward in her chair. She now hung on every word he was saying.

"It was pretty frustrating. When the police got involved, they got me involved, simply because I found the body. At one point, they began asking me some pretty accusatory questions. Turns out, I wasn't even living here in the period they concluded he probably died. So they backed off questioning me about possibly knowing the guy or being involved with his death in any way. Last I heard, they concluded he died of natural causes."

"But they kept me dancing on a string for too long, from my perspective."

Carolyn sat back in her chair, considering what her friend had just said. Her brief silence reflecting a lack of what to say. Conner continued after the brief period of hesitation.

"I can tell you, when something like that happens, it rather reminds you how cold and impersonal life can be. Fortunately, I had some driving time to think this through. I finally realized they were just doing their job. Still, I was really rattled by it. Maybe a little too much."

Carolyn nodded her understanding of his statement.

"I don't blame you. I would be, too."

There was a thoughtful pause before Carolyn continued.

"Have they found out who it was?" Carolyn asked.

"Well, that's the hell of it. Nobody knows who it was. An autopsy was done, and about all the cops could tell me was it was an elderly male. They also felt the guy had been dead for several months."

"And," as I said, I wasn't even living here on the dates they estimated he probably died. They said there were no missing person reports filed. Nobody inquired about lost relatives or friends. None of that stuff." "The last I heard, they concluded he died of natural causes, and that he had no surviving family."

"So, it's over then?"

"I'm not betting on it."

"Have you had any further contact with the police?"

"I have not," he responded.

"I can tell you, I really would have been spooked by something like that, too.."

"It finally occurred to me I just needed to sweep this under the rug and get on with my life,"

As he looked at Carolyn, Conner knew that he hadn't been totally honest with her, and maybe she suspected as much, he told himself. But, he'd have to leave it at that. He wasn't in the mood to share all the other details of the story, and he'd just have to see how it unraveled. At some point in time, maybe the opportunity would present itself to tell her the rest of it. But for right now, that was it.

It was a rather somber note on which to end the conversation. But, for the rest of their time together on this night, the two managed to enjoy each other's company. At the conclusion of the evening, Conner walked his friend to her car and kissed her on the cheek. He then stood and watched as she drove off into the dark, cold night.

CHAPTER TWENTY

The recent talk with Dean Frees at WCU had given Conner renewed confidence and a sense of enthusiasm. He was actually looking forward to getting started in the classroom. It would be a challenge. But, there were exciting new professional possibilities. And, there was the allure of that attractive young woman at the University. The scent of her perfume was still vivid in his memory. The thought of her brought a smile to his face.

Conner forced himself to refocus on the mission for this day. And that was to revisit the bunker and retrieve the rest of the deceased's diaries -- as well as some of the old magazines and other materials that might catch his eye. His hope was that one of these sources would provide further evidence of who the former occupant was.

Over the past few days, Conner familiarized himself with a topographical map, and he discovered a potentially shorter path to the hidden dwelling. Instead of using the logging road entrance, on this morning he'd enter the forest right behind the old White Swan Restaurant, which was at one of the crossroads in Cashiers. He guessed it might have been the same route the mystery man used to occasionally and quietly re-engage with the outside world.

As Conner stepped from his vehicle in Cashiers, he glanced at his watch. It was almost ten o'clock. His gaze then turned to the restaurant. Other than a plume of white smoke rising from the chimney, there was no sign of activity. Even the small, man-made lake just down the hill seemed deserted. Normally, there were a few geese and ducks cavorting around the lake's edge. But the cold weather had apparently driven them elsewhere.

From the outside, the White Swan resembled an old farmhouse. Its weathered siding had a natural -- almost neglected -- look about it. But the place was well kept and there was a certain quaintness about it. The Swan had big windows that looked out over tree-shaded grounds. And shutters beside each window were painted in a pale shade of green, to add a hint of color. Beneath each window was a flower box. During the summer months, these boxes burst forth with blooms of red, white, yellow and purple. Now, they were empty and barren.

Conner parked at the far end of the public parking lot. There were a few other cars scattered here and there. A couple of cars were right across the street from the Swan. He guessed they belonged to restaurant employees who were inside preparing for lunch. It would be safe to leave the Bronco here for the day, he told himself. Plenty of spaces were still available for restaurant patrons. The thought also occurred to Conner that if mystery man owned a car, he conceivably could have parked it here for periods of time.

From the back of the Bronco, Conner retrieved the thermos of coffee, binoculars, his camera and the 9-mm automatic. On this morning, he had brought two backpacks – including an extra to hold the materials he'd be retrieving from the bunker. He threw one of the packs over his shoulder and crossed the heavily travelled road between the lot and the restaurant. His path took him along the lake's perimeter. He noticed that ice had formed around the edge of the water. The presence of ice reminded him how cold it was.

Conner continued past the restaurant into a thicket just out back. He then made his way through the trees to Boulder Creek, which was about 100 feet down the hill. When he reached the creek, one thing immediately caught his attention. And again, the water level was a good foot and a half feet higher than normal.

As Conner proceeded into the woods, the crusted snow crunched sharply beneath each step. He paused and looked around. This two-inch snowfall overnight had added to the already sizeable accumulations. At higher elevations, there were a good 10 to 12 inches of snow on the ground.

Creatures of the forest -- from rabbits and squirrels to turkeys and deer -- would now be more aggressive in their search for food hidden just beneath a blanket of snow. Just weeks earlier, the click of a camera's shutter would have sent them scurrying for cover. Now, determination had replaced fear. Instead of fleeing, a hungry doe foraging for an edible sprout would now stare down an intruder.

Along the way, Conner took advantage of every opportunity he encountered, capturing one compelling scene after another. As he worked, his mood was relaxed -- almost playful. At one point, he focused his lens on three young deer standing in a snow-covered clearing. He stood for several seconds, waiting for just the right shot.

Suddenly, the early morning calm was shattered. At first, the sound was barely noticeable. Then it grew louder and louder. The three deer raised their heads, then quickly bolted into a nearby thicket, irritated by the intrusion. Conner backed away from the shot and looked skyward just in time to see a jet aircraft move into view. Conner reminded himself Cashiers was not exactly on the flight path of airliners travelling between major cities.

What the hell was this plane doing here? he asked himself. And why was it flying so low? He concluded it probably was on approach to Asheville's airport, some 40 miles to the north. The big jet was now directly overhead, and the roar of its engines echoed across the treetops.

From his vantage point, the plane appeared to be moving too slowly to stay aloft. But that was just an illusion. The aircraft's speed was deceiving at this distance. Just then, Conner's mind made an unlikely leap – to the photograph he'd seen on the wall of the bunker. It was the framed picture of a jetliner in flight. He stood quietly for several seconds, trying to make sense of the flashback. Conner watched the plane until it disappeared behind the trees. Then, he looked back at the surroundings and tried to regain his focus.

It took another 10 minutes for him to reach the vicinity of the falls. From this direction, he would not be able to actually see the falls. But, he would hear the sound of the water as it dashed onto the rocks below. And he could see the soft mist that hung above the creek as it spilled over the rocky precipice. Conner continued toward the rim. After a couple of minutes, he spotted the stone crossover about 50 feet ahead.

The big boulders spanning the creek were still visible, though not as prominently as before. Rushing water lapped at each stone, causing them to glisten in the bright sunlight. That meant the surfaces would be wet and slippery. He'd have to be careful as he made the crossing. The last thing he wanted was to fall in this frigid water. Hypothermia was a definite possibility under these conditions.

Conner approached the crossover and paused to secure the knapsack on his back. Carefully, then, he stepped onto the first boulder.

Fortunately, the stones were spaced close together, and he was able to plant each foot securely before shifting his weight. When he finally reached the last stone, he leaped to the safety of the bank. Then he turned and looked back at the makeshift bridge and shrugged. He had passed the first test.

Conner now shifted his attention to the big fir trees standing as guardians for the bunker and the secrets therein.

But, these trees were more than that. They stood there like giant sentries, guarding the secrets of that canyon just beyond. Clearly, mystery man had purposely added them as his first line of defense against intruders. Conner smiled at the foresight the man had shown. But what was it he had wanted to hide?

As Conner stared at the tall trees, a sudden gust caused their big limbs to dance violently in the wind. The sight was chilling -- almost foreboding. It was as if the trees were admonishing him not to go any farther. Conner took a deep breath of the cold air and deliberately pushed his way through the low-hanging limbs.

He continued across the small clearing to the second line of firs. These, too, had been planted by the former resident, Conner believed. After a brief pause, he made his way through the second row, then stepped into the hidden gorge just beyond.

As he moved into the clearing, he felt as if he were an airline passenger whose jet had just climbed through the clouds and emerged into a bright blue sky.

Conner stood for several moments looking out over the sprawling meadow. Everything appeared to be the same as it was the first time he saw it. Only now, the tall brush and wild flowers were gone, replaced by a thick layer of snow. Conner also spotted the unmistakable impressions of animal footprints in the snow. The wind and additional snowfall had partially obscured the prints. But clearly, they were animal footprints.

He then looked to his right, toward the canyon walls rising steeply from the meadow. His eyes followed the base of the canyon until he spotted the mound-shaped structure. It was at least 200 yards ahead. With the heavy blanket of snow covering everything, the structure was more difficult than ever to identify. From this distance it could easily be mistaken as just another rise in the canyon's uneven terrain. But, he knew what he was looking for.

Before proceeding, Conner cautiously looked around him. But, he saw no sign of movement. He then held his breath and listened.

But the only sound was the rush of wind through the big fir trees. Finally, he returned his gaze to the snow-covered mound. It didn't seem that far away.

But, walking straight through the open meadow was out of the question. That would leave telltale footprints. It would be the same as drawing a red line straight to the bunker's location. And it could prove he had been here.

At that point, Conner told himself he was being paranoid. But, what if the police came up here and found out he knew where the deceased lived? And what if they discovered he was systematically removing the deceased man's property. Then he told himself it was best to keep his visits to the bunker unknown. It was important to continue playing it safe, paranoid or not. And it was important to choose a path that was not so conspicuous.

Just then, his eyes locked onto the thin line of trees separating the meadow from the canyon walls. He turned and quickly made his way into the trees. Once there, he proceeded on an irregular path -- as if he had no particular destination in mind. He also walked in shaded areas, where his footprints would be less noticeable. If someone wanted to follow him, they certainly could. But, he wouldn't make it easy for them.

As he neared the bunker, he paused once more. There were no movements or sounds. He then followed the base of the bunker wall to the entrance. The ivy-covered door was pretty much as he'd left it. He could still see where he clipped the shoots to gain entry. But, the cold weather had taken its toll. The vine's dark green color had faded, and the leaves were noticeably withered. Still, it was alive. With the return of warm weather, the ivy would flourish again and obscure the doorway.

Before entering the bunker, Conner used his foot to clear away the mound of snow blocking the door. He then depressed the wooden latch, and the door swung freely toward him. Once inside, he stood for several minutes looking around the big room. Winter had done little to change its appearance. In fact, in this cold mountain air, the bunker's interior had a crisp look about it.

Conner turned his gaze to the small wood-burning stove in the rear of the bunker's main room. It would be nice to crank that baby up and add a little warmth to the room, he told himself. But that was not a good idea. A fire would generate smoke that could be seen for miles. Besides, he could already feel the sun radiating heat through the large glass panels overhead.

After a few moments, Conner felt warm enough to remove his gloves, slip the wool cap from his head and unbutton his coat.

Finally, he removed his coat altogether and placed it on a peg extending from the wall. The makeshift coat hook was another example of the former occupant's attention to detail. Conner stood for several more minutes, refreshing his memory of the dwelling's interior. There were so many things that had escaped his notice before.

But on this trip, Conner knew what he was looking for, and he went straight to the task of gathering up the material and placing it in the backpacks. When he got to the old magazines, he briefly thumbed through the old collection and several piqued his curiosity.

There were about twenty of the dated old publications, and he decided to take them all. As he walked toward the door, he paused and looked around the place again. "Boy, if only the walls could talk," he said out loud.

He then stepped back outside and restored the foliage around the door. He was now anxious to get back home and start digging through this new material.

CHAPTER TWENTY ONE

onner was taking this day off from working. And he was not up to cooking this evening, nor was he in the mood for going out for dinner. He stopped at a local grocery and bought a couple of homemade, pre-prepared meals. Conner believed food stores in the BC area had more locally prepared and tasty selections for their customers than big box stores in large cities.

For this evening, he planned on just hanging out alone at home. And he told himself it was time to do some more digging.

When he finished eating, he slid into the living room chair, and listened briefly to the captivating music engulfing the cabin. Western Carolina was just approaching the short days of winter, and although it was only 6:00, it was totally dark outside, and Conner considered it a perfect night to be at home.

As an afterthought, he retrieved one of the old magazines from the materials he'd laid aside to read. This magazine, in particular, had piqued his interest. It was an oldie, a publication called "Flying," and it was more than 50 years old, according to its published date.

As stated in the publication's masthead, Flying had roots that were traced back to the 1920s, initially as a publication called the Popular Aviator. But the name had changed to "Flying" some 20 years later, in keeping with the transformation of aviation itself -- notably in technology, and in the performance and capabilities of aircraft. The publication's name had remained the same since that time. The magazine was still very popular around the world with subscribers in the aircraft and aviation industries.

The cover of this particular issue of Flying promoted an article on several of the then younger generation of pilots, who were referred to as aviators. And the aviator pictured on this cover was a handsome young man photographed in his flying hat. It was a leather, head-hugging cap of the time, with flaps long enough to cover the ears, and metal-rimmed glasses that were repositioned out of the way and above the aviator's brow.

At that time, goggles were used by pilots who were still flying open-air, bi-wing flying machines covered with fabric.

Planes with aluminum skins were still several years away. Nevertheless, the photograph was a striking picture of the young flyer, whose name was Hans Gerhard Mueller, or Hans Miller.

Miller was the lead test pilot for Hughes Aircraft Company, which was founded in 1932 in suburban Los Angeles, California.

According to the article, before joining Hughes Aircraft, at the age of 20, Miller had served in the U.S. Army Air Force as a combat pilot during the final two years of World War I. He also had served his country in World War II. When Miller completed his military service, he earned a degree in aviation technology from Purdue University, graduating with honors.

As a test pilot at Hughes, Miller had flown several high performance aircraft built by the company, particularly prototypes in the final stages of development for the U.S. military.

The focus of this article was Hughes Aircraft's XF-11, a revolutionary new fighter/bomber, renamed the D-2 during contract negotiations with the government. Understandably, Miller was a staunch supporter of the XF-11. He was quoted as saying the plane's features and capabilities were far superior to other contemporary aircraft under development, either in the U.S. or in other countries. In Miller's own words: "...the XF-11 was a major leap forward in U.S. aircraft technology."

It had a top speed of 450 miles an hour and a climbing rate of 2,025 feet per minute. And it was the first military aircraft to have a pressurized cockpit, which allowed the pilot to fly to an altitude of 42,000 feet – all industry firsts, according to Miller.

The XF-11 was powered by two formidable Pratt & Whitney R-4350 radial piston engines, each of which produced 3,500 horsepower. And each of the engines was equipped with eight-bladed, variable-pitch propellers. This impressive power plant added greater gasoline and bomb carrying capacities to the ship and gave it an impressive flight range of 1,000 miles. This capability, as well, was unique at the time.

The plane was the first military aircraft to have dual fuselages or booms. Some said the dual booms added to the plane's maneuverability during air combat. The XF-11 also was armed with two 20 mm cannons in the nose of the cockpit pod.

"The dual, eight-bladed propellers gave the plane a very menacing appearance," Miller was quoted as saying.

He often boasted the XF-11 "... had the beauty and grace of a swan, but the intimidation and the bite of a shark." Both XF-11 prototypes were painted white, producing something of a futuristic look, Miller also felt.

Conner paused in his reading. He knew a great deal about Hughes Aircraft, particularly after the company's expansion into the electronics and research fields, which occurred during World War II and later. The company was an outgrowth of the Hughes Tool Company, also based in Los Angeles. Hughes Tool's success was a result of the founder's invention of a revolutionary new oil drilling bit – called the Tri-Cone bit - during the Texas oil boom at the turn of the 20th century. The bit still was in widespread use for oil drilling after all these years, Conner believed.

Despite Hughes Aircrafts efforts to get its plane adopted into the Army Air Force's arsenal, continuing delays and requests for on-going modifications of its design and performance took a toll on the company, and Hughes ultimately terminated its dealings with the government. This left the door open, according to Miller, for its competitors --who also were vying for approval with alternative aircraft -- to incorporate the advanced features of the XF-11 in their own aircraft.

After lengthy negotiation, the U.S. Army reimbursed Hughes for its work on the project. And as something of a consolation for losing the contract, a version of the XF-11 would later be selected by the government for a key role in its secretive, high-altitude reconnaissance, or international spying program, industry sources would later confirm.

Sources also quoted in the story claimed a major Hughes' competitor -- Lockheed Aircraft -- had copied the XF-11's design in its similar looking, P-38, which ended up becoming one of the key components in fighter squadron cover, during bombing attacks against Nazi Germany. Like the XF-11, the P-38 also was a dual fuselage aircraft with impressive armaments.

Conner was very much aware of the Hughes Aircraft's sophisticated research, and he felt the company's advanced aviation electronics had set the stage for the birth of the USA's postwar aerospace industry.

Conner also was struck with the eloquence and outspoken nature of this young test pilot quoted in that long ago issue of Flying magazine. He admired his aggressiveness. Miller and his contemporaries were the rough riders of their day, Conner felt. They were pioneers who helped build the U.S. Air Force into the most advanced and powerful airborne fighting force in the world, Conner believed.

After reading the article, Conner placed this young man in the same category as those who followed in their footsteps, young men who demonstrated incredible courage and devotion to country, ignoring the personal risks and uncertainties associated with harnessing the skies for peaceful and patriotic advancement. They were men who set the stage for others to follow -- men such as flying aces Chuck Yeager and John Glenn.

When Air Force ace Chuck Yeager strapped himself into an experimental X-1 rocket plane in October of 1947, he ignored experts who believed man was not meant to fly faster than the speed of sound, which was 662 miles an hour at 25,000 feet. They were convinced the plane would explode. Yeager busted through this target speed of sound, creating the first known sonic boom. And in 1952, he broke his own record, flying at the incredible speed of 1,600 miles an hour.

In a similar attack on the unknown, in February of 1962, John Glenn became the first American to orbit the earth in a spacecraft, orbiting Earth at a speed of 17,500 miles an hour, a record that also was lodged in Conner's memory.

When Conner finished reading the piece, he repeated the young man's name: Hans Gerhard Mueller. He then repeated his initials: HGM. Conner paused momentarily and tried to identify with the young pilot and the achievements of other flyers who had advanced the cause of aviation.

Conner was an acrophobic, which meant he had un-natural fears of heights. Because of this condition, he had great admiration and respect for those heroes who not only had no fear of heights, they also had no fear of the unknown. And this young test pilot seemed to exemplify those admirable traits. Conner spent several minutes thumbing through the rest of the magazine and read excerpts of other articles.

Before placing the publication aside, he repeated the young test pilot's name and his initials, HGM. Unthinkingly, he raised his glass and took another long sip of wine.

At that moment, his thought process exploded with the intensity of a lightning bolt, and he nearly choked on the unswallowed liquid, uncontrollably spewing some of it onto himself. Embarrassingly, he wiped the dripping wine from his chin with the back of his hand and loudly vocalized his excitement.

"I'll be damned!" he shouted out loud. "I'll be damned!" Hans Miller is the mystery man! Hans Miller is the fucking mystery man!"

Conner paused, realizing he was talking to himself. He slid back into his chair dumbfounded. After a few moments, he reached out and picked up the magazine, staring again at the young man pictured on the cover.

"So this is why you hung on to this old magazine all these years?" he seemed to be asking the deceased…because that's your picture on the cover?" Well, I gotta' say one thing for ya'. You were a handsome young sonofabitch!"

Conner chuckled at his reaction. He retrieved a couple of napkins from a kitchen drawer and wiped away the spilled wine as best he could.

"Now, that I know who the hell you are, what the hell did you do? What the hell did you do to prompt you to move to these mountains and live here all those years as a hermit?" he questioned out loud.

It was a question for which Conner had no answer. Frustrated, he returned to the chair and spent several minutes perusing the issue on his own. Why would someone not want to use his or her own name? The obvious answer is he did something that was either against the law, or was so offensive or embarrassing that it would mean total ruin for his future.

The more he thought about the latter scenario the more he concluded that Miller did not seem to have been the kind who would violate ethical or moral issues. If it were one of these two choices, it had to be the former. Miller must have broken the law and wanted to escape prosecution and the strong arm of justice. Even that seemed out of character, based on what he knew, read or guessed .

But that was the more plausible option of the two. Miller had broken the law in some way and wanted to avoid prosecution and incarceration.

The passing thought then occurred to Conner. Miller may have committed a serious or first degree felony, which could include terrorism, treason, arson, murder, rape or kidnapping, to name a few of the most serious crimes. Conner thought about this and, again, he could not imagine Miller doing such things, certainly not murder, rape or kidnapping. Providing his assumption was correct, Conner didn't know any more about Miller than he did before.

From the comfort of his chair, Conner looked over at the stack of diaries on his dining room table. As he stared at the accumulation of old ledgers, he convinced himself the answers to his questions were right there before him, waiting to be discovered.

But in his mind, he had done enough serious thought on this evening, and it was time to put everything else aside and just enjoy the comfort of his home. He poured himself a modest refill of wine, turned the stereo sound up a bit and nestled into his chair.

Sitting there, the image of Carolyn wrapped in that blanket and sitting in this same chair came to mind, prompting a warm smile from Conner.

CHAPTER TWENTY TWO

Over time, Conner had often expressed his dislike of surprises and last minute changes in his life. He didn't mind change, if it were gradual, or if he knew it was coming. But, the next morning, Conner received a letter from the Dean's office, advising staff members the University was advancing its schedule of spring classes by five weeks. This included the Professional Development or Continuing Education Programs.

The letter explained this action was taken to address unavoidable school closures made during the previous semester. The move, they said, would make up for days lost in the school year. But the timing of the announcement threw Conner for an emotional loop.

He was counting on that lead-up time to further develop his curricula for the coming semester. His course, "Fundamentals of Effective Writing," would now begin on December the 12th instead of early January. As he read the announcement, Conner threw up his hands in a faked display of despair that gave way to a forced chuckle. He not only faced course content issues and the pressure of starting a new job, he'd have to handle both on the equivalent of a very short runway.

Conner reminded himself pressure had been a way of life for him at IBM. And he'd just have to count on adrenalin and lotsa' coffee to get it done. The thought brought a smile to his face and helped ease the tension surrounding the scheduling change.

Three days later, Conner pulled onto the WCU campus around 4 p.m. and drove straight to the Fine Arts Center. He needed to confirm his assigned classroom for the evening. A total of 21 students were registered for the class, which would convene on Mondays and Thursdays from 5:30 to 7:30 p.m. He was told the number of students could rise slightly due to last minute registrations. Conner was pleased with this modest class size and felt this would permit more personalized instruction.

A couple of days earlier, Conner had visited the campus for a briefing on his planned use of computers as a class instruction aid. He felt comfortable with that part of his job and looked forward to using technology to provide hands-on involvement with each student. The attendees would be responsible for providing their own, compatible systems. For those not owning computers, WCU would provide the systems at a nominal fee.

After entering the Fine Arts Center on this afternoon, Conner took the elevator to the second floor and proceeded down the hall to room 208. When he stepped inside, all the lights were on, which instilled in him a positive impression of the thoroughness and attentiveness of the department's support crew.

Once in the room, he immediately was drawn to the exterior wall of floor-to-ceiling windows that looked out over the sprawling Smokey mountains in the distance. The day was coming to a close, and the sunset over the mountains was spectacular. He stood for several minutes, admiring nature's incredible beauty.

Conner then walked slowly down the raked stairs of the classroom and paused at the lectern pod up-front. After retrieving his computer and several notebooks from his backpack, he tossed the satchel onto the desk shelving and began reviewing his notes. He guessed he'd have about 20 minutes before the first students began arriving.

Conner turned his computer on and looked expectantly at the large clock on the front wall. It was now just a few minutes past five. Just then, two female students entered the room rather sheepishly and took seats on the last two rows. Conner moved from behind the desk and welcomed them. He continued to make small talk with the two, and then welcomed others who were now filing into the room.

At precisely 5:30, Conner stood before the gathered audience, rubbing his hands together in a show of personal enthusiasm. He quickly scanned the eager faces glued to his every move and began his introduction.

"Good evening, ladies and gentlemen. Welcome. I'm Mitch Conner, and for the next few weeks, I'll be your instructor for this course on effective writing."

The photographer-turned-instructor began walking slowly to-and-from the middle of the room, continuing his introduction as he moved. His voice tone was now one of confidence and enthusiasm.

"I applaud each of you gathered here this evening. Your calling to improve your writing is to be commended. Next to verbal skills, writing skills have done more to advance civilization over time than few other forms of human activity have, in my view."

"Writing in all of its different forms has chronicled the people of western civilizations' emergence from cave life to complex societies . It has helped us understand who we are and where we've been. It has helped us interpret our successes and failures and better understand how to navigate the complexities of a civilized world."

" Simply said. it's the key to our past, our present and our future. It's the glue that holds other forms of societal activity together."

"Unfortunately," Conner continued, "we as a society have not done a good job of sustaining and protecting the written word. And that's having a profound effect on our abilities to communicate with one another, as I see it," Conner said.

"And nowhere is that decline more visible than in the English-speaking countries of the world…particularly the U.S.A."

"In 2011, a nationwide survey revealed only 24 percent of eighth and 12th grade students in the U.S were proficient in writing, and a mere 3 percent were considered in the advanced category," he noted.

As Conner continued his presentation, he took occasional steps across the front of the room, in an expression of subject familiarity and confidence.

"Most educators agree when students are able to write effectively about what they've just learned, it increases their retention and understating of subject matter. Unfortunately, we are not living up to that potential, and these disappointing results are having a profound effect on the learning process in this country."

"That 2011 survey," he continued, "also was a condemnation of our society's dependence on such things as smart phones and other electronic gadgets to do our talking and handle our written communications," he said.

"And this has even led to the creation of a subculture language consisting of three lettered words such as BFF or 'Best Friends Forever.'"

Laughter across the room punctuated the comment.

"So, what do we do about this problem?" he asked.

"To begin, we need to enhance the role of writing as a fundamental part of the broader educational curricula. And we need to offer more elective writing courses such as this one. Granted, this is something of a modest start. But, I say remember the old Chinese proverb: "The journey of 1,000 miles begins with the first step."

Conner paused and leaned against his desk in a more relaxed posture.

"Before getting to any questions you may have, I'll tell you a bit more about my own history and resume," he added.

"You should know I'm a newcomer to WCU, having relocated to Bryson City less than a year ago from Atlanta, where I spent the better part of a 25-year career with IBM."

"In terms of my credentials, I received an undergraduate degree in journalism from Kent State University. I also have a master's degree in journalism from Northwestern University.

During the years I was in college, I worked part-time for daily and weekly newspapers. And early in my 25-year IBM career, I wrote speeches for company executives. I've also written and published three novels and have done some work on a fourth."

"As for this course, our objective will be to build your sense of awareness about your writing. It will not be a refresher course on grammar."

Conner paused at the polite laughter that rippled across the room.

"The grammar course meets down the hall on Tuesdays and Fridays."

Again there was polite laughter.

Nor will I be counseling you on your spelling," he added. If you really need help with spelling, make sure you've got spell check on your word processing program.

"Now, I'm not suggesting grammar and spelling are not important to good writing," he added. "Quite the contrary. All of these things are extremely important. But, we can't focus on each of these disciplines when our focus must be on the writing process itself," he said.

"As writers, we must develop the habit of reading what we're writing. And we must ask ourselves, 'is this really what I want to say?' And when we do this, we often find what we've written is not what we want to say," he continued.

Conner paused, the glow in his eyes reflecting the commitment in his words.

"When I still lived in Atlanta, there was a weather forecaster on one radio station who routinely drove me crazy with the things he said."

"To promote his upcoming weather forecast on the air, he would say the following: 'I'll be discussing whether we can expect snow in five minutes.'"

"Now, this guy was saying there was the possibility it would snow in five minutes. But what he meant to say was: 'in five minutes, I will discuss the possibility of getting snow in the area.'"

"This was pure laziness in my mind," Conner added. "And it was the kind of language that's very misleading to the listening audience. Laziness, or the lack of thoroughness and awareness, are among the cardinal sins of writing. You don't do it!"

"And when we write, keep it simple. Simple…simple…simple. Short sentences are easier to read. And they help us avoid problems that arise when writing gets too complicated.. So, keep it simple."

There was a brief pause before he continued.

"There are other major reasons for this breakdown in our ability to write effectively. They include the complexity and difficulty of this language we call English," he said. "Our native language not only is very hard to learn, there are many, many inconsistencies within it. For example, in America we park our cars on the driveway and drive our cars on the parkway."

There was an understanding chuckle in the room.

"I like what writer Norman Mailer once said on this subject."

"Writing," he said, "is the closest men ever come to childbearing."

Hearty laughs erupted from his audience.

Conner paused and looked thoughtfully at the students.

"So…that pretty well sums up my views on writing," Conner said with a smile.

"In the weeks ahead, each of you will be given common information to arrange on paper – or in our case - on your computer screen. And collectively as a group we'll examine how your written prose may be improved.

And remember this is a learning exercise…and not personal criticism. The good news, there are no tests and no grades handed out."

Relaxed laughter rippled across the room before Conner continued.

"And now that you know who I am, I'd like to know a little bit more about each of you. Let's take a few minutes for you to tell me your name and any other information you'd like to share. What moved you to sign up for this class…that sort of thing."

Conner then scanned the group of students before settling on a perky female in the first seat of the front row.

I'll ask this young lady seated down front here to start us off. And let's just move down each row from right to left. The young woman responded with enthusiasm, setting a positive example for the other students to follow.

Conner used the remaining time with his students to discuss other major contributors to poor writing. He also provided examples of both effective and ineffective writing and described his expectations for student interaction with the computers.

As he gazed around the room, he looked at the fresh faces in the audience, and he guessed at least one, possibly more, were faculty or staff representatives whose presence in the class was to assess his early interaction with his students.

The idea brought a smile to his face. He was not intimidated by those who might be looking over his shoulder. In fact, he rather welcomed such early evaluation. Possibly they could provide tips that would enhance his effectiveness. It was professionalism at its best, in his view.

At this point in his life, such pressure was a motivator, not an inhibitor. He was beginning to enjoy this new challenge. Conner paused before concluding the session, scanning the room with a smile and slight nodding that reflected self proficiency and self confidence.

"Before we adjourn for this evening," Conner added," I have one homework assignment that could be revealing and fun for the next time we gather here."

Conner paused momentarily for both emphasis and effect.

"On November 19th of 1863, our nation's President, Abraham Lincoln, visited the little town of Gettysburg, Pennsylvania, where the Union and Confederate Armies had clashed four months earlier in one of the bloodiest battles of the Civil War. "

"Prior to addressing the crowd assembled before him, President Lincoln had scrawled a 271-word message on the back of an envelope, acknowledging the sacrifice made by those who died on that site. The President's hastily prepared tribute is now considered one of the best-known speeches in American history," Conner added.

"I have copies of the speech for each of you, or you can look it up on your computer, if you prefer. Read it through and ask yourself if you would have said it any differently."

"I look forward to seeing each of you at our next session."

Several students lingered briefly in the classroom to chat with Conner, who remained at his desk to accommodate their interests. It was almost eight o'clock when he finally left the Fine Arts complex.

And as Conner drove from the WCU campus that evening, he continued to replay in his memory highlights of his first day in the classroom. Overall, he was pleased with the lecture and his reception overall. And the students seemed to be suitably engaged, he thought. He also was impressed with the number of students who extended the session with questions and comments when the class ended. But, I can do better next time, he told himself.

CHAPTER TWENTY THREE

Over the next few days, Conner spent considerable time reading and skimming through Miller's diaries. Though interesting, most passages were rather mundane in nature. They concerned Miller's occasional sorties from the bunker into the outside world -- going to nearby stores for necessities or making an occasional visit to a low-profile restaurant -- and the measures he had taken to avoid drawing attention to himself.

On this evening, Conner was reading from journal number eight and he came across an entry that involved a name he'd not seen before. The name was Sarah, and as Conner read, he got the impression Sarah was Miller's first wife. He had mentioned in a very early journal entry there were two loves in his life, both of whom had since passed on. But Hans also referred to the name Amy. She must have been his second love. The date on the entry was September 21st:

Sept. 21st:

On this day, my thoughts are with my dearest Sarah. This was the anniversary of our cherished years together, and ironically, the same date of her passing from this earth. We were both so young –- both only 20 years old – when we exchanged vows in the lovely garden of her parents' home in Portland. Sarah would not have approved of my activities. But the scoundrels deserved what they got. I sometimes look back on the whole affair, and it appears to be a story involving someone else, not me. During Sarah's illness, Amy was such a pillar of support, both to Sarah and me. Over time, she became more of a sister to Sarah and not just a friend. I miss them both so very much. I'm convinced Sarah would have encouraged the time Amy and I spent together after her passing. But memories of each are of great comfort to me. As a friend once told me, the blessing of memories are they allow us to have roses in December.

Conner re-read the touching passage. Then he looked back to the words about his activities and the scoundrels. What were the activities, he asked out loud. And who were the scoundrels?

Conner turned to another journal and his reading continued. It didn't take long before he locked on to another segment, dated Feb. 14th:

February 14th:

At this time of year, my memories always point back to the first conversations I had with Roebie about our joint venture. It was on Valentine's Day. and I remember how receptive he was to my idea, He immediately suggested we meet in person. At the time, Sarah and I were in the process of moving from the Purdue campus in West Lafayette, Indiana back to L.A. I made the necessary travel arrangements, and I still remember the wonderful trip I had on the Santa Fe Railroad and riding the California Zephyr from Chicago to L.A.

February 21st:

My meeting with Roebie exceeded my expectations. He was as excited about the plan as I was…maybe even more. He even suggested ways to guarantee success and make sure we achieved the objectives. I chose not to tell Amy about it, because I didn't want her to be concerned. But, it certainly was in her best interests. To this day, there are some who do not give Roebie the proper credit he deserved for his genius. He probably was one of the smartest and gifted people I've ever known. And throughout our relationship, he always was both generous and appreciative, first as a colleague and then as a friend. Some simply wrote him off as an eccentric nutcase. But they didn't know him as I did.

As Conner pondered the words, he felt as though Miller had recorded these thoughts for the untold side of the story – essentially his side of the story -- presumably after he was no longer around to tell it in person. And although it was very descriptive, it was only revealing when taken in context. But so far, these were just little bits of information here and there. Conner told himself he had to be patient. At some point, the story would all fall into place, he told himself.

———◆———

The sun was just beginning to dip below the horizon when Conner drove through a fast-food restaurant in downtown BC. A quick meal at home on this evening would give him more time for reading. He was skipping his traditional two glasses of wine before dinner. He needed all his senses for tonight's reading.

And he did not want to fall asleep while doing so. Before beginning, he placed a pen and pad on the nearby table and randomly selected a couple of journals.

The first journal had a number of really old entries, an indication Miller might not have been in the bunker yet…or that his living arrangements were not settled. After about an hour, Conner came across another point that seemed relevant. It was dated May 31st.

May 31st:

I choose this date to express my feelings for a friend, a loved one and an American hero – all one and the same. Her life was a symbol of why we pause to say thank you on this hallowed occasion. She did not serve this Country militarily. But she was the recipient of the United States Distinguished Flying Cross presented by the U.S. Congress for her achievements. She also received a gold medal from the President of the United States. Amy Putnam was my loving second wife, She and I not only shared our lives, we shared a deep love for flying.

Conner looked up from the page in awe. Could this get more complicated? he asked himself. He could not answer the question, so his interest quickly returned to the page before him.

I remember well the first time I saw Amy Putnam. She was teaching a class at Purdue University where I was a student, at the time. She had a lively spirit, unshakeable self-confidence, and a very high level of competence. Back then, she was a senior advisor in Purdue's Department of Aeronautics – at the ripe old age of 36. I also knew of the international name she had made for herself through her flying exploits. That included becoming the first woman to cross the Atlantic Ocean solo, which earned her accolades and a friendship with Charles Lindbergh. What impressed me about her, right off, was how approachable this tall, leggy girl from Kansas was, despite her lifetime achievements and world fame. It was at this point she and I, as well as her sister Grace and my wife Sarah, all became inseparable friends. It was a relationship that grew with time, and she and I often flew together. But in her second year at Purdue, she decided she wanted to fly around the world. That was when Roebie and I got involved with her plan to circle the globe. But we purposely withheld our involvement in fear she would resist our assistance. But I knew at some point, we'd have to bring her into the fold.

Conner looked up from his reading. And instinctively, he repeated Amy's name – Amy Putnam. Amy Putnam. He'd never heard of her before. He seemed to have a growing feeling of disconnection with the diary's contents. But he was confident all of this would fall into place at some point.

The plane Amy chose for her 'round the world' trip was the Lockheed Electra 10E, a relatively new model for the company. It was a small, low-wing passenger plane designed to compete with Boeing's 247 and Douglas Aircraft's DC-2. But her Electra 10E was customized to meet her particular needs and included adding four auxiliary fuel tanks, eliminating passenger windows, installing an autopilot system and adding numerous pieces of radio and directional equipment. And, the plane's dual supercharged Pratt and Whitney engines only generated 600 horsepower and all of the extra weight of those modifications reduced the plane's speed to 177 miles an hour. I felt for a time this issue might be problematic but her mechanics and advisors over-ruled me.

Conner paused and gave thought to the aircraft's role in Amy's ambitious journey. Then it occurred to him, this was just history, and he couldn't change history. He returned to the task at hand.

Because of the nature of her excursion, including the flight path she'd pursue, Amy clearly needed a navigator. And her choice was a highly recommended but little-known contemporary by the name of Fred Noonan. Noonan was an accomplished navigator, but he had worked most of his career as a ship's captain. He was best known in aviation circles for developing air transportation routes for Pan American World Airways' fleet of "Clipper" airliners to destinations around the world. About three months after Amy left Purdue University to line up sponsors and make the necessary arrangements for her planned voyage, I received my degree and returned to my job as a test pilot with Hughes Aircraft. At that point, Amy had picked a target date to begin the different legs of her trip. The flight was scheduled for the third week of May. At this point, I had held a number of conversations with Roebie, since there were things on our end that had to be arranged, as well. It was at this point the XF-11 came back in my life. It was such a spectacular aircraft and a fine example of man's genius… Both Roebie and I felt Amy needed a "wing man" to fly along with her because of the many challenges she faced, particularly the large bodies of water she'd have to navigate to achieve her goal. That included the upcoming, 3,000- mile segment over open waters of the Central Pacific Ocean. Finally, three weeks before her departure, I told her of our intentions to accompany her flight. And with all the emotion her Germanic temper could muster; she made her opinion very clear. She adamantly refused to consider the idea. But, I explained to her I would be perfectly invisible and not infringe on any of her decisions or choices during the flight. I emphasized that I would only be an insurance policy in the event of unexpected conditions or developments. That included the unknowns of encountering dangerous weather over the Pacific she'd likely encounter during this cyclone season. I also explained to her I'd be able to document many of the elements of her flight and record as much flying data as I could. After thinking it through, Amy decided it was a good idea and the matter was settled. And by having the XF-11 in my control, I not only could provide backup and security for her, I could showcase the aircraft's many untold capabilities. There were a few modifications and additions made to the XF-11 I'd fly, but not many. To enhance our "eyes in the skies," we added a radar system and additional fuel bladders. During the first week of May, Roebie and I made a trip up to Oakland, where Amy was making final preparations for her journey. Putnam's original plan to achieve her goal was to fly a west-to-east route, but inclement weather over the Pacific at the *last minute led her to switch the direction of her flights, to an east-to-west direction. So, on May 17th she and navigator Noonan lifted off from Oakland and headed for Miami, Florida, almost 3,000 miles away. But a very rough landing during inclement weather at Miami's airport damaged the aircraft and maintenance had been made on the ship. The repairs delayed their departure for several days. But in the early morning of June 1st, Putnam and Noonan left Miami and made a 900 flight to San Juan Puerto Rico.*

Again, Conner paused in his thoughts. This was compelling reading. But it was not very revealing from his point of view. It added nothing to the puzzle, he told himself. Nevertheless, he continued to move ahead.

From Puerto Rico, they flew to Venezuela, then on to Brazil. After a couple of days' delay, they left Natal, Brazil for the 1,900 mile crossing of the South Atlantic Ocean to Dakar, Senegal on Africa's west coast. It took almost three days to overfly the African continent and She and Noonan arrived in Pakistan on June 17 after the 1,000 mile crossing of the Arabian Sea. From Pakistan, Amy and Noonan overflew India, Burma and Thailand before settling in at Bandung, Indonesia for a three-day plane maintenance layover and a much-needed rest. From Kupang, Indonesia, Amy continued another 1,600 miles to Lea, Papua New Guinea, where she would prepare for this risky segment of her journey thus far. And it was at this point in New Guinea that I joined Amy and Noonan in their journey. At midnight on July 2 in deteriorating weather, the two of them took off with the heavily ladened Electra. Their destination: the isolated Howland Island, some 3,000 miles away in the middle of the Central Pacific Ocean. Howland was a deserted coral island that was not much more than a sliver, only 2,100 yards long and 525 yards wide. It was literally in the middle of nowhere and some 1,700 miles southwest of Honolulu. Minutes after Amy's takeoff, I applied full throttle to the XF-11 and quickly climbed through pitch black skies to 35,000 feet. There was a full moon above the weather below and I remember thinking it would be nice if Amy could see this. But, she was flying below me at 15,000 feet and travelling at just under 200 miles an hour in the Electra. Because I was much higher, I was flying in much thinner air, which had fuel consumption and speed advantages. But, I didn't need to fly faster. I had, in fact, throttled back to half normal speed to avoid outdistancing Amy and Noonan. It had been some time since I flew this far solo, and one of my major challenges was staying awake. But, I had a large thermos of coffee and that seemed to help. And from my lofty perch, I could put the plane on automatic pilot and get some relief from the boredom and inactivity. About every three hours or so, I touched base with Amy by radio, and the flight seemed to be going well for her. But as the weather continued to deteriorate, her radio seemed to be less effective, and I'd have to drop below the clouds to reestablish visual contact. When we finally reached the 3/4 mark in the flight, Amy's radio signal completely dissipated, and I was forced to drop down every hour or so to make sure she was okay. When we were only 20 to 30 minutes from Howland Island, I dropped to about 17,000 feet so I could have visual contact with her plane. But, it appeared that Amy was a few degrees off course, and that was very unusual for her. I told myself she probably had lost her compass, and probably the radio, as well. The good news was the sun was rising and we were flying in a decent visual environment again. But the wind speed was at a pretty high level. I decided to fly to the target and circle the Island with all lights on, so she could lock on to me visually. I pulled alongside her plane and flickered my lights while pointing to the target. She seemed to be nodding her head as I increased speed to quickly reach Howland. I continued my circling of the tiny landing site, and instinctively opened the canopy so I could hear her approach. Amy was now about three miles away from touchdown, and I was close enough to hear her aircraft sputtering. I became very concerned and moved closer to her in her approach, maybe four hundred feet. She couldn't be having engine trouble, I told myself as I moved closer to the Electra. Just then the sputtering stopped and both engines of her plane died. I remember the feeling of panic engulfing me as I watched her propellers rotate to a dead stop. Suddenly it dawned on me she had run out of gas. She had no power and the Electra was bouncing around like an un-tethered kite in this fierce wind. Amy was trying to control the ship, but to no avail. I pulled up and circled around her as the big plane went into a 75-degree descent. At the time, she was in close visual contact with the island, I guessed less than a mile away. My entire body went into shock, and all I could do was call out her name, over and over. I was terrified as I watched her plane hit the water. In a matter of a few minutes, it disappeared beneath the waves.

I was devastated, and then suddenly there was movement in the water. One of them, wearing a life vest, popped through the surface, but I couldn't see who it was. Finally, I realized it was Amy in the water. It was Amy in the water, I told myself. Instinctively, I grabbed a small, deflated life raft, pulled the inflation cord and threw it from my cockpit as close to her as I could. I then banked into a landing approach for the island. Within four or five minutes I was on the landing surface and taxied to the closest spot I could, to get a larger raft into the water. Despite the conditions, I could see Amy hanging on to the smaller inflatable, which was being pushed toward the island by the wind and the tide. The weather was now working in our favor, pushing her ever closer to the beach. I guessed she was now less than 100 yards away from me. Once I got the larger life raft in the water, I paddled fiercely toward her. I don't remember all that happened, but at that point, my actions were a mixture of panic and instinct. But I do remember pulling her from the water and into the larger raft. She was pretty messed up from the impact, and clearly Noonan didn't make it out of the plane. I do remember creating a makeshift sling with elements of my parachute. And I was able to hoist her into the cockpit. I then taxied to where fuel bladders had been air-dropped for me on the island. And after retrieving as much of the fuel into my ship as possible - using a hand pump - I taxied to the far end of the island and turned into the wind for takeoff. I had to get Amy to a hospital. With everything buttoned up, I gunned my plane. Within five minutes I was at 45,000 feet and travelling at almost 500 miles an hour. My destination was the small island of Kirimatri, or Christmas Island. With one radio call to Roebie, arrangements were being made for a doctor from Indonesia, only 875 miles from Christmas Island, to meet our plane. Amy's injuries turned out to be pretty serious. She had fractures of both legs, broken ribs and some bruising and damage to the spleen. Under constant care of the Indonesian doctor, she was confined in a small infirmary for six days and then transferred to a hospital in Jakarta. The attending physician also recommended additional hospital treatment for her recovery. Amy's convalescence of nearly three weeks gave her a lot of time to think about her path forward, she later confided to me. The world was waiting for news about her and her navigator. But, she was confused and reluctant to discuss her ill attempted flight. In her mind, she had gone down with her plane, and she felt a deep sense of guilt, particularly about Noonan's loss. She pleaded with the handful of people who knew of her tragedy for total privacy and asked them not to speculate about her situation. The lack of news about her survival became a matter of weeks and then months. Finally, the world concluded her plane and its crew had simply disappeared, with no apparent survivors. And she did not refute or challenge such speculation. In the meantime, I accompanied her when she was released from the hospital in Jakarta. At my urging, she travelled with me to our new home at a secluded area in the San Gabriel Mountains near Los Angeles. For the time being, she would live with Sarah and me. After a few months, her sister, Grace, also joined us. As for Amy's physical health, her convalescence continued to be satisfactory. But mentally and emotionally, she was still in an uncertain state. I knew what she was experiencing, and I did not challenge the decisions she made early on. But from everything I gathered, Amy had no interest in reliving or speculating on what had happened to her. And her compassion for flying seemed to have disappeared with her Electra 10E aircraft, now resting thousands of feet below the Pacific Ocean. In her grief, Amy seemed to be saying if public opinion had already declared her lost at sea, that was fine with her. Her days in Los Angeles turned into weeks and then months, and her personality and demeanor remained noticeably broken and uncertain. She was not the Amy I remembered. She seldom initiated conversations and when she was engaged, her responses were rather brief and indifferent. But I remained upbeat and positive. I knew that same tall and leggy girl from Kansas still existed in her. And I was convinced she would emerge again, given the right amount of time. It was during this period, her younger sister, Grace, gave her a Boston Terrier puppy and for the first time in several months, I heard her laugh again. Amy named her pet after her Electra 10E, calling her new little friend "Lexie."

Conner looked up from his reading and leaned back in his chair. He made something of an exaggerated grunting noise as he extended both arms above his head and yawned. At this point in the evening, he chuckled at his own personal quirks, which seemed to get more numerous and pronounced as he aged. He was reminded of the question his son Kevin had once asked him long ago on the subject of personal mannerisms.

"Dad," Kevin had asked, "why do old people make noises when they sit down?

Then, as now, the question evoked a chuckle and a smile."

Conner realized he'd been reading quietly for most of the evening, and the inactivity had made him sleepy. He had written himself notes on several issues along the way. some of them useful and some requiring more thought. But, it was well after 10 pm, and he decided to call it quits for the night.

Conner pushed himself from the chair and walked straight to the bedroom. He fell onto his bed and within minutes was sound asleep, fully clothed and shoes still on

———————◆———————

CHAPTER TWENTY FOUR

Conner rose early the next morning. He had a busy day scheduled and a lot to get done. His first appointment was with an architect in Franklin. He'd been thinking a lot recently about making major renovations to the cabin, including expanding the living space, adding centralized heating and air conditioning and building a garage or two. And today, he'd take the first step to getting that effort rolling.

He wasn't concerned about the cost of making these changes. When he sold his Atlanta home, he had no mortgage, and he walked away with about half a million dollars. He had paid cash for the cabin, and these improvements wouldn't consume anywhere near the amount he still had from the home sale. Plus he had a sizeable investment in his 401K. So, financially, he felt pretty good about his future.

Through the internet, Conner was able to find three architectural firms at a reasonable distance from BC. The distance he'd have to drive to meet with the firms was an important factor, he felt. And Franklin was only about 45 minutes away. Two of those three firms were in Franklin,. After telephone interviews with all three, Conner chose one of the two from Franklin, the firm of Royce and Associates.

Conner estimated he currently had about 1,200 feet of living space in the cabin. And he hoped to add maybe 1,200 square feet of additional living space. Plus, he wanted to rearrange the overall layout of his home.

Conner spent more time in his first meeting with Royce than he guessed he would, a little more than four hours. But, so far he liked what he heard from the firm's principals. They seemed to be asking all the right questions. He had taken a number of photographs of the cabin. And though they seemed helpful, the firm's associates requested an on-site inspection, to better understand the scope of the project. Before he left the Royce office, a date was set for the inspection and a ballpark timetable was discussed for each major step of the project.

When Conner left the meeting in Franklin, he felt encouraged about the visit and the ideas that were exchanged. And he found himself pleased with the prospects of this major facelift for his home. In fact, he was getting rather excited about the project. And on the drive back to BC, he couldn't help but think about additional questions he had. But, they could wait.

On the return trip to BC, Conner made an unscheduled stop at Eddie Chatworth's gas station. He hadn't seen or talked to the personable mechanic in some time.

When Conner pulled the Bronco into the station, Chatworth was very busy, running from one customer to another. This was a thriving business, Conner told himself.

Chatworth immediately recognized the Bronco and made his way over to the vehicle.

"Hey, mister Conner," he said with a smile. "You havin' some kind of problem with your car?"

"No, Eddie. Nothin' like that. The Bronco couldn't be running better. I love it. I'm here to see if we could do a little more business."

"Sure," he replied. "Whatcha' got in mind?"

"I wanna' hang on to the Bronco. But, I'm interested in buying a second vehicle.

Somethin' a little upscale…you know, a Saturday night kind of vehicle that'll still climb these mountains…Maybe an Audi or a Volvo. Maybe a Land Rover. Somethin' that looks good, has four wheel drive and an engine that gets you where your wanna' go."

"You know what I mean?" he asked Eddie.

"Yessir. Matter fac, one of my customers got a 2018 Land Rover he wants to unload. He's got three or four cars and don't drive that one much no more. He brings all his cars to us for his work, so I can tell you he takes good care-uh his vehicles."

"How many miles on it?"

"I don't recall eg-zackly, but it's maybe 40, 45 thousand. Sumthin' like that. It's less than 50 thousand for shure."

Before Conner could reply, Chatworth continued.

"I think ya' could get it for around 28,000. He might take less, I dunno."

Eddie gave Conner the man's name and phone number and Conner shook Eddie's hand appreciatively.

"Hey, Eddie. I really appreciate your help. Thank you again so much."

"No problem. Glad to be of help."

The car turned out to be a Land Rover Discovery Sport HSE. It was black in color and equipped with everything Conner would want in a car, and then some. Conner thought it was a nice looking vehicle. The owner of the car lived just north of Bryson City in a neighborhood of expensive homes.

Conner took the car for a brief spin and bought it on the spot for $26,500. He considered it a good deal. He also told himself he'd have to do something more for Fast Eddie to show his appreciation.

A couple of days after Thanksgiving, two associates with Royce showed up at the cabin and spent the better part of the day, taking measurements of everything inside and outside his small dwelling. They also stepped off the lot size and closely inspected the entire exterior of the modest structure.

A week later, they came back with sketches and engineering drawings of the project. They even had two renderings of what the front and back of the structure would look like. Conner was very pleased with what they'd done. Essentially the plan capitalized on the way the cabin was positioned on the lot, and Royce blended its design, as best it could, with the surrounding environment.

The front of the house was now the back of the house. And virtually the entire rear plane was now a series of windows and doors, producing a panoramic and unobstructed view of the nearby mountains and the valley below. And what now was the back of the house -but the front of the house in a traditional sense - also had various sized glass windows and double entry doors, to provide an unbridled view of the scenery out front. So, the house had two fronts and no back. Conner liked this idea, as well.

The existing basement level of the cabin had been eliminated and replaced with a bi-level main floor that included an enlarged, two-steps-up living room, a substantial dining room, a half bath, and a small den. The upstairs contained a master bedroom, two other modest-sized bedrooms and two full baths.

An enlarged version of the side door was retained as the primary entry to the house. And a covered breezeway ran from that door to the garages. Hardwood floors were added to the entire downstairs, with carpeting planned for the upstairs areas.

In the midst of the euphoric mood over a new look for his home, Conner told himself he might want to dial his enthusiasm back a notch or two. When the Royce firm saw his excitement, they might decide to raise their fee a bit, he figured, somewhat jokingly.

So, he decided he should find something that would require additional attention. And that something turned out to be a third garage. That probably would increase the cost of the house, but it was a legitimate change. After all, there was always the chance there'd be another car in the family somewhere down the road.

It occurred to Conner the changes he was making could substantially increase the overall cost. But that was emblematic when it came to spending money. You get enticed with buying the low level version of a particular item and end up getting the device with all the bells and whistles. Conner chuckled at the symbolism. He rationalized his actions by telling himself this add-on project would be his Christmas gift to himself.

Two days later, Conners met with Royce and approved their plans with the noted changes he wanted to make. Because of the size of the project, the firm suggested getting four construction companies to bid on the project. Conner agreed and asked that he be allowed to meet with the selected contractor. He also reinforced his thoughts on quality of work and estimated cost comparisons.

Royce agreed with his assessments and committed to its plans to proceed. The company was anxious to get the project underway before the arrival of weather that could interfere with construction.

The following morning, Conner made another trip to Franklin. The people at Royce had chosen a construction company for Conner's project. The name of the company was Walters and Sons Construction, and its proposal was in the mid-range of all the other estimates (a total of $183,000).

The Walters company came highly recommended by Royce. Conner met the owners in the architects' offices, and he, too, was impressed. After a two-hour meeting, Conner gave Royce his approval. Reconstruction of his home would begin within a few days.

And to further speed the project along, the builder agreed to more than double the number of craftsmen and tradesmen on site.

That figure included skilled Amish workers who were accustomed to building techniques that allowed them to raise barns from start to finish in just one day. Conner was impressed with the overall plan, and he considered the meeting very productive.

At least he had the reprieve of a week to make the necessary arrangements and adjustments. At Royce's suggestion, he would need to move out for an estimated 10 days, maybe a few more. And he'd probably be moving into one of the motels in BC. And he could expect to move back after that point, though construction would likely continue around him for a few more days.

To Conner, that was both good news and bad news. He liked the idea that work would begin so quickly. But, he wasn't looking forward to the disruption it would cause in his life. But the end result was worth it, he told himself.

The thought also occurred to him when he finally returned to the house, he'd have to live among the sawdust, construction litter and semi-finished work for some time yet. But that didn't matter. It would be good just to get back to normal.

He had long ago turned his back on living out of a suitcase, which frequent travel and lifestyle interruptions had caused him in the past.

CHAPTER TWENTY FIVE

On this evening, as Conner walked through the cabin tending the stove and turning on lights, he paused and looked around his comfortable little structure. He had grown accustomed to this place. He told himself he'd miss its comfort and familiarity. But, he also was looking forward to an embellished and enhanced version of his home.

Conner's thoughts then shifted to the subject of people like himself who suddenly found themselves in more favorable financial positions or in career changes that unexpectedly enhanced their lifestyles and living standards. He had known such people, and quite frankly, some of them didn't handle those transitions very well, he believed.

All too often, when this happened, such people ended up elevating their own self-image. And they frequently reassessed their relationships with others against those new standards. This resulted in their moving in different social circles, and excluding some friends and acquaintances from their lives. Conner found such behavior unacceptable. That certainly was not something he'd ever do. He saw himself pretty much the same person he had been 20 or 30 years earlier. And that was not about to change, he reasoned.

Conner was thankful for his good fortune and financial independence. And he had vowed not to take them for granted. Typically, behind every successful person, there were advocates who had helped with the heavy lifting along the way. Certainly that was true in his case, Conner believed. . And he also vowed not to forget them. Besides, once you found a true friend, you didn't throw him or her overboard just because you got a pay raise.

After cleaning up for the evening, Conner called Pete Musser. The phone rang a number of times, and Conner was ready to hang up when Musser finally answered.

"Hey, Mitch, you crazy bastard."

"How'd you know it was me?" Conner asked.

"Listen, I was born at night. But not last night." Musser responded. "Your I.D. shows up on my television, fer Chrissake."

"Oh, yeah," Conner said, somewhat embarrassed. Conner was trying to gain control over the conversation, but it wasn't easy when you were talking to Pete Musser, Conner told himself.

"I thought I might buy you a little holiday cheer, if you feel like going out. Plus I've had a busy few weeks I can share with you."

"Listen, when Scotch is on the line, I'm available," Musser added. The neighbor continued without hesitation.

"Is that a new car I noticed in your driveway?"

"It's new for me," Conner said. "I now have a working car, and a playing car," he added jokingly.

"Spare me the envy," Musser shot back.

"Gimme' a few minutes, and I'll walk over to your place."

"Okay." Conner replied.

When Musser arrived, Conner met him at the door before climbing behind the wheel of the Land Rover. Musser slid into the passenger seat of the car and left the door open so he could see the interior.

"I've seen fancy before. But this is damn fancy," Musser said.

"Aw, it's just a car," Conner said, trying to downplay his purchase of a high-end vehicle.

"No. What I drive is just a car. This is a tank with leather seats and ass warmers," Musser shot back.

Conner laughed at his friend's response as he steered the Land Rover down the road to the highway.

"You ever been to a place called The Frog? Conner asked.

"No, but if they sell Scotch , it sounds like a good place to me," Musser replied.

Conner had driven past that small tavern on the north side of town many times, but he had never paid much attention to it. But, The Frog had its own, customized sign out front, instead of having all its visible windows blocked with neon logos of the beers they stocked. There also were a lot of cars parked around the place, all of them with hubcaps and visible signs of being washed in the not too distant past.

Conner felt this parking lot assessment made a lot of sense. Lotsa' cars outside, meant good food inside, he often argued. It was another case of reading the tealeaves.

As Conner and Musser entered the place, they paused to get their bearings. Conner was quick to provide his impression.

"This is my kinda' place," Conner said. "It's quiet. It has enough light for you to read the menu. There are no pinball or shuffleboard machines. And I doubt if there'll be any fights here tonight."

"Sounds pretty damn boring to me," Musser offered.

Conner chuckled and shook his head.

"Muss," I know beneath your gruff exterior… is a gruff interior."

Before Musser could reply, Conner continued.

"So, just step inside and wrap yourself around a glass of Scotch."

Musser dismissed the comment with a flip of his hand and a grunt.

The Frog had two or three large TVs for sports programming, but on this night they were turned off, a subtle way to say the kitchen was in charge.

The restaurant was tastefully decorated and offered a predominance of booths for seating. And along the base of the L-shaped bar was a highly polished brass footrail. Conner thought that added an element of class. The floor throughout was covered with black tile that clicked noticeably when walked on with leather heels. And there seemed to be a number of families in the place.

Conner stepped around Musser and walked to an empty seat at the bar. Musser glanced around before joining his neighbor.

The pair was met by the attractive, middle-aged bartender, who leaned her elbows on the bar and looked up at them expectantly as she spoke, her light brown hair hugging each side of her pretty face:

"Welcome to the Frog, gentlemen," what'll it be tonight?"

Musser didn't hesitate with his response:

"What do I want it to be….or what will it be," he said with an evil grin.

"You know how many times I get a version of that every night?"

Again, Musser shot back.

"Well, if you weren't so damn pretty, you wouldn't have to worry about that," he said.

The bartender laughed spontaneously, throwing her head back and closing her eyes as she did.

Again, Musser steered the conversation.

"I'll settle for a Dewar's on the rocks. And give this crazy bastard neighbor of mine one, too."

"Crazy bastard?" she asked incredulously.

Again Musser shot back.

"Yeah, that's his middle name. The rest of it is Mitch Conner."

"Doesn't he talk?"

All three of them laughed.

"Not when he's talking," Conner shot back, looking at Musser.

All three laughed again.

In an attempt to redeem himself, Conner continued.

"I'm not really this guy's neighbor. He's my father and I get my name from him. He's a crazy bastard, too."

Again the three laughed.

"It's a family name," Conner added.

"I'm his father, alright. And he's my illegitimate son," Musser added.

Again there was laughter.

"Okay guys, I've got to do my job. But is it safe to turn my back on you two for a coupla' minutes?"

"You're safe," Conner said.

"By the way, my name's Helen," the bartender added with a smile, offering a handshake to each customer. She poured two generous drinks for the pair and turned to serve another customer, who had appeared at the other end of the bar. After a few moments of silence, Conner spoke directly to his friend.

"You like Christmas?"

Musser paused and assessed the question before responding.

"Christmas? Well, yeah. I would say yes," Musser replied with some hesitation.

Conner paused, then answered his own question.

"At Christmas time, I'm still 10 years old, and I can't wait to open my presents," Conner reflected.

"That's one way of puttin' it," Musser mumbled.

Conner quickly reacted to Musser's indifferent response.

"I guess the way you feel about Christmas these days is pretty much a personal thing." Conner said.

"But there are a lot of people who think Christmas is too commercial.... all about money. I say the more commercial it is the better. I love drivin' around and seeing all those lawn and house decorations at this time of year, despite how gaudy some of them are," Conner added.

"It's the one time of year when people seem to be nice to each other. And whether it's forced compassion or not, it doesn't matter to me," Conner continued. "It's the time of year when even the Ebenezer Scrooges of the world seem to come out of their cocoons."

"Well, don't be disappointed if you drive around my house and there are no decorations," Musser said with a hint of levity.

"You know what, Muss? You're a walking contradiction of emotions. You call practically everybody a crazy bastard. But, despite what I said about you a coupla' minutes ago, you may be crusty on the outside but inside, you're all gooey," Conner said, looking directly at his friend with a smile.

"Careful now. You're walking on soft ground here. You're trying to ruin my reputation. That's what you're trying to do."

Conner raised his glass to Musser and continued.

"Here's to a good friend. Merry Christmas, Muss.

Musser tapped his glass with Conner's and nodded with a smile.

"And a Merry Christmas to you, too, Bob Cratchet."

Musser paused before continuing his thought.

"I'll tell you one thing. I like the way Northern Europeans celebrate Christmas. I don't' know if you've ever been there around the holidays, but it's somethin' special," Musser said.

"Yes, I have been there. And I agree with you," Conner replied. "Their celebrations are both emotional and spiritual and involve their entire families more than ours do. There's just a personalized and celebratory interchange among them that we haven't mastered yet in this country."

Conner continued and Musser nodded his agreement of what was being said.

Without hesitation, Musser added additional thoughts.

"I particularly love the Christmas Markets Europeans showcase in their town squares… the aroma from gingerbread ovens, the serving of warm mulled wine, and the locals singing traditional songs and carols. Those things really get you into a true Christmas spirit."

The mention of Christmas in Europe brought a smile to Conner's face and triggered treasured memories from his past. But as Musser talked about Christmas, Conner sensed a loneliness that was being suppressed. He didn't know much of anything about Muss' personal life, other than his brief mention of a bad marriage. And he wasn't about to ask. Maybe at some point in the future, Muss would share his story. But then again, maybe he wouldn't.

There was a brief silence between the two. Each appeared to be taking time to scan this cozy tavern and observe all the pre-Christmas stories that were being played out here by patrons on this evening. Conner was impressed that some of the parents had felt comfortable enough with this place to expose their kids to a tavern environment. Musser, on the other hand, probably felt Conner had lured him into a House of Wussies. Conner was the first to resume the conversation.

"As I mentioned on the phone I've had a busy few weeks," Conner said.

"Yeaah?" Musser responded, sounding as though he expected bad news.

But that was not the case. There was no bad news. From Conner's perspective, the news was largely promising, and the tone of his voice projected that.

"It's official," he said 'I've just completed my first teaching session in WCU's Continuing Education Program. And I've also begun coursework toward a PhD in the school's Department of American History," Conner added.

"So, you are officially a professor?"

"No, I'm not officially a professor. Not yet, anyway. In fact, I think my title is senior instructor in the Department of Fine Arts. I'm just another stiff at WCU."

"Sounds like a damn professor to me," Muss shot back. "What was all that stuff you said about teaching journalism?" Musser asked.

"Since I don't have a PhD," I can't teach any "for-credit" classes, including journalism. So, I have to get a PhD before that happens. If it happens. But, it's a start. Currently I'm working with older students, or to be politically correct, more mature students. People who have a little too much time on their hands in the evenings,," Conner suggested.

"Any single ladies?" Musser asked.

"I'm sure there are some," Conner added with a smile.

"Now it's getting interesting. Do you allow outsiders to monitor your classes?" Musser asked.

"Huh uhhr. That would be a no," Conner added, as he shook his head from side to side. "No crazy bastards in my class!"

Conner was pleased with the conversation he was having with his neighbor, and he sensed Musser was enjoying himself as well, despite his gruff pretentions and playful banter. Conner also told his friend about his impending home revitalization project, and Musser was surprisingly supportive and seemed pleased for him.

Musser broke the silence with a deep sigh and a question.

"Well, you been askin' most of the questions tonight, and now it's my turn. Anything new about your mystery man?"

Conner motioned for Helen to pour the two of them another Scotch, and he began updating Muss on other things that had happened since they last talked. He told him about the trip to Atlanta and the meeting with his lawyer friend, Chad Greenlee.

He also shared all he had learned about Hans Miller and his personal frustration with not knowing too much more now than he did at the outset.

Musser listened intently to all that was said before he spoke:

"You know, you have a lotta' stuff on your plate right now. And in a few weeks, you're gonna' have even more, particularly when WCU kicks into full gear. I'm gonna' offer you a little free advice, here. Put everything else aside and tackle this mystery man thing full bore. Pull all these loose ends together. You could be sitting on the edge of a life changing situation, and it's not going to get resolved on a piecemeal basis."

Conner was taken back with the bluntness of his friend's suggestion. But it was both serious and caring.

"You know, I think you're absolutely right, my friend. That's exactly what I need to do."

"Damn right, you crazy bastard!"

For the rest of the evening, the two men continued to engage in civil conversation, and they eventually ordered dinner. Both of them were impressed with their meal choices. And for Musser, it was a two Scotch evening, although he did order wine with his dinner. Conner left the place with an increased sense of belonging in the little town of Bryson City.

CHAPTER TWENTY SIX

Conner's home now was the BC motel room he'd occupied for five days. And even though it had been a long and demanding day, it wasn't over yet. He was tired, but in a good spirits. And his adrenalin level was still half full, he thought. He shrugged off the fatigue, and once in the room, he dialed the phone number of his ex-wife in Atlanta.

The call was for his two children, and he spent several minutes hearing about their excitement over the approach of Christmas and recent activities with schoolmates and friends. As he talked, he apologized for the lateness of the call and expressed his disappointment for not being with them in person.

He continued his conversation for several more minutes, until he noticed a lack of concentration on their part, and a lot of answers to questions with "yes'es" and "no's." After wishing both of them a Merry Christmas, he hung up the phone and sat motionless in thought for several moments. He still had not gotten over how much he missed seeing the two of them regularly.

Conner also felt a little guilty about not having read from the diaries for a couple of days. With such a full plate of emotions hanging about, he decided to treat himself to a Dewar's Scotch but had to settle for a hotel Styrofoam cup as his goblet.

This unorthodox drinking container helped coddle his spirits. It was such a ridiculous contradiction. Here he was drinking a blended, premium Scotch whiskey from a synthetic, plastic cup. He smiled at his temporary change of fortunes. But he reminded himself of the conveniences he'd enjoy once the renovation of the cabin was finished. He had no stereo here at the motel, so he turned on the TV to catch up on the news.

Conner realized he was practically sitting in darkness. And as he stood to turn on more lights, he glanced at the pile of ledgers he'd transferred from the cabin. At that moment, he randomly selected one of the journals, and he realized it was number 24. He then opened it, and was immediately drawn to a Miller entry dated December 24th. As that number rolled around in his head, the thought of the impending Christmas Eve – December 24th – came to mind.

Just then, the numbers seemed to take on a mysterious twist, and he began to repeat the sequence out loud: "Journal number 24, Miller entry on December 24th.

And the approaching Christmas Eve, December 24th. "Was this a symbolic sign? Conner asked himself. Was it serendipity or was it fate?" He wanted to believe it was fate. He took a long sip of Scotch and began reading more fervently.

December 24th.

As I enter the twilight of my time on this earth, I feel the need to reconcile the balance sheet on my life. But so much has happened, I hardly know where to begin. I've tried to live my life by the Ten Commandments and to treat others the way I wanted to be treated. And I owe so very much to close friends and associates I've known over time for helping me achieve the success I enjoyed. In the early fifties, at the urging of my dear Sarah, I resigned my high-risk job as a test pilot and began a career as a senior pilot at Pacific Air Lines, a regional passenger carrier operating primarily in California. And once again, my good friend Roebie made that possible through his ties in the airline industry. The years I spent at Pacific were among the happiest times of Sarah's and my lives. And both Amy and Grace continued to share our sprawling home in the Sierras. We lived as family, not just friends. And throughout those cherished times, Amy continued to give me credit for saving her life. And to this day, I remain reluctant to accept total responsibility for that pivotal event. Of the things I achieved in life, I am most proud of the time I served my country in the military. My eagerness to serve during World War I prompted me to exaggerate my age by three years to meet the 18 years required to serve. At the time, I was tall for my age, and my story and motivation were convincing. I had learned to fly the planes used for crop dusting on the farms of Montana, and joined the military on the condition I would become a pilot in the U.S. Army Air Corps. I flew too many missions to count, but I received several medals for my action during the two years I served in the Ardennes of France. But being a pilot in those years required few flying skills. It was akin to flying a kite with a powerful engine attached. But, when World War II erupted, I did not qualify to fly the more sophisticated planes of that generation. There was no way to transfer my flying skills. The only way I could stay airborne was to become a paratrooper, which I did. But, after several months in the 82nd Airborne Division, I signed up for Officer Candidate School and flight training, emerging as a second lieutenant in the Eighth Air Force. During that war, I was deployed in Europe. And after completing my assigned number of missions, I was returned to the U.S. and discharged when Japan surrendered. Little did I know, the time I spent with the 82nd and the experience I gained would lead me down a path to the FBI's Most Wanted list. But the boys at the 82nd would be proud of me, I can say that. And that's not because I was on that FBI list.

Conner paused again and made a note on the role Hans played in the 82nd. He also noted Hans' being on the FBI's Most Wanted list. Conner then returned to his reading.

As the 60s came to a close, my family and I encountered rough sledding. California's Pacific Air entered negotiations with the much larger Northwest Airlines, and ultimately Pacific became an extension of the larger carrier. For the first time, I became a union member. And from my view, something was lost in this largely forced integration. Fundamentally, those were not happy years with Northwest.

Conner paused, and he now saw a link between Miller and that picture of an airliner on the wall of the bunker. And he seemed to remember the airliner in that picture was a Northwest Airlines plane. He now felt he was approaching the answer to at least one of his questions, and he eagerly resumed his reading.

September 21st:

In the fall of 1969, Sarah was diagnosed with cancer, and after a prolonged treatment program, we received a discouraging prognosis. Doctors told us her only alternative was an expensive and experimental procedure. But Northwest said I hadn't been with the company long enough for her to be covered for this procedure under the medical plan. Unfortunately we lost Sarah on September 21st. Clearly, I have lived a blessed life, with one major transgression against society. One transgression that led to my self-imposed isolation. But, I accept full responsibility for my decision, and I ask neither forgiveness nor special consideration. I fully expect to face my maker for the pain or suffering I may have caused others. But mine was a crime of avarice and retribution. It could have been much worse if I had taken a life, either purposely or accidentally. And although what I did waswrong, through the intervening years I did not carry the burden of guilt in my life's journey. I painfully admit my bitterness that turned to rage and fueled this planned and organized sin of making the evil pay… literally an eye for an eye… to quote a Biblical idiom.

Conner placed the journal down, and a sense of awareness and relief swept over him. He now knew who the real Hans Miller was. And he now pretty much knew what Miller had done to warrant his self-exile.

But there were still a lot of questions to be answered about this whole affair. And he still did not know the true identity of Roebie and the role he may have played. Nor did he fully understand the acclaim and notoriety surrounding Amy Putnam, who eventually became Hans' second wife. There were still major elements of this puzzle that were missing, he told himself. Maybe he was just too close to this thing.

Maybe the answers to those remaining questions were right there before him, he thought. Maybe he just needed another set of eyes looking at this.

The rebuilding of Conner's home was now a couple of days ahead of schedule, and the construction supervisor advised Conner he could move back into the house, if he really chose to do so. But the inconvenience, he told him, might not be worth the bother. Despite the inconvenience, Conner chose to move back in. Several of the subcontractors were already finished with their responsibilities in the rebuild. And others were nearing completion.

On the previous day, Conner had made an unannounced inspection visit to the project, and he was overwhelmed. As he stood in the midst of this on-going maelstrom, he admitted this was no longer a cabin. And it was hard to identify the original structure, since a number of new walls had been added. There also were new concrete sections of the foundation that been poured, creating the base for the new additions.

The central part of the new dwelling was pretty much in place, including the many large glass windows and full-windowed doors. The wooden flooring throughout the house also was in place. But sanding and staining were yet to be done.

He was not looking forward to that. Conner told himself he might be looking at a couple of more days at the motel, if the dust and paint fumes turned out to be a problem.

New concrete slabs had been poured for the garages, from the walkway to the house and for the aprons being added to both the house and the garage entrances. The construction supervisor told Conner the garages would be the last elements to be completed.

There were two heating and air conditioning trucks on site, with at least three workers putting finishing touches on airflow ducts now visible in the labyrinth of support columns and beams. A spokesman for that company said the heating and air conditioning units would be operational by sundown.

The trusty old wood burning stove that had contributed so much to his comfort had already been removed from the house, abandoned on the newly formed terrace in back. The old stove's role had ended, and Conner had decided to give it to mechanic Eddie Chatworth for his kindness and generosity over the past several months.

It was up to Chatworth, Conner told himself, whether to keep the stove for his own personal use or sell it.

Even though he had decided to move into his new house on this evening, he was not quite ready for all the changes that had taken place. But he a liked what he saw, and he knew this new look would grow on him. And the most important thing was he'd be sleeping in his own bed again.

After entering the house, Conner dusted off his stereo and tuned to a station carrying the Mormon Tabernacle Choir's pre-Christmas concert. With that program in the background, he poured himself a glass of wine and relaxed in one of his few remaining pieces of furniture – those being his leather chair, the stereo, and his bed.

CHAPTER TWENTY SEVEN

onner glanced at his watch. It was almost six o'clock in the evening as he took to the road and drove east on State highway 107, continuing another 10 miles past the WCU campus toward the little town of Tuckasegee.

It was dark, and a light rain was falling. Forecasters had predicted the rain would turn to occasional snow flurries later in the evening, and Conner was driving very carefully on this very erratic roadway.

The 1,800 residents of the tiny community of Tuckasegee - like many other small towns and cities in Western Carolina and North Georgia – had grown up along the banks of the area's many streams and rivers, including the Tuckasegee River. This was true of Native Americans who first occupied these lands, and it became true for the invading white man who replaced them, as well.

In recent years, residents of Tuckasegee were largely employees and staff at nearby Western Carolina University. But the early settlers of this land were people of the earth. Not only did they regard the flowing waters in these mountains as a major source of transportation, but the water was Manna that supported life itself, in their beliefs.

They knew without water, there would be no life for plants and animals alike. And they relied on the flowing power of rivers to sweep bass and trout into their fishing nets. Clearly, they were ahead of their time in treating these waters with the appropriate reverence and respect they deserved, in Conner's view.

And in keeping with Indian language, their choice of words was literally descriptions of what was being named. And the name Tuckasegee was first used to describe the River. It meant "Turtle Place." And it later became the name of the Cherokee settlement on this site, before the white man took ownership of the land and sent the Cherokee Nation packing.

As Conner thought about this information he obtained from the internet, his mind settled on Cynthia Henchel, the psychologist he'd met at the Fryemont Inn a couple of months earlier. She was now a resident of this historic little village known as Tuckasegee. Conner wondered if she knew the origin of her new community's name. Being an academic and a student of history, she probably did, he told himself.

During their most recent conversation, Cynthia had invited Conner to drop by and see her new home in Tuckasegee, prior to their going to dinner together. Conner had graciously accepted her invitation.

As Conner approached her home, he reduced his speed to make sure he found her address among the many others posted on roadside mailboxes. He spotted the right house and pulled into the gravel driveway.

Before killing the lights, Conner gazed at the car parked in front of the garage. As his eyes focused on Cynthia's car, he reacted instinctively at what he saw in his headlight beams.

"Oh no!" he mumbled to himself.

"She drives a Prius."

That was a dead giveaway, in Conner's mind, that Cynthia Henchel was a liberal

He shrugged and smiled at the thought.

"Maybe it's just a loaner car," he told himself.

"Or, maybe she's the one in a million Prius owners who is not a liberal," he thought.

He smiled at the absurdity of the idea. But, he'd find out soon enough.

Cynthia's new home looked rather small, but it had a cozy or warm appearance to it. All of the lights in the front of the house were turned on, which helped create that appearance. Overall, it was an attractive house, he felt. The house also appeared to be much the same as other homes in the area, having a back-to-nature, or woodsy feel to it. Because of the darkness, Conner couldn't tell exactly what color it was. It appeared to be a muted shade of green, and it was trimmed in white. Overall, it was an attractive house, he felt.

Conner paused momentarily at the front door, deciding whether to knock or ring the doorbell. He chose the bell, which chimed with a two-note tone. That's a good sign, he told himself. "the doorbell works," he mumbled to himself.

As Conner waited for the young woman, he could hear her walking toward the door, her heels clicking on the hard surface of the floor inside.

When Cynthia opened the door, Conner was frozen at her sight. She was as pretty in this subdued light as he remembered her from two previous encounters.

Conner guessed Cynthia to be in her mid-thirties or early forties. She had beautiful long black hair that hung down to her shoulders.

And she wore a bright red lipstick that accentuated her pretty face, which was enhanced by dimples and a petite pug nose.

"Is this the residence of Dr. Cynthia Henchel?" Conner asked with a broad grin.

"It is indeed," she said with an amused chuckle.

"Come on in out of the cold," she said, her hand in a sweeping motion guiding him inside.

"Thank you."

Conner stepped inside and gazed about the small foyer that opened onto an adjacent and nicely decorated living room, to the left. It appeared very comfortable and inviting. To his right was a dining room with a sparkling chandelier suspended over a modest, oval-shaped table.

"I like your home," he said with a nodding approval.

"Thank you, sir." she replied with a smile.

"Let me take your coat," she added.

As Conner replied, his speech appeared to be rushed, reflecting a bit of early evening nervousness. He paused briefly before continuing.

"The day I saw you on campus, I got the impression your home was a work in progress. But either you're a very fast worker, or you're a perfectionist. Your home has all the appearances of a showplace," he said.

"I guess I'm a little of both," she replied with a smile.

Conner noticed a sparkle in her eyes and acknowledged her comment with a nod.

"Incidentally, I made our reservation for seven. Was that okay?" Conner asked.

"That's fine. That'll give us a little time to visit. Besides, the restaurant is less than 10 minutes from here. I think you'll like it," Cynthia replied

"Can I interest you in something to drink?" she asked.

Conner hesitated in thought before replying.

"Sure. Why not? We've got plenty of time. Do you have Scotch?"

"I do."

"Make it on the rocks," he said.

"Mmm," she acknowledged.

"Come on back to the kitchen," she added, as she turned and led the way.

Conner followed Cynthia down the short hallway to the back of the home. He was immediately drawn to a large, windowed door that looked out on the area in back. Floodlights illuminated a sea of ivy that blanketed the entire area, with spotted flowerbed islands, and an occasional flowering tree here and there.

A winding, stone covered path ran through the ivy and led down to the banks of a rushing stream below.

The floodlights captured the white capped water dashing around boulders and over rocks in an unbridled display of nature's fury. Conner was moved by what he saw.

"You've got a beautiful view out there," Conner said as he continued staring at this compelling image.

"Thank you," she said, as she handed him the Scotch ."That view really sold me on the house. And it's even more impressive during the day," she added.

"You know, I had precisely the same feeling when I first saw my house in BC. Except I live on a mountain ridge and look down on the valley. I call it my million-dollar view."

"I can imagine," she responded, adding her pretty smile.

Conner smiled and tapped his glass to hers.

There was a brief silence between the two until Conner spoke.

"Here's to a Merry Christmas," he said.

"And Merry Christmas to you," she replied.

"Why don't we go back to the living room?" she suggested. "Unless you'd like to stay here in the kitchen?"

"Let's just stay here," Conner replied, his tone now more confident.

There was a small island in the middle of the kitchen, and Conner slid onto one of the four stools around the elevated table. Cynthia joined her guest from the other side. Conner took a long sip of Scotch before continuing.

"You know, the night we met at the Fryemont, we didn't have much chance to get to know each other. So, I gotta' ask you…"

"What's your story?"

"What's my story?" she asked with laughter.

Both of them laughed before Conner continued.

"Yeah, you know. Do you rob banks as a hobby? Do you abuse animals. Do you redeem coupons at grocery stores? You know, stuff like that," he teased.

Cynthia blushed as she laughed and looked into her glass of wine.

"I'm afraid I have to say no to all of those things. I guess that makes me pretty dull, huh?"

Both of them laughed again.

"Well, I'm gonna' let you off the hook, but I wanna' come back to that later," he said.

"Particularly because you're a psychologist, I want to share a story that may or may not be relevant to our getting to know you better here," he said.

"As you might have guessed, Conner explained, "I'm single. And shortly after my divorce a few years ago, I asked the real estate agent who was renting me an apartment if she'd like to join me for a drink?"

"She said yes, and in the course of a coupla' hours, she started telling me about what a jerk her ex-husband was. And as she talked about him and told me all the things she didn't like about him, it occurred to me she wasn't talking about her husband. She was talking about me. All the things that she didn't like about him were things I might have done as well. I can tell you one thing. It certainly was an eye opener. And I certainly didn't reach out to her again."

Cynthia chucked at the remark, as Conner continued.

"Now, I'm not looking for advice or anything. And I don't have any guilt feelings about being divorced. But I do feel bad for my two young kids' having to go through that experience. My only hope is that I'll be able to make it up to them someday, particularly when they're at an age where I can talk to them as adults, and establish a good relationship with them."

"That was an interesting experience," Cynthia added, "and I can see where that could have been awkward," she said. "But I applaud your goal with your children."

Conner smiled at his companion and winked at her.

"Okay, that's part of my story. But, what about your story?" he asked again.

Cynthia laughed under her breath and blushed at his question.

"Okay. So, it's my turn in the barrel…that's what you're saying," she replied.

Conner responded with a "yes." nod.

"I, too, am divorced. I was married for six years. But we had different values. We just grew apart. I'm an only child, and I'm originally from Evanston, Illinois. My father is a doctor and my mother is a psychiatrist. They wanted me to go into medicine, but they let me make my own choice. I'm very close to my parents, and I see them as often as possible. And as I told you on the night we met, I'm also very close to my grandparents."

"That's a lot of different information in one package," Cynthia continued. "But that's basically 'my story,'" she said, slowly moving her head in an up and down motion for punctuation.

"Well, it's a brief story but a nice story," Conner said, shaking his head in the same way to mimic her display of emotion.

His response evoked laughter from both.

"Whatta' ya' say we head down to the restaurant? Conner asked.

The Orchard Restaurant, which Cynthia had recommended, was just a few miles down the road from her home. It was a converted old farmhouse that would have fit nicely in a Norman Rockwell painting. It had a chimney on both ends, largely covered by grown-over British ivy. And the quaint old house was situated in a large grassy field that boasted an old well with its covered roof and a walkway to the dwelling's entrance. Conner felt as though he was stepping back in time when he first saw it.

The inside of the restaurant was as quaint as the exterior. Old hard-wood planks covered the entire restaurant floor, and tables and chairs placed throughout the place were covered with large white tablecloths. Candles on each of the tables provided soft lighting for the interior.

The couple was quickly seated at a table near the restaurant's log crack-ling fireplace. Conner sat and gazed at the flames for several moments before looking back at his companion.

"I love this place." he said.

"It's one of my favorites," she added. "And the food is very good."

With Cynthia's concurrence, Conner ordered a bottle of white wine from selections on the menu.

As they waited, the waiter placed large, red wine glasses on the table, before returning with the bottle and carefully pouring a sample into Conner's glass. Conner took a quick sip and nodded his approval. The waiter then poured an appropriate amount in both glasses and nestled the bottle into an ice-filled bucket before leaving the table,

Conner waited until the waiter was out of earshot before speaking.

"You know, I think having wine with dinner is a valued tradition. And I love wine. But, I really don't know that much about it. I can't tell the difference between a Merlot and a Cabernet Sauvignon, and I'm afraid I couldn't tell a ten-dollar bottle of wine from a fifty-dollar bottle. I feel a little impervious about this whole wine selection protocol in restaurants. I think it's pretty much Kabuki Theatre. I mean, what can you tell by sniffing a cork?"

Cynthia put her hand to her mouth to control her laughter.

"There," Conner said. "I've revealed the soft side of my underbelly."

Cynthia laughed again before responding.

"I appreciate your honesty and admire your willingness to discuss your shortcomings," Cynthia added.

Conner raised his wine glass toward Cynthia and took a small sip of the tasty liquid.

"I'll tell you one other anecdote and then I'll shut up and let you talk," he added.

"I'm kinda' like my daughter was as a child. One time she refused to eat her scrambled eggs at breakfast, and I asked her why."

"She told me, Dad, there are two kinds of scrambled eggs. The kind I like and the kind I don't like. These are the kind I don't like." he said.

Cynthia laughed at the story. And Conner continued his point.

"I feel the same way about wine, of which there are two kinds…the kind I like and the kind I don't like," Conner concluded.

"And the wine we're drinking is the kind I like, by the way. It's nice and dry."

Again Cynthia chuckled and dabbed her eyes with the table napkin.

Cynthia then picked up on Conner's comments with a story of her own.

"I think there's a pretentiousness about dining in formal settings of restaurants," she said. "And sometimes, I don't really understand people's motivations in what should be a simple enjoyable experience," she added.

"I had a friend in Baltimore who regularly sent food back in restaurants, for what reason I don't know. Maybe it made her feel more powerful, more discriminating or more worldly in the eyes of others. But I can tell you, it got to be embarrassing for me, and I quit having dinner with her."

Conner nodded at the comment.

For the remainder of the evening, Cynthia and Conner continued sharing personal stories. He told her about his first appearance in the classroom in WCU's Continuing Education program. He also shared his uneasiness and commitment for re-engaging in the learning process through the PhD program.

Conner then spent considerable time telling her about the cabin and the major renovation that was nearing completion. Cynthia offered her advice and assistance for any redecoration challenges he might encounter. Conner suggested she visit the construction site with him sometime and help him celebrate its near completion. She seemed enthusiastic about the idea.

As Conner dropped her off at home, Cynthia turned before stepping inside. "I enjoy your company," she said. "You make me laugh."

She gave him a "Christmas hug" and a kiss on the cheek.

Conner smiled at her and walked to his car for the unwelcomed drive home. It was beginning to snow, ever so lightly.

CHAPTER TWENTY EIGHT

More than a week had passed since Conner ventured into the forest on a photographic shoot. He had gotten into something of a routine with his photography, and he rather missed being out in the elements with wildlife. He told himself it was safer out there among the raccoons and bears than on the streets in downtown Bryson City. He chuckled, somewhat facetiously, as he balanced the risk in both environments.

But for this morning, he decided to split the difference. He'd take on the streets of BC, and, in a sense, he'd venture into the wilderness, as well. But his photographic target for the day would be the historic old train that took tourists on a scenic round trip from BC to Nantahala on a daily basis.

It was a 44-mile adventure through fertile valleys, an old tunnel, across river gorges, and along a winding riverbed. The old train was powered by a vintage steam locomotive, given a reprieve from the scrapheap and afforded the opportunity to thrill yet another generation of young passengers.

And as a workup to Christmas, the train had been decorated with appropriate holiday finery and temporarily renamed "The Polar Express." They even had a Santa Claus conductor on board. This seasonal promotion alone had attracted more than 91,000 passengers during the previous year's celebration of Christmas. On today's trip, Conner was able to get several shots of the train, including some as it snaked its way around the curving river bed of the Nantahala River. And he was anxious to review what he'd taken.

When Conner dropped off his disc at The Scarlet Letters, he sought out Carolyn in the store to say hello. She seemed very friendly and a couple of times she acted as though she wanted to say something. But there was only silence.

"Well, in case I don't see you before then, I hope you have a nice Christmas." Conner said to her as he turned to leave.

"Maybe we could have a Christmas lunch," she added quickly.

"Lunch would be great," he replied. "I'll call you."

Carolyn nodded her head and smiled as Conner left the store..

Christmas was only a few days away, and Conner was still adjusting to being back at home. There were still a lot of finishing touches being added to the house, and he was still stepping around construction clutter. But, he was pleased to be sleeping in his own bed again and pleased he'd be in his house for Christmas.

Conner also was delighted the county had responded so quickly to his request to refinish the road that provided access to his and other houses along the way . The work was now complete, and it made a significant difference in the ride up and down the mountain. Everything seemed to be coming together for him, he thought.

On this day, the streets of downtown Bryson City were cluttered with last minute shoppers and out of town visitors waiting for the next departure of "The Polar Express." Conner had never seen this many people in downtown BC before, and all the activity was exhilarating.

But with so many people walking the streets, it was difficult to find a parking space. He finally pulled into an open slot, about two blocks from the popular downtown eatery, Millie's Mountain Diner. Conner had eaten there on frequent occasions, and today he was meeting Carolyn Biggs there for a late lunch.

It was almost 1:30 in the afternoon as Conner approached the diner and spotted Carolyn standing out front.

"Hey, you. How's my favorite jogger?" he asked.

"Your favorite jogger is just fine. How's my favorite photographer?"

"He's just great, thank you. And a Merry Christmas to you Scarlet Letters Lady."

Conner gave her a prolonged hug, and she hugged him back. Carolyn smiled at him and nodded her head as she replied.

"And to you as well, Mitch Conner."

"Millie said we're next on the list, so it shouldn't be more than a few minutes," Carolyn added.

Before Conner could reply, Carolyn continued.

"I hear you're putting that addition on your house," she added.

"Yup. In fact, it's all but finished. I moved back in yesterday. I chose to abandon my BC motel paradise a mite early – despite living amongst sawdust, candy wrappers, glaring radios and all. But, this means I won't have to spend Christmas in a motel," he added, smiling.

"By the way, you seem to have a great information source," Conner said to her kiddingly.

"You have to remember that I work with Gretchen and Camden Dunner. And apparently they know a lot of construction workers in town."

"Oh yeah," Conner replied with a laugh.

Just then a group of people left the restaurant and Millie motioned through the plate glass window that a table was available. The couple was ushered to a booth near the back of the restaurant.

The Mountain Diner was frequented mostly by locals, but it also managed to get a lot of walk-in traffic from tourists, particularly during the summer months and on holidays and other special occasions. The restaurant was known for its small town friendliness, its tasty, down-home cooking and its generous portions. Conner liked to say the diner's pancakes were the size of manhole covers. And the waitresses, as well as the owner, Millie Castro, called everybody "darlin."

After ordering lunch, Conner looked at his friend and smiled, handing her a small, professionally wrapped box.

"I wanted to get you a little remembrance for Christmas, but I always have problems buying people gifts," Conner told her.

"Gifts," she replied. "I didn't buy you a Christmas gift."

"That's not important. Remember, it's better to give than receive," he replied.

"Merry Christmas," he added.

Carolyn wrinkled her lips in an exaggerated pouting look.

"Okay, then I'll buy your lunch," she suggested.

"Nope, lunch is on me," he insisted.

Carolyn proceeded to open the gift and expressing delight as she recognized the brand of perfume Conner had purchased for her.

"Perfume," she said. "I love this stuff." she exclaimed

"I don't know much about perfume," he told her. "So, I went to the internet and inquired about hot selling brands this holiday season. That name popped up. But, I couldn't pronounce it, so I had to look that up as well."

Carolyn interrupted him with her comment.

"It's a great new Italian perfume, and it's called 'Boolgaadee', although you might have trouble pronouncing it by reading the label BVLGARI, she said.

"Thank you so much, Mitch." she said with an enthusiastic smile.

"You're welcome," he replied. "I'm glad you like it."

Carolyn removed the bottle from its box and sprayed a small amount on her wrist, which she rubbed on her neck.

"I like that scent," Conner added.

There was a brief silence before Conner continued.

"When you have some free time, I'd like to take you out and show you what we've done to the house," Conner said.

Carolyn paused briefly in thought before responding.

"When I left the store this afternoon, I mentioned to Gretchen I was going to lunch and might do some shopping, and she told me to take the afternoon off. So, I could do it this afternoon, if you're not busy."

"That works for me," he replied.

As Conner drove up the mountain to his house, Carolyn looked at him several times with her pretty smile. When he caught her in a stare, she quickly looked away somewhat embarrassed..

"I've been on this road only once," she said. "But it seems there are fewer bumps than before."

"You're very perceptive," Conner said. "And you're right, there are fewer bumps. The County road crew just re-graded and refinished it a few days ago. It makes a big difference, doesn't it?"

"It does indeed," she replied.

As Conner pulled up to the construction site, Carolyn's reaction was immediate.

"Woww," she said. "It looks like you've built a totally new house. It's beautiful," she exclaimed.

"I'm very pleased with the results," he replied. "They've given me more than double the floor space I had before. And I've added centralized heating and air. No more wood stove. I've also added three new garages, too."

"Three garages?"

"Yup," he said. "I already have two cars. And who knows what the future holds. I could just turn it into a workshop."

Carolyn smiled at the little boy at Christmas tone of Conner's voice.

Conner then took her on a careful walk-through of the layout, stepping over scattered pieces of lumber, nails and trimmings from the metal roof. He also pulled out the architectural drawings and renderings of the new home.

"Mitch. This is magnificent. You already have a million dollar view. Now you have the house to go with it. I'm very happy for you. It's going to be just great," she said with a smile.

Conner returned her smile and squeezed her hand. When they arrived back downtown, it was almost five o'clock, and at her request, he dropped her off in the middle of town.

He spoke to her as she turned to walk away,

"By the way," he said to her. "I've never seen your place. That would be nice to do before the holidays are over.

"I'll see if I can arrange it," she teased.

CHAPTER TWENTY NINE

I t was snowing again when Conner made his way through town and headed northeast on Route 74, which was a four-lane highway toward Lake Junaluska. Conner had never visited Carolyn's home, but she had given him directions, and he knew generally where she lived. The home was in the unincorporated township of Whittier, NC – about six miles northeast of BC

Conner exited the four-lane, as it was commonly called, and took a mountain road leading east. Like many of the highways around BC, it was a winding mountainous roadway requiring the driver's full attention. Conner was getting close to his destination when he spotted a roadside sign that read, "Dangerous curves ahead."

Conner chuckled out loud and made a mental note to mention this to Carolyn.

As Conner approached his destination, a big smile transformed both his face and his mood. He verified the address on the mailbox and immediately broke into haughty laughter. His reaction was one of surprise and admiration at Carolyn's unorthodox and gutsy choice for a home. It was an old grist mill that probably dated back to the early 1900s. Good for her, he said to himself.

In Conner's mind, one of the most appealing attractions of this century-old, wooden structure was its color, deep gray from ages of non-painting. It was topped with a durable slate roof, which gave the mill an appearance of being both durable and contemporary.

But the most compelling feature was the mill's gigantic water wheel, which dipped into a cascading tributary of Glade Creek. And it was still operational -- turning ever so slowly and dependably. It was this same water wheel that long ago had supplied the power to grind corn into meal for nearby residents, friends and neighbors. Conner laughed again and shook his head spontaneously at Carolyn's choosing the mill for her home.

But he also was impressed with her noticeable talent with landscaping. The majestic old structure was surrounded by flowering trees and shrubbery that totally transformed the site's overall appearance. It was another interesting facet of this fascinating woman, he mused.

Carolyn was standing in the open doorway of her home as Conner approached. The broad grin on her face seemed to mirror her playful mood.

And her expression seemed to be saying, I know you're surprised at the nature of my house, which he was. Conner realized the look on his face was one of total surprise, and he made a concerted effort to avoid a jaw-dropping facial expression. But, Carolyn knew what he was thinking.

"Come on in," she said, smiling. "And welcome to my home."

Before Carolyn could comment, Conner again expressed his surprise.

"I'm really....really impressed.," Conner said sincerely. And what a home it is!" he added.

"Thank you," Carolyn replied.

As Conner talked, he stepped inside the old mill and took his time scanning the many touches Carolyn had added to make the mill's appearance so exceptional. She had salvaged, restored and incorporated old mechanical devices into the décor to reinforce the mill's role in local history.

Other touches included original pieces of historical art for the walls, and a few authentic tools and devices used by area craftsmen from many years past. Such examples were period representative and not just clutter designed to disguise open spaces of the walls, Conner felt. Carolyn had transformed a one-time industrial building into an attractive and seductively inviting home.

Carolyn continued to stand closely behind him, waiting for his reactions. Conner was openly impressed with her creativity throughout the place, and the more he saw, the more he nodded his head and pursed his lips. The expressions clearly were acts of approval and admiration. They were reactions she did not overlook.

Carolyn then provided her guest a brief tour of other parts of the house, beginning with the rest of the downstairs. An overly wide stairway that was covered with an attractive, light colored carpeting, led to a three-bedroom upstairs that was equally impressive to Conner.

"Carolyn. I'm speechless. I'm downright, bona-fide speechless. And that is not because I didn't expect much from you. I just didn't know what incredible talents you had."

"But I have a question for you. How much restoration did you have to deal with?"

"Let me put it this way," she replied. "When I decided to buy this place, there were holes in the building that were more suited for a star-gazing observatory than a house."

"There were quite a few structural issues that had to be fixed, but I had a friend who knew a lot about construction, and his prices were very reasonable."

"The fact is, it needed quite a bit of work to make it livable. That was the key reason I could afford it. And that was almost six years ago."

"Well, I think you've done a helluva' job. I'm really impressed."

Carolyn's proud smile reflected her delight with Conner's compliments. Before she could express herself, Conner continued.

"One of my brother's friends once converted an old dairy silo into a house that, needless to say, was totally vertical in nature."

"And what he did with the space and spiral stairways was magical," he said. "But that house couldn't hold a candle to what you've done with this old mill."

"Thank you kind sir," Carolyn added.

There was a brief pause before Carolyn continued.

"Okay. So, tell me. What is so urgent that you needed to talk to me?" she asked.

Conner paused before answering.

"My mystery man isn't a mystery man anymore. I know who he is."

"That's great news," she responded. "That's great news, isn't it?"

"Yes," he replied. "But, there's more to it than just his name."

Conner shared his concerns with her. They included his desire to know more about Miller's mysterious plot, the identity of Roebie and several questions regarding both of Miller's wives."

Carolyn's look of confusion reflected her not being able to fully understand everything Conner had said. Plus, she didn't know exactly what he wanted her to do. Conner sensed this and continued his comments.

"Do you remember the conversation we had a couple of weeks ago about whether you were good at trivia?" Conner asked.

"Yes," she replied, her voiced traced with curiosity. Before Conner could respond, she added to her answer.

"I said I liked trivia, and I had a good memory for dates and things," she said. "I think I also said I know a lot of stuff."

Both of them laughed at the response.

"That's exactly right," and the fact you remembered what you said back then proves you have a good memory," Conner said.

'Yes?" Carolyn replied again, somewhat expectantly.

"I also asked you if it would be okay to call on you sometime as an additional source," Conner continued. "And you said, 'yes,' if you were still around," Conner added.

Both were silent, thinking of that last statement.

"Well, you're still around, and I'm still asking you if you'd be my additional source on this mystery man thing," he said. "I'm asking you to look at the information I now have on this character, and his cohorts, and see if there are things I didn't catch or things I'm overlooking," he added.

"Well, yeah. I guess so. When would you want to do it? she asked.

"What about right now? he responded.

Carolyn paused briefly in thought before responding.

"Sure. Why not," she replied, shrugging her shoulders in a show of indifference.

"Okay! Okay!" Conner repeated excitedly. He then excused himself and hurriedly retrieved several items from the Beast, including his computer and a file folder he'd compiled on Miller. He was a little out of breath when he rejoined Carolyn inside.

"I brought a few things with me in the event you'd say yes," he said, looking somewhat apologetic.

"Why don't we go to the study," Carolyn suggested. "I keep my computer and reference materials in there."

"Fine," Conner replied, as he stood and followed her to a small room near the rear of the house. The quaint little room had two large windows that overlooked the wooded area in back and afforded a view of the stream powering the mill's imposing water wheel.

Carolyn cleared a small table beneath one of the two windows and moved a second chair in place for Conner. Since Carolyn used the table as a desk, all of her reference sources, records and her computer were already in place or reachable from the desk. Conner retrieved notes from his valise, placed his computer on the table and signed on to the internet.

"Okay. Let's start with Hans Gerhard Mueller, or Hans Miller," Conner began. "What we know is he grew up on a farm in Montana. As a youngster, he was captivated with crop dusters who sprayed crops in his father's fields and those of adjacent farmers. Somehow, he talked his way into the cockpits of those planes at the early age of 14. He was a natural born flyer," Conner pointed out.

"And at the age of 15, Miller lied about his age and joined the U.S. Army Air Corps. He became a combat pilot in both World War I and World War

II. Miller also spent some time as an enlisted man in the 82nd Airborne Division. It was during this period Miller met and married his first wife, Sarah."

"After military service, Miller earned a degree in aeronautical engineering from Purdue University, graduating with honors. Purdue, by the way, is where Miller met his second wife, Amy Putnam," Conner pointed out.

"During Miller's years at Purdue, he and Amy developed a very close bond over their love for flying. They not only flew aircraft together, Amy, Hans and his wife Sarah became lifelong friends. It was a relationship that soon would embrace Amy's only sibling, her sister, Grace. Hans and the three women would become inseparable.

"That sounds like trouble waiting to happen," Carolyn mused with a chuckle.

"Based on what I've read in the journals, the friendships seemed legitimate," Conner responded. "The four of them seemed to be cut from the same cloth, compatible in virtually every way," he pointed out. "Otherwise, there's no way they would have stayed together…stayed so close…for as long as they did," Conner added.

Conner paused briefly and looked seriously at his friend before continuing.

"Following Miller's graduation from Purdue, he was hired by Hughes Aircraft as a test pilot. Not too long thereafter, he became the company's Chief Test Pilot, a job he would hold until he became a senior pilot for California-based Pacific Airlines.

"Miller's wife, Sarah, had asked him to find a job that was less risky than being a test pilot. Responding to her request, Miller discussed his dilemma with his good friend Roebie. And Miller credited Roebie for getting him the job at Pacific Airlines.

Roebie was not only a big muckity muck at Hughes, he was very influential in the airline industry. But I don't have a clue who Roebie really was," Conner pointed out.

"In the late 1960s, Pacific Airlines merged with the much larger Northwest Airlines in something of a hostile takeover. And Hans Miller's life changed dramatically. For the first time, he was forced to join a union, and he was no longer a select and valued employee. He was just one of thousands," Conner suggested.

"Some years later," Conner explained, "Miller wife, Sarah, was diagnosed with a serious form of cancer. Her doctors recommended a very promising but expensive new treatment for the disease. But her claim was denied due to a Northwest insurance policy technicality. Shortly thereafter, she died."

"And here's where it gets interesting," Conner continued, as he looked at Carolyn and smiled. "Something I'm about to describe happened about the same time you were born. But maybe you've heard of it anyway," he added with a smile.

"On November 24th, 1971, an unknown person, who went by the pseudoname, D.B. Cooper hijacked an airplane as it prepared for a flight from Portland, Oregon to Seattle, Washington.

Cooper claimed to have a bomb strapped to his person, and he threatened to detonate it if his orders weren't followed. Cooper also demanded a quarter of a million-dollar ransom and multiple military parachutes. And, according to public records, he then demanded all passengers depart the aircraft and a limited crew fly the plane to an unspecified destination," Conner explained.

After the Airline delivered all that money, made up of bundled packages of large denomination bills, Cooper taped it all to his body.

"The guy really knew what was necessary to pull this thing off," Conner suggested. "He was no ordinary criminal. No dummy. He chose a plane that allowed him to easily jump during flight - much the same as he would have done in the military."

"And he demanded they provide him with military parachutes, which were stronger and more maneuverable than recreational chutes. Even the FBI later said he would have had a better chance of success by using military parachutes," Conner explained.

Carolyn again nodded her understanding.

"I've read about that over the years because it was such a brazen stunt," Carolyn explained. The name D.B. Cooper is familiar. But, I don't remember many details about the event," Carolyn added.

"It was brazen alright," Conner responded. "But in Miller's writings, he admits he did something terribly wrong."

"But he doesn't come right out and say what he did, how he did it and to whom he did it. All I've had to go on was pretty inexact references. And the blanks were filled in with unverified statements from law enforcement officials," Conner said. "I suspect Miller was the famed D.B. Cooper. But I don't know that it would hold water in court," He added.

"I don't agree it's not strong evidence," Carolyn interjected. "It's circumstantial, but it's strong circumstantial," she added. "He mentions the name Northwest Airlines, as I recall, in the same context of his writing about guilt and wrongdoing."

"Yes, he did say that," Conner agreed. "In fact, there's something else Miller said in his writing that ties him to the hijacking. In view of the fact he parachuted from that plane in flight, Miller made the statement 'the boys from the 82nd would be proud of me," Conner pointed out. "That was a very telling statement that verified his actions."

"And it verifies the jump was successful," Carolyn observed.

"There's another point," Conner continued. "In a separate document, Miller corrected the ransom amount to about half a million dollars, not a quarter of a million as the media reported."

"According to the pilots of the hijacked aircraft, the jump was made somewhere in the vicinity of Amboy, Washington, an isolated little town in the foothills of Mt. St. Helens and only 50 miles due north of Portland, Oregon.

"Miller had lived in Portland," Conner continued, "So he was familiar with the landscape of that whole Columbia River Basin. It's rough country, forested by giant fir trees, and he would have used that to his advantage in the landing and escape. I'd bet a month's pay there was somebody monitoring the flight and locked on to Cooper's recovery and escape," Conner said.

"At the time of the high jacking, Miller was married to his second wife, Amy. It was possible that either she or her sister, Grace, could have helped.

Both were devoted to the perpetrator -- Amy more than Grace. But this scenario was unlikely," Conner felt. "At the time, both women were elderly and physically unable to handle strenuous activities. But a more likely candidate would have been Miller's friend, whom we know only as Roebie," Conner continued.

"I think you're right," Carolyn suggested. "If you buy his success in bailing from an aircraft flying at a couple of hundred miles an hour and half a million taped to his body, you have to agree his getting away with the money was a piece of cake, particularly if he had help on the ground."

Conner slowly nodded his agreement.

"I agree with that, as well," Conned added. "I first thought someone could have just left a vehicle at an agreed-to location. But Cooper's escape seemed to be well orchestrated. And there had to have been someone on the ground monitoring the flight who could react to a very fluid situation."

"The FBI later said they didn't think Cooper survived the jump. When he left the plane through the rear stairwell, they claimed, he encountered winds of some 200 miles an hour," Conner said. "Plus they said he had to deal with the cold weather and hazardous terrain below. But, the FBI found no trace of Cooper, dead or alive. That's because his jump and escape came off without a hitch," Conner concluded.

"Personally, I think those FBI statements were nothing more than covering their ass because they found nada," Conner said with a smirk.

"You're adding to your evidence," Carolyn interjected. "And you're winning your case. I think the guy wanted to say he hijacked that plane," Carolyn added.

"I don't disagree with that," Conner added.

"And, I accept your assessment," Conner admitted. "I agree there's sufficient evidence to conclude, without a doubt, Miller was the legendary D.B. Cooper, which was the name he used to buy his ticket on the Portland to Seattle flight." Conner reiterated.

"The only question remaining is what did Roebie do. And who the hell is he?" Conner asked again.

Without responding, Carolyn engaged her computer and began typing.

"What are you doing,?" Conner asked.

"I'm retrieving a list of Hughes Aircraft's executives from the late 1960s and 1970s," she replied, her attention now focused on the information appearing on the computer screen.

"The Chairman and CEO of Hughes Aircraft was a guy by the name of Donald G. Whitfield. No way to get "Roebie" out of that name," she said. "There was an executive vice president by the name of Bud Charles Jansen."

"No Roebie there either. And there was an aircraft division president by the name of Richard C. Clay. No Roebie."

"There also are names here of several other vice presidents, but nothing on the surface would lend itself to the name or nickname: "Roebie," she added.

Carolyn leaned back in her chair in thought, looking intently at her computer screen. Then slowly, she placed her hands on the keyboard and entered another name. The name was Howard Hughes, the billionaire owner of Hughes Aircraft. Howard Hughes' name popped up on the screen, along with a lengthy article and several pictures. The look of anxiety settled across Carolyn's face, reflecting her impatience. She paused again, then placed her hands back on the keyboard and made another entry: "Howard Hughes full name."

A split second delay occurred as the computer responded to the command and displayed the requested information: "Howard Robard Hughes"

Instinctively Carolyn clasped her hands over her mouth and emitted a muffled squeal, reflecting her unbridled excitement.

"That's it!" she exclaimed excitedly. "That's it! Roebie is Howard Robard Hughes." she repeated. "They are one and the same," she said confidently. "Roebie is the nickname for Robard,"

Conner spun his head around to read the screen for himself.

"I'll be damned," Conner uttered.

Carolyn continued to read from her computer screen.

"Howard Robard Hughes was the namesake of his father, Howard Robard Hughes, Sr. And "Roebie" was the nickname the son was given by friends and close working associates over the years," Carolyn read aloud.

"So, Roebie was the big dog at Hughes Aircraft?" Conner reflected.

"Over the years, Miller had endeared himself to Hughes, and Hughes was instrumental in advancing Miller's career and capitalizing on opportunities for him. He also went to bat for Miller's wife, Amy, during her daring attempt to fly around the world."

"Hughes was like that, based on what I've read about him," Conner added. "He had lots of enemies. But he also had a lot of friends in high places," Conner shared. "And like Miller, he also loved flying and was nearly killed once when he pushed the edge too far in one of his company's new and unproven aircraft."

"There was one other reason for Hughes' getting involved with Miller's act of vengeance," Conner added. "Northwest Airlines was a fierce competitor of one of Hughes' companies. At the time, Hughes owned Trans World Airlines, or TWA."

"And Northwest was something of a thorn in the side of TWA, particularly on international flights," Conner pointed out.

"Howard Hughes also was a tough-minded businessman, looking for any advantage he could find to advance his businesses interests. And teaming with Miller against Northwest could have been an appealing opportunity to stick it to this predator. There was no way of verifying that. But I think the odds were good that's what happened," Conner concluded.

Carolyn nodded her agreement.

"I think you're right," Carolyn suggested. "If you buy his success in bailing out of an aircraft flying at a couple of hundred miles an hour and half a million dollars taped to his body, you have to agree his getting away with the money was a piece of cake. Particularly if he had help on the ground."

I'm comfortable with this conclusion," Conner added.

"The final question I now have involves Amy Putnam, Miller's second wife," Conner added.

"What do you wanna' know about her," Carolyn asked.

"Pretty much everything," Conner replied.

"Miller wrote in his diaries she had become a national hero before she attempted to fly around the world. That effort on her part, incidentally, turned out to be a disaster," Conner added. "I don't know a lot about aviation history. Maybe Charles Lindbergh was a national hero. But everybody knows about him. As for Amy Putnam. Nothin'" Conner confessed. Never heard of her before this," he said.

Carolyn shrugged her shoulders, indicating she too didn't know who Amy might have been.

"Well, my trusty computer came up with the answer before. Let's try it one more time," Carolyn suggested.

Once again, her fingers danced across the keyboard, as she entered the name Amy Putnam. Almost instantly, an image appeared on her screen.

"Hmmm," Carolyn said out loud. "There are more than 40 hits on that name."

There was a long pause as she began reading the backgrounds associated with each name. After a couple of minutes, she paused and looked at her friend.

"Their professions and affiliations are like that doctor, lawyer, Indian chief song," she said. "Lots of doctors, lawyers, accountants, teachers, professors,

But no Indian Chief," she observed. "Nothing here that would suggest any of these people are what we're looking for," she added.

"I would have guessed this information would be readily available and easy to find," she added.

Then Carolyn went silent as she returned to her computer. Without saying more, she made another entry into the system: "Famous women in flying history."

One name instantly appeared on the screen. It was "Amelia Earhart."

Carolyn looked at Conner without speaking. Instead, she entered Earhart's name and a lengthy article appeared on the computer. She immediately began reading, mumbling to herself as she skimmed through this plethora of information about the world famous female flyer. Conner was not close enough to her screen to read the material. Instead he sat quietly and relied on Carolyn for her commentary.

Just then, Carolyn stopped reading.

"Wait a minute," she said out loud. "Wait a minute," she repeated. "Amelia Earhart was married for several years to a man by the name of George Palmer Putnam, who was a noted American publisher, author and explorer back some time ago. And Amy, it seems, was the given name she preferred instead of Amelia. Amy Putnam was definitely Amelia Earhart!," she called out.

"Amelia Earhart?" Conner asked in astonishment.

"Yup!" Carolyn confirmed. "We've found Amy Putnam. Or Amelia Earhart, whichever you prefer," Carolyn exclaimed excitedly.

Before Conner could respond, she continued.

"I would guess she just kept the last name, for whatever reason who knows? But, didn't she die in a plane crash?" Carolyn asked as an afterthought.

Conner paused thoughtfully before responding.

"To answer your questions, 'no' she didn't die in a plane crash, which was widely reported and believed," Conner responded. "In fact, in one of Miller's journals, he described her final flight in great detail. Her plane did indeed crash, and her navigator was killed. But, she survived, thanks to Miller's heroics. She also suffered serious injuries, both physical and emotionally. After that, she just disappeared. She apparently decided she didn't want to be Amelia Earhart anymore, I guess. And she never flew again," He added.

"In his writings about the incident, Miller had doubts whether she would ever be the same again."

"But after considerable time passed, as Amy Putnam she found happiness in total seclusion with Hans. And it's understandable why she might have wanted to do that," Conner concluded. "Interesting that both Amy and Miller lived out a good portion of their lives in anonymity," he said. "And both had become famous in their own rights.

That's a sad story," Carolyn said.

Conner nodded his agreement.

"Maybe sad. But everything seemed to have turned out right for her," he added. .

"Okay. Now that you seem to have all the pieces of the puzzle on the mystery man, what are you going to do with it? Carolyn asked.

"Well, I guess you'll just have to keep in touch with your favorite photographer to find out," Conner said with a chuckle. "By the way, I'm deeply in your debt for being such a help. Maybe we could have dinner."

"Maybe we could," she replied with a smile.

Conner approached his friend and gave her an embracing hug.

CHAPTER THIRTY

The following day Conner left home early, heading for Atlanta and his lawyer friend's office. He had called ahead two days earlier. But this trip was far different from the first meeting he had with Chad Greenlee. On this morning, Conner arrived with the energy of a tropical storm approaching warm waters. And as he approached Greenlee's office, even his walk reflected confidence and enthusiasm.

Conner had reclaimed one of his mothballed IBM suits from the back of a bedroom closet and laced himself into a pair of long-ago abandoned Florsheim wingtip shoes. To the casual observer, Conner looked like the rest of these men of jurisprudence who walked these halls. But this lawyerly image was purposeful on his part, and it contributed to his sense of self-assuredness.

After greeting Greenlee's secretary, Conner followed her into Chad's office and immediately gave his friend a big smile and an enthusiastic handshake.

"Good morning counselor, It's great to see you again. And thanks for seeing me on such short notice," Conner said.

"Counselor?.....Counselor? Well, ain't we hyped this morning. And don't we look very IBMish, as well?"

"Yes. I guess you could say I'm a little hyped this morning. And I am dressed kinda' upscale. But it's only because I'm in the presence of greatness."

The two friends laughed.

"Have a seat, and tell me what's been going on," Greenlee began.

Before Conner could respond, Greenlee continued.

"I gotta' tell you, Mitch, after our last meeting I was a little worried about you. But today you seem to have gotten your second wind. You're loaded for bear, if you will."

"Well, I can tell you a lot has changed since we last talked," Conner responded

As Conner eased into a nearby chair, he gazed around the office as if it were his first trip there. Then it occurred to him, he probably was in something of a haze during that previous visit. And he was, indeed, seeing Chad's office for the first time.

"Most of the questions I had a few months ago now have answers," Conner began. "I know a lot more about this situation in the mountains than I did then."

"But there are several loose ends, and a coupla' new issues for which I need resolution…and maybe even representation,"

"Sounds serious. Let's start with the new issues," Greenlee responded.

"The most important development is I now know the real name of the mystery man who died out there in the Carolina wilderness. His name was Hans Miller. Probably you remember him by his infamous pseudonym, D.B. Cooper. He's the guy who hijacked an airliner in flight, and bailed out of the plane with a hefty ransom strapped to his person.

"Sunnovabitch!" Greenlee exclaimed loudly. "Yeah, of course I remember. FBI never found a trace of that guy. But, you found 'em!"

"Yep. And that's a story within itself," Conner continued. "But there were other well-known characters involved with this thing, making it even more bizarre," he added.

"First, there was Miller's second wife, Amy Putnam. She turned out to be Amelia Earhart. She didn't die in a plane crash, as was reported and popularly believed. She did get seriously hurt in her last flight, however. Damn near died, But, as a result of that mishap, she totally walked away from flying and from her whirlwind lifestyle. She also married this guy who had high jacked a passenger aircraft, and she followed him to a foreboding hideaway in the Mountains of North Carolina."

"I can't believe that," Greenlee shot back. "You're saying Amelia Earhart did not lose her life in a plane crash? You've got to be kidding."

"No. I'm not kidding. And yes, I'm saying Amelia Earhart did not die in a plane crash. She probably died of old age," Conner reasoned. "And in the Carolina mountains.," he added. "And the free world never heard from her again."

"I still find it hard to believe!" Greenlee responded, while continuing to shake his head.

"Well, there was another famous name in this strange yarn. It was Howard Hughes. He and Hans Miller became very close friends. And the two of them got involved financially, in backing Miller's escapades, and in helping save the life of Earhart," Conner added.

Greenlee quickly responded to Conner's comments on Hughes.

"There's not much you could tell me about Howard Hughes shenanigans over the years that would surprise me. And as he got older, he became a total whack job. He was nuts," Greenlee argued.

Conner interrupted to get back on track.

"But, Miller was the center of attraction here. And it's his activities that brought me back to your office today," Conner said.

"Whatta' ya' mean by that?" Greenlee asked.

"As you remember, Miller gave me the Power of Attorney, in absentia, which provided me unquestioned access to his personal effects and gave me the authorization to make decisions I considered, or will consider, beneficial to him," Conner continued. "That was a critical element in this whole exercise."

"Yes, I do remember, and I do agree, as strange as it was." Greenlee replied.

Conner held the will in his hand and jiggled it overhead as he discussed its contents.

"And the will made me an absentia recipient of Miller's estate, which I now quote verbatim 'I hereby bequeath all of my property, my wealth and financial assets, real, personal or mixed, of whatever nature and situation, to the unknown bearer and holder of this will, and in the presence of subscribing witnesses on this 23rd day of October, 2017. Signed by Winston Cryder, Attorney at Law, Asheville, North Carolina."

"Then, his address and so forth followed, And there were two witnesses, whose names and identities are not important," Conner added.

"Yes, I remember that as well.," Greenlee replied.

Conner acknowledged the response and paused briefly before continuing.

"In my view, these two occurrences clearly identify me as both recipient and executor of the will and give me the authority to do what I think is in the best interests of the Testator – or in this case, Miller."

"At this point, I can't disagree with any of that. But I'd have to explore it in greater detail to be certain of it all." Greenlee responded. "But I think that statement is generally correct," he said.

"The reason I'm revisiting the will is to clearly establish the rules of the game from my perspective," Conner concluded. "And that was one of the things I wanted to achieve today," Conner repeated.

Greenlee slowly nodded his head in approval

"But, there is one thing I originally thought was peculiar about this will. But I clearly understand it now. The will did not include Miller's name nor signature. At first I didn't even think about that, because I didn't know his name anyway. I didn't raise the issue. But it became very apparent when I found out who he was. I'll bet Miller's attorney, Winston Cryder, covered that omission in a separate addendum to make it a legal part of the document. That's something we need to find out, because it could affect the will's legitimacy."

"Right," Greenlee confirmed. Conner paused, then continued

"Among the items included in the paperwork I discovered at Miller's residence was the name of his bank."

"It was the Bank of America office in Asheville. And, as you know, it's a nationwide, if not international, institution…one of the big ones. I'm sure Miller picked that bank because of its history of stability and longevity."

"And I'm sure he figured the institution would still be in business after he passed on," Conner pointed out.

"A few days ago, I got in touch with the lawyer who prepared the will, Mister Cryder of Asheville, and we actually talked a bit on the phone. By the way, you and he agree this will is the most bizarre ever."

"After my chat with Cryder, I drove over to his office in Asheville, which was about an hour away. We had an interesting couple of hours. I gave him your name and said you'd be representing me on this issue. He agreed that would be advisable. Cryder also said he had several meetings with Miller over a period of time, and he told me he grew very fond of him…said he was a gentle and compassionate man."

"Funny thing. I had the same feeling about Mister Cryder," Conner said. "He, too, was a gentle and compassionate man."

"Incidentally, I never mentioned to Cryder I knew exactly who Miller was and what he had done during his lifetime. He didn't ask, and I didn't tell," Conner admitted. "Now maybe he was just being discreet, as I was. Or maybe he was being lawyerly and couldn't violate the lawyer/client privilege," Conner added.

"The latter is probably correct, Greenlee replied.

Conner paused briefly, then continued.

"I've also done a little research on inheriting substantial amounts of cash. And from what I've read, there is no inheritance tax in North Carolina…no gift tax. So it would appear my situation is not a State of North Carolina financial issue but an issue with the Internal Revenue Service. So, if I decide to accept this money, I need the wise counsel of a Certified Public Accountant to deal with anything raised by the IRS. And I'm hopeful you can find the appropriate people to handle that part of it," Conner said, looking seriously at his friend.

Greenlee nodded his agreement.

"There's another issue that should be addressed here," Conner pointed out. "It concerns the local law enforcement, the people who tried to implicate me in Miller's death. Although I think it's a non-issue, I'm not so naive as to ignore possible police interest in this story, once it gets out. And I'm convinced it will get out," Conner said.

"Yes, you're right. We'll just have to wait and see how it develops and then deal with it," Greenlee responded.

"But now, for the sixty four dollar question," Conner added. "And this one is for you the lawyer, not you the friend."

Again, there was a pause as Conner carefully chose his words.

"Should I even consider taking this money from a man I never knew?" he asked.

Greenlee paused as well, and he briefly spun his chair around and gazed momentarily out at the imposing Atlanta skyline. Just as quickly, he spun back around to face his friend.

"I certainly understand your dilemma…your hesitation. But what's your gut feel? Can you justify taking gift money that might have been illegally obtained?" Greenlee asked.

Conner's eyebrows arched at this difficult question.

"What we may be overlooking here is some portion of that money could have come from the estate of Amelia Earhart," Conner added. "She was Miller's second wife, and I understand, there were no surviving relatives from that side of the family."

Greenlee shrugged his shoulders at the statement.

"What's the alternative if I don't take the money?" Conner asked. "Does it go back to the public trust? Does it go to the police fund? Does it go to politicians and their favorite causes? Or would it go to some airline conglomerate?" Conner asked.

Before Greenlee could respond, Conner continued.

"From what I read, that money has long since passed the statute of limitations," Conner added. "Plus, the victimized company doesn't even exist anymore."

"Those are appropriate question, as well," Greenlee said before continuing. "But, I think this keeps coming back to the fact a sizeable portion of Miller's wealth was obtained through an unlawful act…and that's Chad the lawyer responding to you."

There was a long pause as Conner reflected on Greenlee's statement.

'Before I go any further, let me say that Mister Cryder was very understanding and very cooperative."

"At my request, he called the bank, and verified I was the sole heir of the will. Apparently, Cryder is well known and widely respected in Asheville. And based on his verification of my claim, the bank was perfectly willing to tell me the amount of money Miller had accumulated in a Roth IRA. And I can tell you, it was well over a million dollars…damn close to two million."

"And, in fact, I had to try very hard not to show the shock I felt when I heard how much was involved," Conner added.

"To go back to your question, Conner responded. "I have to say I have mixed feelings about taking the money. I've said this to you before, on another issue, but I think it's what he would have wanted to happen. He's not here to defend himself. Not here to tell us what he'd like done. But I think he had a sixth sense about things. And he was right, from my point of view," Conner said. "I certainly have a lot of compassion for him and the price he paid for what he did."

"And believe me, he paid in his own way, over a period of some 30 years. And by the way. I looked it up, and the typical sentence for armed robbery these days is 20 years on the high end."

"There's one thing for sure I can tell you about Miller after reading most of his journals. He would not have wanted his financial assets – including some of the monies he acquired legally - to be surrendered to any public system and certainly not to any existing airline."

Greenlee nodded slowly at the comments. But Conner continued.

"Now that I know who the guy was and what he did, I can say I might have done the same thing under the circumstances," Conner suggested. "I dunno.' Put yourself in his shoes. Could you have done that?" Conner asked.

Before Greenlee could respond, Conner continued

"You know, there are a lot of people who think D. B. Cooper was a hero.," Conner said. Each year, thousands gather to pay tribute to him. They look at him as a current day version of Robin Hood, who took it to the Big Man when there were few other options for him to pay for his loss. He seemed to have grown up in a rough-and-tumble era that believed, 'if you take a swing at me, I'm going to take a swing at you."

"In some senses, I feel like fate played a role in my stumbling on his story. And as for the money, it's like I found a lot of money in the woods, with nobody around to claim it. I now have an opportunity to do something good with that money."

"Maybe it's contributing to the fight against cancer, the disease that took Sarah Miller's life and prompted his actions. Maybe it's creating some kind of tribute to this Robin Hood of the forests who fought for his country in two separate wars and never got credit for it. He never got a 21-gun salute. He never had taps played over his grave and never had a word of thanks directed toward him…And I have the opportunity to do some of those things that could make a difference.

"You know, I think I'll take that money in the name of D.B. Cooper and Hans Miller," Conner concluded.

Greenlee smiled a big smile before responding to Conner's thoughts.

"You know, champ, you've convinced me that's the right thing to do. That's Greenlee the friend talking. Let's go for it," Greenlee said eagerly

CHAPTER THIRTY ONE

I t was late afternoon when Conner arrived back in BC. Before leaving Atlanta, he had picked up the tab for lunch at one of Atlanta's most exclusive restaurants. And he had enjoyed lunch with his friend. It was a time of unwinding, more for him than for Chad. But his recollections of the meeting and the questions posed continued to dominate his thoughts during the drive back home.

Chad was a true friend, and Conner appreciated his honesty and his friendship. He also was reassured Greenlee would now be at his side to handle the kind of issues that helped make him one of the city's best attorneys. And Conner felt good about that.

There were other things that had needed to be handled on this day, but Conner decided to take the rest of the day off. It had been a trying and emotional session with Greenlee, and he decided to spend some time in his new home. A cleaning crew had been in his house for a second day. And he was anxious to check their progress. Conner still had not gotten over thinking he was living in someone else's home. But he loved the way the remodeling turned out. And he was anxious to make it his home again.

But, now that the construction clutter was gone, the house felt empty. And it was. Most of the furniture from the cabin had been discarded or given away. And he certainly needed help in getting the right pieces, a mixture of comfort and décor. He needed a soft touch, he told himself. And that was not a difficult thing to achieve.

Instead of taking the shortcut around downtown BC, Conner headed for The Scarlett Letters shop. This was not a business call. He needed to unwind. He needed to share the pressures he had already faced on this day. And he needed to share the pressures he was about to face in the coming weeks. He also needed to loosen his tie and take off these damn wingtip shoes, he told himself.

For no apparent reason, Conner suddenly wanted to see his favorite jogger, Carolyn. The mere thought of her instilled in him feelings of serenity and security.

Once inside the store, Conner spotted her in the book section again. She was seated on the floor arranging stock at the lower shelf levels. Several strands of her longish yellow hair had separated from the rest and hung over one side of her face, partially blocking her view.

Conner smiled at that image as he approached.

She was totally occupied with her work and didn't look up to see him. When she did feel his presence, she was caught by surprise and slightly startled.

But her expression quickly turned into a big smile, as she brushed her hair aside and stood effortlessly in front of him.

"Heyyy," she exclaimed. "You're all dressed up! I like it."

Conner was happy to see her, and he reached out and put his arms around her. Unexpectedly, she pulled away and a serious frown transformed her face."

Conner was puzzled by her action.

'Is something wrong?" she asked, pulling slowly away from him.

Conner was thrown off guard by this serious reaction. But, after a moment, he began to laugh, and it prompted laughter from her as well.

"No. No. Not at all. Nothing is wrong. In fact, things are almost perfect."

"Well, what would make them perfect?"

"If you'd have dinner with me tonight," he replied with a smile.

"I'd love to," she responded.

"Great," Conner replied. "I tell you what. I just got back from spending most of the day with a lawyer .in Atlanta. And I wanna' get outta' these stuffed shirt clothes and into garments that hang loosely and shoes that fit," Conner said. "I can get back here at quitting time and take you home to change, if that's okay with you. Shouldn't take me more than 45 minutes."

"Take your time. I'll be waiting for you outside." she responded, her blue eyes mirroring her enthusiasm.

It took Conner about seven minutes to drive home. When he pulled up out front, he sat momentarily in the car, looking at the finished structure. He was delighted with what he saw. He wished he could spend more time getting to know the place again. But he knew it would be a long-term process that deserved his full attention. As for right now, picking up Carolyn was the more pressing issue on his agenda. And she deserved his full attention, also," he told himself.

As he entered the house, Conner chatted briefly with the cleaning crew that had completed their job and were packing up. After they left, he took a quick shower, slipped into a pair of Jeans, a slightly oversized cotton shirt, his favorite dark grey sport coat and the most comfortable casual shoes he owned. He then headed for the Land Rover.

When he reached the highway, only 33 minutes had elapsed. From there, he made the trip back to Scarlett Letters in five minutes, thankful that he had not encountered any Sheriff's Office cars along the way.

Carolyn was standing in front of the Scarlett Letters, her purse hanging loosely in front of her. When Conner pulled up, she squinted to see through the slightly tinted windows.

Conner quickly rolled down the passenger side window and smiled, which brought her rushing to the vehicle. Before getting inside, she stopped briefly to admire his car. She then swiveled onto the seat and closed the door.

"I really like your new car. It's very nice," she said.

"That's nice of you to say so. I like it, too," he replied.

As Conner pulled away, she ran her fingers across the leather seats in a childlike move, smiling almost mischievously. The car was still new enough that her action produced a muffled squeaking noise.

"Did you sell the other one?" she asked.

"Heavens no," Conner responded. "I couldn't live without the 'Beast.' It's my workhorse. It gets me to places that are difficult to reach. Places where I need to be. Even places I shouldn't be."

Both of them laughed modestly at the remark.

"As for this one, it's my get dressed up and 'go out' car.," he said. "I also take it on long trips and to the offices of attorneys when I've got serious business to do.."

Carolyn nodded and smiled.

"I would think if the Bronco was so important to you, you'd come up with a name for it that's a little kinder," Carolyn said playfully.

"Nawww. The Beast is the perfect name. And, when I say it, it's with fondness and great respect."

Carolyn laughed, then continued.

"Well, I'd hate to ask what you call me when talking to others."

"What makes you think I talk about you to others?"

Carolyn laughed out of embarrassment and glanced at him with a forced look of hurt feelings.

Conner smiled at her and laughed at that feigned look of rejection.

He paused briefly before responding.

"Actually, I've told a few people about you. I haven't come up with a pet name or anything like that. Not yet anyway. Not yet. But, I typically refer to you as a very pretty, very smart and fun lady to be with."

Carolyn blushed and waved her hand toward him in an act of dismissal.

"Well, mister Conner. there's one thing I must say about you. When you change your life, you really change your life," she kidded. "New house. New job. New car. What's next?"

"I guess we'll just have to wait and see," he replied, punctuating the remark with a palms up gesture.

Carolyn smiled at him, before quickly turning her attention to the passing scenery en route to her home. Conner glanced at her. Her profile was accentuated by the setting sun, and there was an orange glow about her face. Damn she's pretty, he thought to himself.

Carolyn noticed his stare and responded.

"What?" she asked.

Conner shrugged and look back at the road.

"Nothing," he replied. "I was just admiring the scenery."

There was a momentary silence before Conner looked back at her.

"With your approval, I recommend we drop in at this little place I discovered not too long ago. It's called the Frog. Are you familiar with it?"

"Yes, I am. The Frog would be great," she responded. I've been there on a couple of occasions, and I was impressed with the atmosphere and the menu. It's a family kind of place. Quiet but not boring."

"I agree," Conner said with a nod.

When Conner arrived at Carolyn's home, she quickly unlocked her front door and led her guest into the house. Conner followed and watched her as she moved around, disposing of her coat and bringing the house to life.

"I'll get some lights on and run upstairs to get ready," she said. "Make yourself at home, and I'll be down in a bit," she said with a smile. "And if you'd like a drink while you wait, there are beer and wine in the refrigerator, and there's Scotch in the cabinet to the left," she called out as she hurriedly made her way upstairs.

Conner moved to the kitchen and found the liquor supply cabinet, as explained. This was a Scotch night, and he immediately spotted a large new bottle of Dewar's on the bottom shelf. "Well," he mumbled to himself, "the lady either has a good memory or she's lucky. I'll bet on the good memory," he said to himself.

Conner's reasoning continued.

"My favorite Scotch and a large sized bottle? Interesting, he thought. She would not have gotten a large bottle if she wasn't expecting more than just one casual serving."

"Conner chuckled to himself as he moved the whiskey from its place and poured himself a moderately sized drink. He then wandered back into the living room and took a seat in a comfortable-looking, oversized chair. Conner treated himself to a long sip of Dewar's and let his eyes roam around the room.

Wherever he looked, he saw evidence of Carolyn's personality and attention to detail. Her choice of furnishings was more about comfort, warmth and taste and not about flamboyance or ostentation, he decided. There also was a definite element of compatibility throughout the room. It was not a museum. It was a living room. It was exactly the kind of furniture he hoped to get for his home, he concluded.

Carolyn had turned on her stereo before running upstairs. And the volume was very subtle. Hmmm, he thought, she likes classical music. Conner took another sip of Scotch, closed his eyes and leaned back into the chair. He was totally relaxed for the next several minutes. "Woah," he said softly to himself and adjusted his posture to more of an upright position. I could fall asleep here in a nanosecond, he realized. "That would not be good," he reasoned.

Conner then took a longer sip of his drink and unthinkingly glanced at his watch. He was surprised a little more than ten minutes had already passed. He could now hear scurrying noises from upstairs, which meant Carolyn would soon be down. Looking at his glass, he noticed there were only one or two sips left. And Just then, Carolyn shouted down a status report on her readiness in something of a sing-song manner.

"I'm almost ready," she said. "Down in a sec."

"No need to hurry," he replied. "We've got plenty of time."

Conner pulled himself from the chair, downed the rest of his Scotch and headed to the kitchen, where he put everything back in order. He headed back toward the living room just as Carolyn began a rapid descent of the stairs. Conner looked at her and once again, she looked great, he thought. She was dressed in a white blouse, a black sweater overwrap, with matching skirt, and 3/4 length high heel shoes. "I was right," he told himself. She looks great in high heels. " It helps that she has great legs," he thought with a smile.

When Carolyn reached the bottom step, she paused and reached out to him. Conner put his arms around her and kissed her. She smiled at him, and gave him a pecking kiss, for good measure.

"Okay," I'm ready if you are," she said. "Shall we go?"

"Yes," he replied. "I'm getting hungry."

The Frog Restaurant and its surroundings were just as Conner remembered. When the couple stepped inside, he requested a booth, which he preferred over a table.

As they walked past the bar, Conner spotted the bartender, Helen, and waved to her. She returned the wave with a smile.

"She seems to know you," Carolyn said.

"Yup," Conner replied. "I was here a short time back with my neighbor. Pete Musser. He made a big impression on her, as he does with most people he meets. I'll have to introduce you to him some time. He's a real piece of work."

Carolyn nodded as she continued to follow the maitre'd who took them to their table. Carolyn slipped into her seat and Conner eased on the same side, right next to her.

She looked at him and smiled.

"Here we are again", Conner said. "Faced with the choice of beverages…. beer, wine or whatever," Conner said.

"Sometimes I just hate making decisions," Carolyn said. "And tonight, it's neither light outside nor dark outside. So, I guess we have our choice. I think I'll have wine," she decided.

"I think that's a good choice," Conner said. "I've had a Scotch already...my high octane beverage for the night. So I think I'll go with the wine, as well."

After the waitress delivered their beverages, Conner proposed a toast.

"Here's to the future, whatever it may bring," he said tapping her raised glass with his.

"To the future," she repeated, before taking a long sip from her goblet.

There was a short pause before Conner continued.

"I'm glad you were available tonight. I enjoy your company," he admitted. "And I didn't feel like spending the night alone. Besides, with the exception of three items, I don't have any furniture in my house these days...just the stereo, that old leather chair and my bed."

Carolyn responded in kind.

"I'm glad you stopped by the store. And I enjoy your company as well. You know, it's kinda' nice at times to do things at the spur of the moment. I think that helps keep life interesting."

"I agree," Conner replied.

"And while I'm on that subject of furniture," Conner continued, 'I desperately need help in that area. And from what I've seen in your home, I think you're the perfect choice to provide such assistance. I'm also prepared to pay you handsomely for your expertise," Conner added in something of an exaggerated voice.

"I'd be delighted to help spend your money. And for you, there's a special rate: Nothing!"

"I was serious when I said I'd pay you handsomely."

"And I was serious when I said my rate would be: nothing!"

Carolyn punctuated her statement with a modest giggle and a response to Conner.

"I think I told you this, but as a younger man my father worked in a furniture manufacturing plant near Franklin," Carolyn added. "But, he was one of thousands in the Carolinas who lost their careers and lifestyles in the late 1900s. The industry was devastated by China and other low-wage countries who turned furniture buying into a matter of simply price with no concern for quality and craftsmanship."

"He never got over losing something he really loved doing," she recalled. "He tried hard to start his own business, but he was a master craftsman and not a businessman."

Conner showed his sympathy with a look of disappointment.

"But I think the industry is on its way back in the Carolinas," Carolyn suggested.

"I found a wonderful source of custom-made furniture over in Boone. The company not only has an incredible showroom with beautiful and quality pieces, they offer tours, which, alone, is worth the trip. It's about a two and a half hour drive from here…about the same distance as Atlanta. It's called Charleston Forge Furniture Company."

"I definitely would like to go there," Conner said. How about tomorrow?" he teased.

"I'm serious," Carolyn countered. "I have to work tomorrow."

"Alright, then let's go when you don't have to work."

"That would fine," she said.

There was a brief silence between the two before Carolyn continued.

"Well, I think we've talked enough about me. Tell me about you," she said. How did that meeting with your lawyer friend go?"

Conner paused for several moments thinking about his response.

"I'm hesitating," he said, "because of the way this whole issue has developed in recent days and the legal issues that have surfaced. I have you to thank for my having a pretty complete picture of what went on with the late Miller. But, it seems the more we discover, the more complicated it gets."

"The good news is Chad Greenlee is a very good lawyer. And I have the utmost confidence in his ability to resolve most — if not all - of these issues in our favor."

"The bad news is there are still major sticking points involving a will I found in Hans Miller's dwelling. That's at the forefront of everything else."

"It was an open ended will that left all of Miller's worldly possessions to whomever found the document out there…or as the will stated…I hereby bequest all of my wealth and financial assets, real, personal or mixed, to the unknown bearer and holder of this will…. I've read that so many times, I memorized it," he added.

"So, because I found the will, I became the recipient of the man's total estate. And right now, that's issue number one," he told her.

"Under normal circumstances," Conner continued, "that would be good news. But in this case, we're talking about an estate that contained a lot, and I mean a lot of money. And there are a lot of people, including government agencies, who might just want to get their hands on that money," he said

"You see, this guy took a big gamble. By leaving all of his assets and worldly possessions to some unknown person, he gambled this stranger would look kindly on the way his life and reputation had unfolded…the life of Hans Miller – A.K.A. - D.B. Cooper. And he also gambled the recipient would tell his story in a favorable fashion. And damned if he wasn't right!

"Today, I think I made the case with Greenlee why hijacker Miller had already paid his price to society when he died alone and without fanfare there in the woods. End of story. And Chad seemed to agree with what I argued."

"But, there also is the matter of possible law enforcement involvement once this story gets out," he added. "And it will get out, because that's the way we've got to do this thing.."

"I've already begun a book that tells this whole story…along the lines of "whatever happened to D. B. Cooper?""

"And at some point, maybe when the book is complete, I plan to hold a press conference and reveal the story of my involvement. That could turn out to be a bumpy ride," he said with a chuckle. It would make the trip up the old road to my house child's play."

"And there's one more thing, depending on the way this thing shakes out. I just may find myself out of a teaching job at WCU. Who knows how the University would view my involvement with such a controversial issue.' he explained.

"Doctor Frees, the Dean of Fine Arts, seems to be a practical and fair-minded man. But who knows how he'd look at this?" Conner asked.

Conner paused, and Carolyn's response was to the point.

"Wow…" she said quite simply.

"Yeah, I know," that's a lot to swallow. But you did ask," he reminded her.

Conner looked away, with a stare through one of the restaurant's big windows. He remained silent for several moments before Carolyn broke the silence.

"Professionally, I prefer to look at the bright side of issues," Carolyn reasoned. "And I believe what you say about your friend being a great lawyer. And great lawyers do great things. I do believe he will do an outstanding job of defending you in any possible legal confrontations."

"As for this story being controversial, it's just history. And as I see it, you'll be getting an advanced degree in history soon. And it would appear to me you're simply expanding your knowledge of history. As for the book you're writing, it could turn out to be a best seller, and the University would surely be happy to have a best-selling author on its staff who teaches writing."

Conner chuckled at her narrative and raised his glass.

"Here's to the future," he said as he smiled at her and raised his glass to hers.

Conner turned and kissed her softly.

"You just made my day perfect," he said.

"I'd say my day has been about the same," she added.

"Waiter, we'll have another wine and then we'll order."

Carolyn reached over and squeezed his hand, keeping it in her grasp until the waiter approached the table with their wine.

CHAPTER THIRTY TWO

Dusk had begun to settle over the mountain and shadows were replacing rays of sunlight around Conner's new home. Because of his lack of furniture, he and Carolyn were seated on the top level flooring of his new, two-steps-down living room. Conner excused himself for interrupting their conversation and moved toward the entrance and the wall-mounted light switches.

Overhead lights immediately washed the entire area in light. Conner reached down and retrieved his telephone from the floor and dialed the number for Pete Musser, who answered promptly.

"Hey Daddy Warbucks," Musser responded.

"Would you quit calling me that?" Conner asked.

"Got it. Hey you crazy bastard," Mussed replied.

Conner laughed at his neighbor.

"Hey, Muss. If you're not busy, I'd like you to stumble over here and meet a friend of mine. It's Carolyn Briggs from the Scarlett Letters," he explained.

"Okay if I bring my dog,?" he asked.

"Sure. Blitzen is always welcome," he said.

When Conner opened the side door, Musser and Blitzen were standing together on the newly added portico outside the main entrance. Conner's attention was immediately focused on the dog sitting quietly next to his master.

"Hey Blitzen," Conner said enthusiastically. "Hey, boy."

"And hey to you, too, Muss."

"Boy, I can tell where your priorities are," Musser countered.

"Well, you don't bite," Conner said. "At least not yet."

Musser ignored the comment and stepped inside, followed closely by the big dog, who looked at Conner again and wagged his tail. Blitzen then turned his attention to Carolyn, and he trotted directly to her.

Carolyn met him half way and knelt on one knee to greet him. Blitzen immediately began licking her face. Carolyn giggled at the animal's affection and rigorously rubbed his head and ears. The dog responded to the attention and dropped to the floor right beside her.

"Boy, he really likes you," Musser observed.

"I love animals," Carolyn responded. Blitzen raised his head and attempted to lick her face again, but Carolyn restrained his affection this time. Blitzen resumed his position on the floor next to her and continued to wag his tail.

I've never seen him react to a stranger like this," Musser said.

Conner used the brief pause for introductions.

"Pete Musser, this is Carolyn Briggs. Carolyn works up at the Scarlett Letters shop," Muss.

"Nice to meet you Carolyn. And that's my dog, Blitzen," Musser added.

"Nice to meet you, too," she replied. "So, you're the crazy bastard man?" Carolyn blurted out.

Musser laughed out loud before responding.

"Yes, I'm the crazy bastard man. But I would never call you that. Maybe I'll just call you C. B," he added.

"C. B. Would be fine,' Carolyn replied politely. "I've been called worse, as they say."

Before either of the other two could reply, Carolyn continued.

"It's nice to finally meet you. Conner has told me about you often."

"I'll bet he has," Musser added.

"No, I'm serious. He's very fond of you. And he refers to you as his friend, which I think is one of the nicest things anyone can say about another person.:"

"Well aren't you nice?" he said. "It's clear what he sees in you. But what redeeming values do you see in him?"

Both Conner and Carolyn chuckled at the remark.

"This conversation is gettin' a little personal, so let's change the subject," Musser blurted out.

Musser then turned his attention to Conner.

"You got yourself a nice house, here," Musser observed. "Doesn't look anything like that little shack you lived in before," he added.

"Shack?" Conner shot back. "I liked that little 'shack!"

"Whatever," Musser replied, waving his hand in Conner's direction.

"You still got a liquor cabinet?"

"I do still have a liquor cabinet. A new one. And I'll get you a glass of Scotch before you show signs of a convulsion," Conner added.

"Thatta' boy," Musser replied.

"Since I only have one chair and you're the oldest one in the room, you can have that old leather chair over there," Conner suggested as he walked toward the kitchen area.

"Damn if I'll turn an offer like that down," Musser replied as he walked over and slid into the old chair favorite.

Musser continued to direct his remarks to Conner, raising his voice to reach the other side of the house.

"I understand you've put together all the pieces of the mystery man puzzle," Musser said in a raised voice.

Conner failed to hear Musser's comment, since he was determining what Carolyn preferred to drink. She decided on having a Scotch with the guys, much to Conner's surprise. The host returned to the other two, carrying the drinks on a serving tray.

"I'm sorry I couldn't understand you from the kitchen, Muss. What were you saying?" he asked.

"I was talking about your mystery man. I understand you've pretty much put all the pieces of the puzzle together."

"Well, that was one of the things I wanted to tell you this evening," Conner replied. "Carolyn and I kinda' put the finishing touches on it together, just a copula' days ago. Who told you about it?"

"Is this really something you want to talk about openly? Musser asked as he nodded toward Carolyn and her presence in the room.

"As I said," Carolyn and I worked on the final pieces together. I would trust her with my life," Conner added in a serious tone.

"Well, nobody told me about it. I just knew what was going on," Musser stated.

"And I knew sooner or later, you and I would have this conversation. But, I've been involved with this thing for quite some time. In fact, I had a few encounters with Hans Miller before his death. And I must say, he was an incredible person. He was very personable. Very bright. And he lived an incredible life. I really liked the man," Musser said.

Conner was stunned, and his surprise was clearly evident from his facial expression. Carolyn's response was very similar to Conner's. She was shocked at Musser's comments, as well.

"You knew Hans Miller?" Conner asked.

"Yes, I did," he admitted. "I also know the lawyer, Winston Cryder, and I've worked with him, as well. He's also a helluva' guy."

Again, there was prolonged silence among the three. When Conner spoke, there was a hesitancy in his voice.

"Have you been in touch with my friend, Chad Greenlee?" Conner asked.

"The answer is yes. I talked to him a couple of days ago. When he contacted Cryder, he became a part of the equation," Musser replied. "I was impressed with him, as well. You're lucky to have him as a friend."

"Damn Muss. I'm a little surprised you didn't tell me any of this before."

"Would you have done anything differently?"

"No, probably not."

"Well, I didn't see the need to make this process even more complicated than it already was. And I didn't want to impose my priorities on you. You seemed to be doing all the right things. And in the right order. The most important point is you dug for the information you needed. And you came to your own conclusions along the way."

"If Miller was alive today, I think he'd be pleased with what you've already done and what you plan to do."

"Well, I gotta' ask you, 'why didn't Miller simply pick you to be the recipient in his will?"

"Let's just say, it wouldn't have been a good move for me. And certainly, I didn't care about the money. It was a matter of my personal situation. I didn't need the kind of exposure this story will generate," Musser added.

"Based on my conversation with Greenlee, I understand you're writing a book on your experience, and I admire that. However, I would ask you, Mitch, not to reveal my true identity. Or a character that would identify my true identity. You have a good imagination, and I'm sure you can come up with some other dull guy other than me."

"I consider you a good friend, Muss. And I think you know I wouldn't do anything to damage that friendship. You can count on it, Muss."

Musser responded with a nod and a serious tone of voice.

"I'm going way out on a limb in discussing this with you and Carolyn. But I trust you both as friends who wouldn't betray me. After meeting Carolyn, I'm convinced I can trust her, as well."

Carolyn nodded and smiled.

"You can count on me, as well, Pete," Carolyn added.

"Mitch, I know in recent weeks, you've agonized over the possibility this story could have a negative effect on your life. I would suggest you have nothing to worry about. I have well placed friends. And that extends to local and federal government agencies. Just trust me when I say, if you continue on the path you're now pursuing, this will add to your future and not detract from it."

Musser paused briefly before continuing.

"You may just come out of this being a national hero. Who knows? And I'll be able to say I knew you when…"

Conner raised his glass to both Musser and Carolyn.

"Here's to your futures," Conner said to each of them.

Musser looked directly at Conner and smiled.

"And here's to your future, you crazy bastard."

Indeed, right here in these mountains, one life had ended quietly and unnoticeably. But in these same mountains, another life had just begun, neither quietly nor unnoticed.